ISLAMIC EXTREMISM

ISLAMIC EXTREMISM
Causes, Diversity, and Challenges

Monte Palmer
and
Princess Palmer

ROWMAN & LITTLEFIELD PUBLISHERS, INC.
Lanham • Boulder • New York • Toronto • Plymouth, UK

ROWMAN & LITTLEFIELD PUBLISHERS, INC.

Published in the United States of America
by Rowman & Littlefield Publishers, Inc.
A wholly owned subsidiary of The Rowman & Littlefield Publishing Group, Inc.
4501 Forbes Boulevard, Suite 200, Lanham, Maryland 20706
www.rowmanlittlefield.com

Estover Road, Plymouth PL6 7PY, United Kingdom

British Library Cataloguing in Publication Information Available

Library of Congress Cataloging-in-Publication Data

Palmer, Monte.
  Islamic extremism : causes, diversity, and challenges / Monte Palmer and Princess
Palmer.
    p. cm.
  Includes bibliographical references and index.
  ISBN-13: 978-0-7425-5517-4 (cloth : alk. paper)
  ISBN-10: 0-7425-5517-8 (cloth : alk. paper)
  ISBN-13: 978-0-7425-5518-1 (pbk. : alk. paper)
  ISBN-10: 0-7425-5518-6 (pbk. : alk. paper)
  1. War on Terrorism, 2001-   2. Islamic fundamentalism.   3. Jihad.   4. Islam and
politics.   5. United States—Politics and government—2001-   I. Palmer, Princess,
1952-   II. Title.
HV6432.P345 2008
973.931—dc22   2007026060

Printed in the United States of America

♾ ™ The paper used in this publication meets the minimum requirements of American
National Standard for Information Sciences—Permanence of Paper for Printed Library
Materials, ANSI/NISO Z39.48-1992.

For Nikki and Katie

Contents

1

America's Struggle against Terror

Who Is the Enemy?

T HE GREATEST THREAT facing the United States today is jihadist terrorism. The jihadists are a self-appointed collection of Muslim fanatics who have launched a holy war, a jihad, against the United States and everything American.[1] They have also declared war on Israel, Europe, and anyone else who opposes their vision of a world governed by Islamic law. Ironically, the foremost target of the jihadists has been the Muslim world itself. Most Muslims reject the jihadists' rigid interpretation of Islam, and few relish the austerity of jihadist rule. It is the Muslims who have borne the brunt of jihadist terror, with the past decade claiming more then 150,000 lives in Algeria alone. The jihadists might be Muslim, but few Muslims are jihadists.

The September 11, 2001, terrorist attacks on the United States killed nearly three thousand people when two planes crashed into the World Trade Center twin towers in New York City; a plane crashed into the Pentagon in Washington, D.C.; and Flight 93, heading for the White House, was diverted and crashed into a Pennsylvania field. These terrorist attacks on American soil made Osama bin Laden's al Qaeda network the focal point of world attention. The jihadist movement, however, is much larger than bin Laden and his al Qaeda network. Jihadist groups flourish throughout the world, plotting violence and fueling civil unrest whenever the opportunity presents itself. Some jihadist groups have formed temporary alliances with al Qaeda. Others have not. Most of the groups are small and fluid, appearing and disappearing, splintering and reemerging in new alliances. Adding complexity to the picture has been the splintering of the al Qaeda network itself. Rather than facing one bin Laden, the United States might now be facing several.

But what about the more moderate extremist groups such as Hizbullah,

Hamas, and the Muslim Brotherhood? Are they any less lethal than the jihad-ists? The answer to this question depends upon whom you ask. For many Muslims, the Muslim Brotherhood, Hizbullah, and similar groups represent the only viable hope for confronting the oppression, incompetence, corrup-tion, immorality, and foreign domination that afflict the societies. The Israe-lis, in contrast, find them to be one and the same. Staunch American allies such as Egypt have made a truce with the jihadists only to declare the Muslim Brotherhood a threat to the security of the Egyptian state.[2]

Many people believe that the United States is locked in a war of religions with Islam. How, they ask, could the September 11 attacks have been put in place by a jihadist enemy who represented a minute segment of the world's Muslims? The answer seemed obvious. It was the broader Islamic community who had made the attacks possible. By all appearances, the jihadists wanted for neither money nor protection. Weapons abounded and supply lines transversed the world.

The American government denies that it is at war with Islam, but the world's Muslims remain unconvinced. Perhaps the impression that America had declared war on Islam was created by the wave of emotion that followed the September 11 attacks. President Bush, himself, referred to America's war on terror as a "crusade," a turn of phrase that seemed to imply that the United States had renewed Christendom's conquest of the Holy Lands. He later apologized. Italian prime minister Silvio Berlusconi was particularly blunt, saying, "We must be aware of the superiority of civilization . . . in contrast with the Islamic countries," a comment that seemed to suggest that Muslim were barbarians.[3] The European Union rushed to denounce Berlus-coni's comments as unfortunate. Jerry Falwell weighed in on CBS's *60 Min-utes* by calling the Prophet Mohammed a terrorist. Falwell's comments triggered protests throughout the Islamic world, with some observers blam-ing his statements for the victory of Islamic parties in Pakistan's subsequent elections.[4] Falwell later apologized.

Somehow lost in the shuffle was the fact that most of the world's 1.3 billion Muslims abhorred the jihadists. It was they, after all, who were the primary victims of the jihadist terror. Also ignored was the fact that most Muslim fundamentalists, extremists if you like, were not wild-eyed terrorists any more than most Christian fundamentalists supported the bombing of abor-tion clinics or formed vigilante groups holed up on remote mountaintops. They, like fundamentalists of all religions, were attempting to make sense of a world in turmoil by returning to the basic tenets of their faith. Did Islamic fundamentalists want more religion in government? Absolutely, but few were interested in the cruel repression of the Taliban, or even the repressive

Islamic doctrines of Iran or Saudi Arabia. For most, Islam had become the one beacon of hope in a world of despair and repression.

The situation remains much the same today as it did in 2001. Jihadist terror continues to stalk the world. Bin Laden and al Qaeda remain at large and have spawned more clones and imitators than the West can keep track of. The Taliban fanatics who were chased from Afghanistan in the aftermath of the September 11, 2001, terrorist attacks have reasserted their influence and spread their venom to the large areas of neighboring Pakistan, a key American ally in the war on terror. Bin Laden's al Qaeda network has joined them. The war on Iraq, the cornerstone of America's war on terror, has served only to increase terror and extremism. Such, at least, was the conclusion of America's sixteen intelligence agencies.[5] Rather than becoming the cornerstone in America's war on terror, Iraq is emerging as the key element in a Shi'a triangle that links Iran with radical Shi'a groups in the Gulf sheikhdoms, Saudi Arabia, Syria, and Lebanon. The United States, for its part, has now renamed the war on terror the "long war." In the meantime, Iran, the world's foremost supporter of terror and extremism, is pursuing its goal of nuclear weapons.

The more moderate varieties of Islamic extremism have fared even better. A moderate Islamic party rules Turkey; a pro-Iranian religious coalition governs in Iraq; Hamas scored a stunning victory in the 2005 Palestinian elections; the Muslim Brotherhood might have done the same if the Egyptian government had not used brute force to keep Brotherhood supporters from the polls; and Hizbullah defeated Israel in their brief war of 2006 and is clearly the strongest force in Lebanon. The message is clear. Free elections will lead to an increase in the power of the more moderate extremist groups in the Middle East and other areas of the Islamic world.

There can be little doubt that a new Middle East will be forged in the coming decades. The present configuration of aging dictators and curious kings forged at the end of World War II is no longer viable. What will the new Middle East look like? Will it be a democratic and prosperous Middle East that welcomes Israel and bows to the awesome power of the United States? Or, will it be a Middle East reshaped in the image of Islamic extremism? Current betting is on the latter. This does not mean that it will be a Middle East addicted to terror, but it does mean that millions of Muslims are turning to their faith in an effort to stem decades of corruption, oppression, mismanagement, and foreign manipulation. Islamic fundamentalism is not going away anymore than Christian fundamentalism is going away. The return to religion is a global phenomenon as people seek to find security in a world that has run amuck.

The United States and its allies, for their part, are no closer to coping with Islamic extremism, jihadist or otherwise, than they were on the eve of the

September 11 attacks on the United States. Now, as then, they continue to squabble over what to do and how to do it. World public opinion is bitterly hostile toward the United States, believing that George Bush is the world's second-greatest threat to world peace. Bin Laden is first. Even the Israelis are beginning to have their doubts about American policy, with only one in four Israeli voters believing that the Bush administration has made the world a safer place to live.[6] The U.S. Army and Central Intelligence Agency (CIA) are attempting to reinvent themselves to better fight terror, and the Department of Homeland Security is in disarray. One can only wonder what the next much-predicted terrorist attack on the United States will bring. Will it be the heroism of the New York firefighters or will it be the chaos that followed the Hurricane Katrina disaster in New Orleans?

The crusader dimension of the war against Islamic extremism has also intensified. In 2006, Yom Kippur, the Day of Atonement, witnessed three hundred million Christian evangelicals worldwide praying for the security of Israel and, ipso facto, against an Islamic extremism that claims Israeli lands for its own. Israelis also estimate that approximately sixty million American evangelicals stand by the side of Israel and that U.S. evangelicals constitute one-third of the tourists who visit Israel on an annual basis.[7]

The question is not whether one applauds or condemns the crusader dimension in the war against Islamic extremism. The important fact is that sixty million Americans who support anything constitute a major force in American politics regardless of the political party in power. Christian fundamentalism has become a key influence on the way Americans view Islam, Islamic extremism, and terror. Fundamentalist emotions on both sides are increasing and could well transform the war on terror into a war of religious fundamentalisms.

It would also be a mistake to suggest that Christian concerns with Islamic extremism are limited to the evangelicals. In September of 2006, Pope Benedict recalled that a fourteenth-century Byzantium emperor had referred to Islam as "evil and inhuman." The Islamic world erupted in anger as political leaders competed with Islamic extremists to condemn the pope's presumed slur on Islam. The pope later clarified that these words were not his own and apologized for the pain that his comments had caused to the world's Muslims. Some Muslim clerics accepted the pope's apology, while others found it evasive and inadequate. The point to be made is that the Muslim world is acutely sensitive about threats to its faith regardless of their intent. Attacks on Islam, however inadvertent, strengthen the forces of Islamic extremism.

What precisely, then, is the line separating the jihadist fanatics who have launched a war of terror on the United States and the Western world and the less violent forms of Islamic extremism? Is Islam really a seamless pyramid of terror, or is it, like most religions, a vast mosaic of diverse groups and institutions struggling to find the best way to serve God? While a fuller discussion of this topic must await the next chapter, suffice it to say that Islam is, indeed, a vast mosaic of groups and institutions struggling to find the best way to serve God. The struggle is bitter, and conflict between Muslims is often far greater and far more violent than conflict between Islam and its sister faiths.

Whatever the confusion surrounding Islam and Islamic extremism, it is now evident that the United States cannot win its war on terror without the cooperation of the world's 1.3 billion Muslims. They are natural allies of the United States in the struggle against the jihadist terror that is engulfing the world, and it is they who must deprive the terrorists of the support that they need to survive. At present, this is not happening. The vast majority of the world's Muslims are hostile to the jihadists but do not share America's hostility toward lesser extremist groups such as the Muslim Brotherhood, Hamas, and Hizbullah. They are also bewildered by what they firmly believe to be an American crusade against Islam. To cite the title of a recent discussion on *Al Jazeera*, a leading Arab television network, "War of Religions: Coming or in Progress?"[8]

The United States might have no other choice but to deal with the Muslim Brotherhood, Hamas, Hizbullah, and other less extreme elements of the Islamic movement if it intends to stem jihadist terror and have productive relations with the Islamic world. They are the most dynamic force in the politics of the Middle East and have dominated virtually every reasonably fair election in the region including those arranged by the United States in Iraq. Efforts to crush them by force will merely increase their radicalism and pose an even greater threat of terror. This, at least, has been the lesson of Middle Eastern history since the advent of the first crusades.

This is the cruelest of choices, for an extremist Middle East will be far less conducive to U.S. and Israeli interests in the region than the puppet regimes that the United States has kept in power for the past several decades. There certainly can be no guarantee that moderately extremist regimes will remain moderate.

With the above thoughts in mind, the purpose of this book is to provide an understandable portrait of the world's diverse extremist currents, their strengths and weaknesses, and the reasons why efforts to contain them have failed.

We approach the task from four different perspectives. First and foremost, a few words are in order concerning the nature of the Islamic faith, its internal conflicts and its relations with Judaism and Christianity, its sister faiths. This accomplished, the discussion moves to an analysis of the Muslim Brotherhood, Hamas, Hizbullah, Turkey's ruling Justice and Development Party, and other radical-moderate groups confronting the United States in its efforts to shape the politics of the Middle East. From there we move to the jihadists and their allies, America's main opponents in the war on terror, the "long war." We conclude by examining why efforts to contain Islamic extremism have failed. A few suggestions are also offered for ways of coping with the threat of Islamic extremism. This is hazardous, but these are hazardous times.

Notes

1. It is important to note that the word "jihad" possesses a variety of meanings ranging from war in the name of God to the individual's internal struggle against evil. We have debated alternative expressions to characterize the narrow band of extremists who commit terror in the name of Islam but find jihadists to be the least offensive. The term jihadist also finds extensive use in the media of the Islamic world. We do not use the expression "Islamic extremists" or "Muslim extremists" to imply terrorists, for most extremists in the Islamic (Muslim) world are not terrorists.

2. "Mubarak Says That the Brotherhood Constitute a Danger to the Security of Egypt" [in Arabic], *Al Arabiya*, January 11, 2007, at www.alarabiya.net/ (accessed January 11, 2007).

3. "EU Deplores 'Dangerous' Islam Jibe," *BBC Online*, September 27, 2001, at http://news.bbc.co.uk/2/hhi/europe/1565664.htm (accessed December 7, 2002).

4. Todd Hertz, "Riots, Condemnation, Fatwa, and Apology Follow Falwell's CBS Comments," *Christianity Today*, October 14, 2002, at www.christianitytoday.com/ct/2002/140/41.0.html (accessed December 7, 2003).

5. See the discussion of Iraq in chapter 14.

6. Julian Glover, "British Believe That Bush Is More Dangerous than Kim Jong-Li," *Guardian*, November 3, 2006, at www.guardian.co.uk/ (accessed November 3, 2006).

7. Etgar Lefkovits, "1/3 of U.S. Tourists Evangelicals," *Jerusalem Post*, October 9, 2006, at www.jpost.com/ (accessed October 9, 2006).

8. Hasan As-Sasrrat, "The War of Religions: Coming or in Progress?" [in Arabic], *Al Jazeera*, November 12, 2006.

2

Islam, Muslim Extremism, and Anti-Americanism

MANY AMERICANS find the link between Islam and violence to be self-evident. This is not the case. The overwhelming majority of the world's 1.3 billion Muslims want nothing more than to live their lives in a normal and peaceful manner. While most would welcome a greater role for religion and morality in their societies, few support violence as a means for achieving that end. In their view, the jihadists are an aberration of Islam who offer little more than oppression, religious police, veiled women, and disavowal of modern science. This is not how the majority of Muslims want to live.

Why, then, are anti-Americanism and religious extremism rampant in the Islamic world? The objective of the present chapter is to shed light on this most perplexing of questions. We begin by examining Muslim relations with Christians and Jews as well as the tremendous diversity that exists within the Islamic faith. This accomplished, we examine differing levels of religiosity among Muslims. A few Muslims are secular. Others, also few in number, exhort the faithful to violence. The overwhelming majority of the world's Muslims occupy various stages between these two extremes. Levels of religiosity have much to say about who supports the jihadists and who opposes them. Rough estimates are provided for each category. Finally, we look at the broader causes of anti-Americanism in the Islamic world. Anti-Americanism has a religious component, but it is so much more. Focusing on religion alone will not solve America's problems with the Islamic world.

Muslim Relations with Christians and Jews

Most Christians and Jews will be relieved to find that they already know more about the Islamic experience than they realize. Islam builds upon Judaism and Christianity, and a clear line of progression exists between the three religions.[1] Much as Christians believe that God sent Christ to correct the deviations of the Jews, so Muslims believe that God sent Mohammed, his final prophet, to correct the deviations of the Christians. Islam acknowledges the major prophets of the Jews, including Adam, Noah, Moses, and Abraham. Christ is recognized as a major prophet but not as the Son of God. Islam does, however, accept the virgin birth of Christ, and the Koran, the revealed word of God, devotes an entire chapter to Mary.[2]

Not only do Muslims worship the same God as Christians and Jews, but the Islamic experience parallels that of the Christians and Jews. Much like Christianity and Judaism, Islam is a religion of many parts. Islam is a creed based on the revealed word of God. It is also the clergy (*ulema*) who interpret that creed and a multitude of schisms resulting from those interpretations. Above all, Islam is a body of faithful attempting to achieve salvation by living in accordance with the will of God.

The institutions of Islam also parallel the institutions of Christianity and Judaism. Muslims are linked to their clergy by a network of mosques that differ little from churches and synagogues. Islamic schools, charities, and religious societies are similar to those of their sister faiths. Much like Christianity and Judaism, Islam is also an identity, a way of life, and a symbol of hope. Muslims, like Christians and Jews, struggle to find a proper means of expressing their faith. For many members of all three faiths, the struggle has found expression as religious fundamentalism. A very small minority of all three faiths promote violence in the name of their religion. In Islam, these are the jihadists, the sworn enemy of America.

The holy book of Muslims is the Koran, a compilation of God's laws as revealed to the Prophet Mohammed by the Angel Gabriel. Mohammed is revered by Muslims as a prophet of God rather than as an extension of God. He was a mortal being chosen by God to receive his message of peace and enlightenment and, as such, possessed no supernatural powers. In addition to the Koran, Muslims seek guidance from the Sunna or "way of the prophet." When early Muslims encountered issues not fully addressed in the Koran, they sought guidance by consulting the traditions of the Prophet Mohammed and his associates. This process was quite effective during the years immediately following the Prophet Mohammed's death but led to abuses as memories grew dim.

Much like the Torah and the Bible, the Koran provides Muslims with a guide to salvation. The Koran, however, far exceeds the Bible in instructing Muslims on the ordering of their political, economic, and social lives. The Prophet Mohammed was a political leader, and the Koran has much to say about how to organize a well-run society in a manner that will promote peace and justice. Unlike the Christian tradition, Islam does not draw a clear line between the sacred and the profane. Indeed, many Muslims find it absurd to separate religion from government. Why would human law be placed above the law of God?

The Koran refers to Christians and Jews as "people of the book." Christians and Jews, from the Islamic perspective, had been converted to the one God by earlier prophets but refused to accept the teachings of the Prophet Mohammed, God's final prophet. As believers in the one God, both Jews and Christians are allowed to live in peace among Muslims.[3]

Islam calls on its adherents to protect their faith, as do all major religions. Barring this, there would be no faith. In Islam, protecting the faith is referred to as a jihad, an Arabic word used to sound the call for a holy war.[4] It is this, but so much more. Sheikh Atiyyah Saqr, an eminent Muslim scholar long associated with Cairo's venerable Al-Azhar Mosque, offers the following clarifications.

> The word "jihad" means exerting effort to achieve a desired thing or prevent an undesired one. . . . Among the types of Jihad are struggling against one's desires, the accursed Satan, poverty, illiteracy, disease, and all evil forces in the world. . . . Jihad is also done to avert aggression on the home countries and on all that is held sacred, or in order to face those who try to hinder the match of the call of truth. In Islamic Shari'ah [law] Jihad in the Cause of Allah means fighting in order to make the Word of Allah most high and the means for doing so is taking up arms in addition to preparation, financing and planning strategies.[5]

Islam's relations with Christianity and Judaism, then, operate on a dual axis. One axis stresses tolerance toward Jews and Christians who live in their midst. Historically, the record of Muslim tolerance toward people of the book has been exemplary. It has certainly surpassed the Christian treatment of Jews in Europe.

The second axis centers on the Koranic scriptures enjoining Muslims to protect their faith and to bring nonbelievers into the fold. Conflict between Islam and the West has centered on this second axis and has occurred whenever Jews and Christians have challenged Muslim dominance in the predominantly Islamic countries of the world. This occurred during the Crusades, and it has been a recurring theme in the violence that has devastated the Islamic world since the colonial era. Many Muslims believe that Christian and Jewish attacks on Islam are now reaching a level of fervor unknown since the Crusades. They also believe that those attacks are being spearheaded by Israel and the United States. Does this require a jihad? If so, what kind of jihad? These matters have yet to be resolved. Most Muslims see little need for a holy war. The jihadists believe that there is no other option.

Regardless, a long history of tolerance between Islam and its sister faiths has been strained by an upsurge of fundamentalist views in all three religions. Cooperation between Christians and Jews has surged as Christian evangelicals honor the biblical injunction to support Israel. Evangelicals also appear moved by biblical texts prophesying that Armageddon will see Jews embrace Christ as the Messiah or perish.

No similar bonds exist between Christianity and Islam. The Bible preceded the Koran and, as such, does not acknowledge its existence. For many evangelicals, Islam takes on demonic overtones as the oppressor of Israel. Christians, in general, know little of Islam, and few seem aware of the fact that the three faiths share a common God. Many evangelicals find this proposition to be blasphemous. If one believes in God, they ask, how can one reject the Son?

Muslim extremists reciprocate Christian and Jewish hostility and fuel fears of an American crusade against Islam. Christian communities in the Middle East face increasing hostility from their Muslim hosts, and many are leaving the region. Interfaith dialogues between clergy of the three faiths exist but are largely an academic exercise. Popular emotions are driving the two sides toward confrontation. This is unfortunate, but it is one of the forces shaping the future of the Middle East.

Unity and Turmoil within Islam

The evolution of Islam parallels the evolution of Christianity. In each case, a simple message of hope and faith was revealed to the masses by a messenger. In the case of Islam, it was the Prophet Mohammed. In the case of Christianity, it was the Son of God. Organizational structures, such as they were, consisted of the prophet, a small band of disciples, and a gradually expanding body of the faithful. The evolution of Judaism was somewhat more complicated, but the basic principle was the same.[6]

With the passing of the founding prophet, simplicity gave way to complexity as a class of priests became the guardians of the faith, bickering over fine points of doctrine and preparing the way for eventual schisms. In the case of Islam, the most devastating schism occurred in AD 656 when Ali, the fourth caliph, or successor to the Prophet Mohammed, was challenged for the leadership of Islam by Muawiyah, the governor of Damascus. Ali was assassinated, giving way to a schism of enduring bitterness. As described by Yahya Armajani,

Failing to establish their claim by politics or by war, the Shi'is separated perma-nently from the majority and founded a religion of their own complete with theology, philosophy, government, and ethics. Religiously, Shi'ism has Zoroas-trian, Nestorian, and other overtones, and has supplied Islam with mysteries, saints, intercessors, belief in atonement, and a spirit of high cult all of which are repugnant to the majority of Sunnis. The Sunnis consider the Koran infalli-ble, while the Shi'is place infallibility in a man, the Imam, who is sinless and has been considered as a man-God. The Shi'is believe in the doctrine of the Return. This has many things in common with the return of the deliverer of Zoroastrianism, the coming of the Messiah in Judaism, and the "second com-ing" of Jesus in Christianity. The majority of the Shi'is believe that there were twelve imams and the twelfth, the Mahdi (messiah) has disappeared and shall return at the end of time when he will bring the whole world under the jurisdic-tion of Shi'i Islam.[7]

The Shi'a belief that the Hidden Imam would reappear to lead the Muslim community to salvation resulted in the evolution of religious leaders empow-ered to rule the Shi'a community until the time of the Imam's return. Such individuals, often referred to as ayatollahs, were imbued with spiritual pow-ers similar to if not greater than those of the pope.[8] These powers have enabled the Shi'a clergy to control their followers by promising entrance into heaven for religious sacrifice.

In sharp contrast to the mysticism of the Shi'a, the Sunnis follow a more literal interpretation of the Sunna, or way of the Prophet. There are no Hid-den Imams, nor are Sunni spiritual leaders imbued with supernatural pow-ers. Aside from the caliphate, now vacant, the religious elites of Sunni Islam consist of learned scholars or *ulema*. The most senior of these are the *mufti* (senior religious judges), the directors of waqfs or religious endowments, and the rectors of Islamic universities such as Al-Azhar University in Cairo. Other than these positions, Sunni Islam lacks an overarching organizational struc-ture, and each congregation more or less selects its own preachers (*muazin*) and prayer leaders, albeit with help from the government. In effect, the schism between the Shi'a and Sunni shares much in common with the schism between Catholics and Protestants.[9]

Each of the two main branches of Islam has generated diverse schools of thought, each with a multitude of interpretations. Some interpretations are liberal, allowing Muslims a large degree of freedom in ordering their daily lives. Others are severe, attempting to re-create life on earth much as it existed during the days of the Prophet. The Taliban in Afghanistan clearly fell into this latter category and created a society that forbade every symbol of modernity, including music and soccer. The Wahhabi interpretation of Islam applied in Saudi Arabia is also renowned for its severity. While soccer is a national passion, women remain veiled, and calls to prayer are enforced by religious police.[10]

The points of doctrine that separate Sunni and Shi'a are dwarfed by popular misunderstandings and emotions, many fueled by political and religious leaders. The 2006 war between Israel and Hizbullah, for example, saw the emergence of a *fatwa* (religious decree) issued by a Saudi religious leader declaring the Shi'a to be non-Muslims (*kafirs*) and unworthy of Muslim support. Coincidently, the Saudi government chose this moment to blame Hizbullah, a Shi'a movement, for the war. Egypt and Jordan followed suit, with Egypt's government-controlled press portraying Sayyed Hassan Nasrallah, the Hizbullah leader, as a wild-eyed extremist who, along with bin Laden, was attempting to hijack Islam. Egyptian religious leaders joined the fray by warning that Shi'a agents were attempting to infiltrate Egypt and subvert it from the way of the Prophet.[11]

To their dismay, Israel's war against Hizbullah turned into a fiasco, and the Saudis hastily retreated. A spate of religious *fatwas* were issued proclaiming to one and all that Shi'a were, indeed, Muslims. The earlier *fatwa* was denounced as being outdated, erroneous, and totally unrelated to the Israeli-Hizbullah War.

Al Arabiya, a leading Arab language television channel, published a long rejoinder by Shi'a clergy from Saudi Arabia and Lebanon denouncing the Saudi *fatwa* excommunicating Shi'a.[12] This said, they also acknowledged that ignorance and emotionalism reigned among the Shi'a as well as the Sunni, and urged the leaders of both sides to unite in the face of the U.S. onslaught.

Few people, it seems, were listening. Open violence flares between Shi'a and Sunni in Iraq, Pakistan, and Afghanistan, and hovers beneath the surface in Lebanon, Saudi Arabia, and the Gulf sheikhdoms.[13] Indeed, the main point of cooperation between Islam's two main sects appears to be in Palestine. Some cooperation between Shi'a and Sunni extremist groups also exists at the international level, a topic to be discussed in later chapters. For the moment, suffice it to say that American and Israeli hostility to Islam is one of the major forces uniting what is otherwise a deeply divided religion.

The Evolution of Islamic Extremism

The evolution of all major religions has witnessed the emergence of extremist groups vowing to purify the faith. Islam is no exception. Indeed, extremism in Islam returns to the earliest days of the faith and was spawned by the debate over who should succeed to the leadership of Islam after the passing of the Prophet Mohammed. Many of the faithful believed that successors to the Prophet Mohammed should be drawn from his lineage and particularly that of Ali, the fourth caliph. This view was opposed by the Kharijites, who believed that the successor to the Prophet Mohammed should be selected by egalitarian and democratic procedures. Those who opposed their views were killed as heretics.

The roots of modern Islamic extremism are often traced to the works of Ibn Taymiyyah, a Muslim thinker who lived in Damascus during the thirteenth and fourteenth centuries. Ibn Taymiyyah lived in an era in which Islam was in danger of being dominated by the Mongols, and his writings are often credited with rallying the Arabs against the Mongol invaders. The Mongols had legitimized their rule by converting to Islam, but they had done so in an imperfect manner that mixed the creeds of several religions as the moment dictated, not the least of which was hailing their leader, Genghis Khan, as a prophet of God. Ibn Taymiyyah declared the Mongols to be infidels (*kafirs*) and, as such, unfit to rule. Only the followers of the Salafiya—the Koran and teachings of the Prophet Mohammed, his followers, and their followers—were true Muslims and fit to rule. All others had to be resisted. Among Ibn Taymiyyah's justifications was the following saying of the Prophet: "The best of mankind is my generation, then those who follow them, and those who follow them."[14]

Far from being obscure, Ibn Taymiyyah's logic has long been used by Sunni extremists to justify attacks on groups whose lax interpretations of Islam didn't conform to the Koran and the Sunna (Salaf).[15] For example, in the early eighteenth century, the Wahhabi doctrine emerged in Saudi Arabia. Abd al-Wahhab, a charismatic religious leader with a broad following in the region, joined forces with the founder of the first Saudi dynasty and used Ibn Taymiyyah's earlier teachings to purge the Saudi kingdom of mystical beliefs, not the least of which were those of the Shi'a.[16]

The fortunes of both the Saudis and the Wahhabis ebbed and flowed over the ensuing centuries and surfaced again with the founding of the present Saudi kingdom at the turn of the twentieth century. Ibn Saud, the founder of modern Saudi Arabia, used Wahhabi teachings to fire his troops with holy zeal but was himself threatened by the zeal of the Wahhabi extremists, known as Ikhwan or brothers. As Robert Lacy describes these zealots,

> The Prophet condemned personal osternation, so the Ikhwan shunned silk, gold, jewelry and ornaments, including the gold thread traditionally woven round the dark bhisht or mishlah, the outer robe and they also cut their robes short above the ankles. This was because the Prophet had declared clothes that brushed the ground to be an affectation, and the same went for luxuriant moustaches. So the Ikhwan clipped the hair on their upper lip to a mere shadow of stubbiness while adopting a different rule for the hair on the chin. In this case,

they argued, it would be affectation to trim and shape, so beards must be left to grow as long and to straggle as far as God might will them.[17]

The most recent crisis in Islam was provoked by Western colonization of the Islamic world, a process that was well under way by the end of the nineteenth century. While science and industrialization had transformed England, France, and Germany into world powers, the Islamic empires of old collapsed of their own weight. The Ottoman Empire, the remaining Islamic power at the time, survived largely because the European powers had already begun to fight over its corpse, each fearing an advantage for the others.

The power of Europe forced Muslim intellectuals to acknowledge that the Islamic world was in decay. The issue could not be dodged. Something had to be done, but what? Enlightened voices called for the accommodation of modern science within a religious framework. Science, as all things in life, they argued, was the will of God and should be accepted as such. Islam would enjoy the best of both worlds: scientific advancement provided by the West and the moral strength provided by the Islamic empire long in decay.

Not all in the Islamic world shared this enlightened view. Conservative theologians feared that modern science would lead to secularism and eternal damnation. It was not the science of Europe that had led to the decay of Islam, they argued, but the perversion of basic Islamic teachings that had occurred over the course of Islamic history. Attempting to "modernize" Islam would weaken the Islamic faith, not strengthen it. The only solution to the decay that had beset Islam, in the view of the conservative theologians, was a return to the fundamental principles of the Koran and the way of the Prophet Mohammed. Everything not based on the fundamentals of Islam as preached by the Prophet would be eliminated.

Theologians debated while the Islamic world fell ever deeper under the control of the European colonialists. The crisis came to a head in the aftermath of World War I, when the entire Arab world, with the exception of Saudi Arabia and Yemen, fell under Western control. Turkey and Iran, the two non-Arab powers of the region, escaped Western domination but had become so dependent on Europe for arms and commerce that the result was much the same.[18] The time for debate had passed. It was time for action.

It was not the Islamic theologians who acted but rather secular generals. Stung by defeat and fired by national pride and the lust for power, it was they who plotted the future of the Islamic world. Muslims, in their view, had been defeated by the science, industrialization, and secularism of Europe. The countries of the Islamic world, they reasoned, could only defeat their adversaries by following suit. Islam, in their view, was passé, and an obstacle to development. Nationalism, not religion, would be made the opiate of the masses.

The forced secularization of the Islamic world was spearheaded by Mustafa Kemal, a Turkish general who had seized power in the waning days of World War I in a desperate effort to prevent the dismemberment of Turkey by the allied powers. Soon renamed Ataturk (Father of the Turks), Kemal used the power of the army to forcibly transform Turkey into a clone of Europe.[19] Forced industrialization became the order of the day and was matched by the forced secularization of Turkish society. Islamic law was replaced by the Swiss legal code. Family names, a rarity during the Ottoman Empire, became mandatory. The fez and other forms of religious dress were forbidden. Latin script replaced Arabic script, the script of the Koran, as the medium for writing Turkish. Religious schools were also secularized, and religion was relegated to the role of personal salvation. Did Ataturk succeed? This is an interesting question and will be examined at length in chapter 7.

Particularly distressing to Muslim theologians was Ataturk's abolition of the caliphate in 1924. For some five hundred years, Turkish monarchs had ruled their massive empire as both sultan and caliph. Ataturk had shattered the unity of religion and state. Political leaders of the Muslim world continued to pay lip service to Islam, but the religious elites were on the defensive, their power fading much as the power of Christian leaders had faded in the Europe of an earlier era. Presidents and kings appointed religious leaders compatible with their views and changed them at will. The role of the Muslim *ulema* was to justify a secular regime, not oppose it. In the final analysis, the modernizing generals posed a greater threat to Islam than the colonial invaders.

It was in this environment that Hassan al-Bana, an Egyptian school teacher, launched the Muslim Brotherhood, an organization designed to encourage Egypt's youth to follow the way of the Prophet Mohammed. Indeed, the initial name of al-Bana's organization was the Young Men's Muslim Association. The solution to Egypt's woes, according to al-Bana, was not secularism but rather a return to the basic principles of Islam and a system of government modeled on the Koran. As al-Bana's emphasis on basic principles seemed to have much in common with Protestant fundamentalism, it soon became common for Westerners to refer to groups such as the Muslim Brotherhood as fundamentalists.

Muslims have never been particularly comfortable with the term "fundamentalism" and believe that it is the obligations of all Muslims to follow the way of the Prophet. The Muslim experience was also far more complex than Protestant notions of redemption and rebirth. Muslims are born again every time they testify that "there is no God but Allah and Mohammed is his prophet," something that can happen several times a day. In contrast to Christian fundamentalists, the basic issue confronting Muslims is not the rededication of their faith but rather agreeing on the best way to serve God. Were prayer and good works adequate, or did their faith require political action?

Many chose political action. The Brotherhood flourished and became the largest and most dynamic fundamentalist organization in the region. Henceforth, the Islamic faith would be divided between two Islams: an "establishment Islam" consisting of religious leaders appointed by the government and a "fundamentalist Islam" that sought to recapture the state.

The road, however, was not easy. The very success of the Muslim Brotherhood placed it in conflict with a new generation of secular generals intent on building a modern Arab empire. During the mid-1950s, the Brotherhood made an abortive attempt to assassinate Abdul Nasser, the president of Egypt and successor to Ataturk as the driving force of secularism and modernity in the Middle East. Nasser retaliated with vengeance. The Brotherhood's leaders were either killed or jailed, and the organization was driven into remission. Visions of westernization and modernity reigned supreme.

The Middle East, however, is a region of startling change. The Arab-Israeli War of 1967 saw the armies of Nasser humbled by Israeli forces in less than a week. The war is often referred to as the Six Day War, but the humiliation of the Arabs took only four. The promises of secular modernity had proven hollow and left the Arabs bitter and devoid of hope. Their despair was shared by the Muslim world as a whole, for the defeat of the Arabs was also a humiliation for Islam. In whom could Muslims place their faith and trust?

The Muslim Brotherhood provided the answer. "God is the Solution," proclaimed their slogan. It appeared everywhere: in mosques, on pamphlets passed from hand to hand, and on the walls unprotected by the watchful eyes of the police. The Muslim Brotherhood might have been in remission, but it was not dead.

The Brotherhood, however, had also changed. The Muslim Brotherhood that emerged in the ashes of the 1967 war was a chastised Brotherhood that stressed reform rather than assassinations and violence. Nasser and the generals had proven too powerful to be overthrown by a religious organization. Henceforth, the Brotherhood accommodated the secular leaders of Egypt and other countries on the condition that it would be allowed to pursue an Islamic revival not terribly different from the Christian revival sweeping the United States. Reform based on teaching, preaching, and good works was to be the key to success. Once the spirit of Islam had been revived among the masses, so the Brotherhood's new strategy went, the political leadership would follow suit. They would have no choice.

Again, however, there were problems. The new moderation of the Muslim Brotherhood attracted a following with views so diverse that they defied incorporation into a single organization. The question of strategy was particularly divisive. Was it better to work within the system, as advocated by the new strategists of the Muslim Brotherhood, or to destroy it, as advocated by Sayyid Qutb, a leading Brotherhood thinker during the 1950s and 1960s? According to Qutb, Muslim society had been corrupted beyond the point of salvation and differed little from the era of ignorance that had prevailed in Arabia prior to the arrival of the Prophet Mohammed.[20] Just as the Prophet Mohammed had imposed the teachings of Islam on the citizens of Mecca by force, Qutb argued, so the obligation of today's Muslims was to reclaim Islam by force. There was no other choice. Working within the system served the devil and corrupted the faithful. A holy war, a jihad, had to be declared against secular regimes and those who supported them. Secular Muslim leaders had become infidels and were no longer fit to rule.

The jihadists excelled in zeal and violence but found unity elusive. Some observers in Egypt charted the existence of some ninety Islamic jihadist groups of one variety or another. Rare was a country in the Islamic world that did not have several.[21] A majority of the Egyptian groups were small and short lived. A few larger groups such as the Islamic Group and Islamic Jihad affiliated with international jihadists networks such as bin Laden's al Qaeda network or developed their own international branches.

How well do the Muslim Brotherhood and the jihadists cooperate? We'll discuss this in detail in later chapters. For the moment, suffice it to say there is little consensus on the issue. Some find the inherent tension between the Brotherhood and the jihadists to be a window of opportunity for defeating the jihadists. To strengthen the Brotherhood, they argue, is to weaken the jihadists. Others argue that the Muslim Brotherhood and the jihadists are merely two sides of the same coin: one possesses a seductive ideology of reform and democracy while the other intimidates its opponents with threats of violence and mayhem. The goal, they note, is the same: an Islamic state.

As things currently stand, both the Muslim Brotherhood and the jihadists have branches throughout the Arab and Islamic worlds, including the Muslim communities of Europe and North America. Parallel fundamentalist movements, some violent and some nonviolent, evolved in Pakistan and Iran, many with a broad international reach. The Iranian-sponsored groups represent the Shi'a branch of Islam and are heavily supported by the government of Iran.

The Sources of Muslim Discontent

Not only has fundamentalist Islam developed a global reach, but also it has become the most vibrant political movement in the Islamic world. It could not be otherwise, for the forces that gave rise to Islamic fundamentalism in the early years of the twentieth century have increased exponentially. For more than five decades, the peoples of the Middle East and Islamic worlds have lived in a vortex of social change. Once rural if not tribal, they now seek a better life in megalopolises so polluted that the very act of breathing is dangerous to their health. Except for the wealthy minority, there is little but squalor. The extended families, that massive network of parents, grand-parents, brothers, sisters, uncles, aunts, and cousins extending to the fifth degree that once provided the foundation of Middle Eastern society, are beginning to crumble. Families remain the focal point of individual loyalty, with many individuals devoting some 50 percent of their salaries to helping relatives. Life, however, has become too complex and demanding to be sus-tained by families alone.

Social despair is paralleled by economic despair. Middle Eastern universi-ties are bursting at the seams, but there are few jobs for graduates. Those jobs that are available go to relatives of the influential or are allocated as a form of political patronage. Little of the region's legendary wealth finds its way to the poor countries of the Islamic world, and even the pampered residents of Saudi Arabia and the Gulf States are now being asked to put their shoulders to the wheel.[22] Sadly, they don't know how. Their whole lives have been spent receiving government handouts while guest workers got things done.

With governments as oppressive and ineffective as they are corrupt, it is only natural that many Muslims have sought salvation in their religion. In the parlance of Christian fundamentalism, "they are hurting." They are look-ing for a savior. Tragically, there are few avenues for peaceful change in the Islamic world. Secular reformers are condemned as tools of the United States, and Muslim reformers are condemned as terrorists. Political parties exist here and there as window dressing, but the only voice that counts is that of the regime. The Islamic movement is the only effective opposition to the pol-itics of the Islamic world as presently constituted. The choice, by and large, is between radical reformers such as the Muslim Brotherhood and Hizbullah on one hand, and various strains of the jihadist movement on the other.

Globalization now threatens to accelerate the pace of change and despair to the breaking point.[23] Satellites, DVDs, and the Internet assault this most conservative of regions with seductive and unrealistic images of Western cul-ture. Many are lured by the promise of westernization. The devout have recoiled in fear that traditional Islamic values are being irrevocably destroyed. Both sides are fearful and frustrated, the former by what they can't have and the latter by what they might lose. The battle is more than a contest between groups. It also rages within individuals torn by diametrically opposed visions of society. Most want both: westernization and the security of their faith.

If cultural globalization is seductive and subtle, economic globalization has pounded the Islamic world with the force of a sledgehammer. Virtually all Islamic countries have practiced some form of socialism, with most people, aside from peasants, being employed by the government. Huge bureaucracies gave employment to endless streams of college graduates, while most urban workers labored in government-owned factories. Not much was accomplished, but most people had a job, a pension, and rudimentary health care. Wages were abysmally low—until recently a professor in Egypt made about two hundred dollars per month, a school teacher about half that much—but food, health care, and housing were all subsidized. One got by.

That now has changed. The World Bank, International Monetary Fund (IMF), and World Trade Organization have decreed that capitalism will do a better job of curing poverty and violence than government welfare programs. This view is wholeheartedly seconded by the United States and other major donors of foreign aid. The poor countries of the Islamic world remain skeptical but have little choice. Most cannot survive without loans from the IMF and the World Bank. State-owned industries are being sold off, jobs jettisoned, overblown bureaucracies trimmed, and social safety nets dismantled. This seems to make good economic sense, but it sows panic among populations that have long survived on government handouts. A narrow class of merchants, land speculators, and industrialists has become inordinately wealthy under the new economic order, but the masses have not.[24] Things have become worse, not better. The gaudy lifestyle of the nouveau riche rubs their noses in the collective misery of the poor on a daily basis. Are the poor bitter? Absolutely.

Ironically, America's war on terror and Islamic extremism has added the element of military globalization to the instability of the Middle East. As a U.S. general admitted, it could not be otherwise with the stationing of more than three hundred thousand mainly American troops in the region.[25]

Tragically, political globalization has lagged far behind cultural, economic, and military globalization. Much-ballyhooed promises of democracy and human rights remain little more than empty slogans. Not only are Muslims locked in a vortex of change and economic chaos, but their political systems are locked in a vortex of decay. Rather than offering hope for a better life, they offer little but oppression and despair. There is no democracy in the Western sense of the word. Corruption is endemic, human rights are honored in the breach, and the quality of services is dismal. Health and welfare services for the destitute are provided largely by the Muslim Brotherhood or similar religious organizations. Ironically, the one area in which the leaders of the region excel is their ability to cling to power and pass it on to their sons. As a result of enhanced technologies in intimidation and repression, peaceful change in the region has become a virtual impossibility. Indeed, a region once renowned for its coups d'état has now become a region renowned for its aging dictators.

The situation of Europe's large Muslim population is not markedly better. While most Muslim immigrants to the United States are middle class and well integrated into American society, the Muslim immigrants to Europe are overwhelmingly low-level workers from rural backgrounds. Education levels are low, and poverty and unemployment are rampant. Most immigrant families, many extending for more than three generations, cluster in run-down neighborhoods that are Muslim in culture. This makes it easy for immigrant populations to cling to their rural traditions, and many remain more culturally linked to their countries of origin than with the culture of their European hosts.[26] Added to the equation is the hostility of Europeans who blame Muslim immigrants for escalating crime, drug, and unemployment rates, all of which are hovering at record levels. Immigrant bashing has become standard fare of right-wing politicians across the continent as well as some left-wing-inclining politicians anxious to solve the concerns of their working-class constituents.

For all of the present woes, Muslims have a deep sense of history and are intensely proud of their past. It was they who provided the cradle of civilization. It was also they who set the standard for science and enlightenment during the dark ages that descended on Europe following the collapse of Rome.

It is that very pride in their past that makes the humiliation of the present so bitter. Much like Islamic thinkers of an earlier era, Arab and Muslim intellectuals of today relentlessly debate the cause of their malaise, most placing the blame on colonialism that swept the Islamic world during the nineteenth and twentieth centuries. The Islamic world was fragmented. Each mini-country, some no larger than a postage stamp, was endowed with a mini-king subservient to the West. The era of independence that came after the end of World War II was merely replaced by a more insidious form of economic and cultural colonialism that threatened to transform the very roots of Arab and Islamic society.[27]

Of all of the insults to Arab and Islamic pride, none was greater than the creation of Israel. The crusaders, from the Islamic view, had returned, laying claim to the third-holiest shrine in Islam. War after war found the Arabs humiliated by a small Jewish state, itself no larger than a postage stamp. How could so few Jews defeat so many Arabs and Muslims? To accept the possibility of Israeli superiority would be to admit that a fundamental flaw existed in the Arab and Islamic view of the world, an admission that would threaten the very foundations of the faith and the Arab psyche.[28]

Gauging Popular Support for Muslim Extremists

If the peoples of the Middle Eastern and Islamic worlds share a common despair, they differ violently over the cure. Some, a minority, have adopted Western secularism with a vengeance. Others, also a minority, seek salvation in religious governments that impose servitude in the name of Islam. Between this vast and unbridgeable chasm lies the majority of the world's Muslims. Most would prefer a balance between Islamic morality and modernity. Of these, some are moderate in their religious views, while others incline toward extremism. For those concerned with the relationship between Islam and the war on terror, the obvious questions are (1) Who is who? and (2) How many are there of each?

Unfortunately, it is difficult to gauge the intensity with which Muslims embrace their faith. Some researchers have attempted to measure the intensity of Islamic religious emotions by monitoring levels of attendance at mosques or observing the number of people who participate in religious celebrations such as the Hajj.[29] Regardless, the results are awesome. Mosques are overflowing. Millions of Muslims attend the Hajj each year and return to joyous celebrations among friends and families. The 2006 celebration of Biswa Ijtema (three days of prayers and teaching on the banks of the Turag River in Bangladesh) drew a reported two million worshipers from some eighty countries.[30]

Other observers have focused on the explosion of Islamic dress that began in the late 1970s and early 1980s. Beards, long a symbol of religious piety, became a statement of opposition to the secular regimes of the Islamic world. The late President Anwar Sadat of Egypt banned beards, only to see their numbers multiply. He was assassinated by jihadists in 1981. Religious dress among women has become ubiquitous. Billboards in Egypt and elsewhere advertise the latest in Islamic fashions, many designed in Paris. Even women traffic police officers in the Middle East have begun to wear Islamic head scarves tucked neatly beneath their military caps.

How does one interpret this phenomenal upsurge in Islamic dress? Is it an expression of piety, a show of support for religious extremists, or a message of defiance to corrupt and oppressive regimes? For many Islamic men, it is some of each. Deciphering the explosion of Islamic dress among women is far more complex, being variously interpreted as a symbol of piety, support for the Islamic revival, a statement of political opposition, a signal of purity to perspective suitors, submission to family pressure, conformity to the latest style, a means of deflecting overaggressive males, relief from lengthy hairdos, and even reverse sex appeal.[31]

Both the American government and leaders of the Islamic world are deeply concerned by the growing number of religiously based protests against American policy in the region. Participating in protests is a far clearer expression of political involvement than praying in a mosque, and such demonstrations are routinely videotaped by the police for future reference. Demonstrations against the U.S. invasion of Iraq and Israeli policies in the Occupied Territories have been particularly emotional. Most participants in anti-American demonstrations are drawn from the region's universities and high schools and do not necessarily reflect the general sentiment of the population. It's also not clear whether the protests are a manifestation of religious zeal or an expression of nationalistic resentment against U.S. policy— probably some of each. Regardless, they are part of the puzzle.

Yet another piece of the puzzle is the results of the region's fraudulent elections. Candidates of the Muslim Brotherhood scored surprising victories in Egypt's 2006 parliamentary elections and might have won the elections were it not for massive fraud and police brutality. The picture has been much the same in Morocco. Islamic fundamentalist parties have emerged victorious in the recent Turkish, Palestinian, Saudi Arabian, Iraqi, and Afghani elections. How ironic that democracy has become the enemy of the United States. Are people voting for Islam, or are they protesting against corrupt and oppressive governments? Again, the answer is some of each. President Husni Mubarak of Egypt tends to attribute the growing popularity of Islamic parties to the region's lack of experience with democracy. As he explained to the U.S. Congress,

> This country was under pressure for years and years, and when you open the gate for freedom, you will find many terrible things taking place. If you have a dam and keep the water until it begins to overflow, and then you open the gates, it will drown many people. We have to give a gradual dose so people can swallow it and understand it. The Egyptians are not Americans.[32]

Yet another way to assess levels of Islamic religiosity is to simply ask people how religious they are, a procedure that is routine in the West. Our colleagues and we have experimented with public opinion research in a variety of Middle Eastern countries with varying degrees of success. Respondents in Egypt and Lebanon, countries with long intellectual traditions, were quite forthcoming with their responses, while respondents in Saudi Arabia all responded that they were deeply religious. It is dangerous to be tepid about religion in Saudi Arabia.

Particularly surprising was the willingness of some 50 percent of the Egyptian respondents to indicate support for the Islamic revival, an oblique reference to the Islamic fundamentalist movement. Of these, a hard core of around 14 percent indicated very strong support for the revival. The Lebanese results paralleled those of the Egyptian respondents. More than 90 percent of our Egyptian respondents expressed either strong or very strong support for religion in schools, with the latter category exceeding the 65 percent mark.[33] In much the same manner, more than 70 percent of the Egyptian respondents supported religious censorship of the media. Again, the results among Lebanese Muslims were similar.[34]

Particularly alarming from the American perspective were the spate of opinion polls that followed the September 11, 2001, terrorist attacks on the United States. A *Times* of London poll conducted shortly after September 11 found that approximately 11 percent of Britain's two million Muslims believed that there was some justification for bin Laden's attacks on the United States; some 40 percent of the respondents disagreed with bin Laden's means but agreed that his war against the United States was justified. Sixty-eight percent indicated that their faith was more important than "being British." The results were based on interviews with 1,170 Muslims conducted outside British mosques.[35] In the same period, the *New York Times* reported that a classified Saudi intelligence survey found that 95 percent of educated Saudis supported bin Laden's cause.[36] The director of Saudi intelligence reportedly acknowledged the survey but attributed its results to Saudi anger against the United States for its support of Israeli oppression in the Occupied Territories.[37] Gallup polls in the Islamic world conducted in 2002 and 2003 registered high levels of anti-Americanism among Muslims, as did a parallel survey sponsored by the Saudi-backed Arab Thought Foundation.[38] A congressional study conducted in the summer of 2003 found that "the bottom has indeed fallen out of support for the United States."[39] Similar results were forthcoming from broader cross-national polls such as those conducted by the Pew Research Center for the People and the Press. By and large, hostility toward the United States focused on American policy in the Middle East and particularly U.S. support of Israel. The spread of American culture was also a concern throughout the Islamic world as well as in much of Europe. Only the Japanese, it seems, are particularly fond of American culture. Interestingly, Muslims retain a high regard for American democracy and freedom.

The beat goes on year after year in poll after poll. A 2005 poll conducted by researchers at the University of Maryland found that respondents in Jordan, Lebanon, Morocco, Saudi Arabia, Egypt, and the United Arab Emirates believed that U.S. policy in the Middle East was primarily concerned with protecting Israel (76 percent), dominating the region (68 percent), and weak-ening the Muslim world (63 percent). Only 6 percent of the respondents believed that the United States was interested in promoting democracy or human rights.[40] In much the same manner, a 2006 Pew Global Attitudes Project indicated that Muslims viewed the West as selfish, greedy, violent, and fanatical. Westerners returned the favor, viewing Muslims as fanatical and violent.[41]

Assessing public opinion in the Islamic world remains more of an art than a science, and the data reviewed are merely suggestive. Their consistency, however, is alarming and constitutes a clear warning that American efforts to win the hearts and minds of Muslims have failed miserably. Anti-Americanism is not terror or even Islamic extremism, but it does make people indifferent to America's plight. It also makes it difficult for their governments to cooperate with the United States. In much of the world, it is the Americans, or at least the American government, who are viewed as the bad guys.

Levels of Islamic Religiosity

Taken collectively, our surveys and those of our colleagues suggest that the Islamic community might conveniently be viewed as consisting of six basic levels based on the intensity of their religious beliefs, their vision of an Islamic state, and their predisposition toward violence. These levels are nonbelievers (*kafirs*), minimalists, practicing, devout, publicists, and fanatics.[42]

To be a *kafir* in Islam requires that one disavow the existence of God and the role of the Prophet Mohammed as his messenger. Merely losing interest in one's faith is not grounds for excommunication. There are few avowed nonbelievers in the Islamic world, most being leftist intellectuals who eschew religious violence and are staunch advocates of a secular state.

This said, many Muslims, like many Jews and Christians, are minimalists. They are Muslim in identity and culture but are lax in the execution of their religious obligations. Those who do attend the mosque often do so in response to social pressures rather than deep conviction. The minimalists also eschew religious violence and are staunch advocates of a secular state. Based on the research discussed above, this group would probably constitute about 15 percent of the world's Muslim population, although that figure might be unduly optimistic. Most are intellectuals, but that is not to say that most intellectuals are secularists. Indeed, many jihadist leaders possess dazzling intellect as do the leaders of more moderate groups such as the Muslim Brotherhood and Hizbullah.

A third major category of Muslims might be called practicing Muslims. They try to fulfill the basic religious obligations as best they can, some being more successful than others. Religious concerns are important but compete with a broad range of social, economic, and political interests. Practicing Muslims worry about the lack of morality in government and society but are essentially secular in outlook. They reject religious violence. Practicing Muslims probably constitute about 30 percent of the Muslim population.

The next rung in the hierarchy of Islamic religiosity is occupied by concerned Muslims, a group that approximates the moral majority in the United States. Concerned Muslims are far more likely than practicing Muslims to attend religious lectures, participate in study groups, associate with religious societies, and otherwise make religion a major focus of their own lives. Most, however, view religion as a personal affair and incline toward moderation in their political views. Morality, however, is high on their political agenda. They, too, condemn religious violence. The research reviewed above also suggests that concerned Muslims constitute nearly 30 percent of the Muslim population.

The fifth category of Muslims we have termed publicists. Unlike concerned Muslims, publicists believe that religion is far more than a personal affair. Islam, in their view, is a public affair. They display their religiosity via Islamic dress and other signs of piety, and they actively encourage others to behave in a religious manner. They are doers rather than talkers and openly advocate a religious state. Most do not advocate violence, but they often support doctrines considered inflammatory by the United States. Our limited research in Egypt and Lebanon suggests that the publicists constitute approximately 20 percent of the Muslim population, a large percentage given their propensity for action. Judging by their statements, they would feel quite comfortable living in an Islamic theocracy.

Topping the hierarchy of Islamic religiosity are the fanatics. As with fanatics in all faiths, they are driven by a zeal and singleness of purpose that blinds them to all but the narrowest of doctrines. The Islamic fanatics share a common vision of a pristine Islamic state that differs little from the Islamic state established by the Prophet Mohammed in seventh-century Arabia. If anything, it is more extreme, lacking the humanity, flexibility, and enlightenment that characterized the rule of the Prophet. While the Prophet Mohammed looked to the future, the Islamic fanatics look to the past.

Even the fanatics, fortunately, are not of a single mind. The jihadists advocate terror to achieve their goals, while other fanatics have turned to asceticism and are minimally concerned with the political affairs of the temporal world. An interesting example of this phenomenon is the al-Ahbash of Lebanon, a Sufi group that has openly confronted the jihadists, occasionally with violence.[43] As such, they pose an appealing alternative to the jihadists for fanatical Muslims troubled by Islamic injunctions against the killing of Muslims and innocents.

Fanaticism, then, does not of itself lead to violence. In reality, the jihadists represent an infinitesimally small number of the world's 1.3 billion Muslims. It is their fanaticism that makes them so dangerous. The Central Intelligence Agency (CIA) estimates suggest that al Qaeda can draw on a global base of six to seven million fanatical Muslims. Potential fighters are placed at 120,000.[44] These are roughly in line with our own estimates.

The six groups form a simple bell curve, the two extremes of which are the nonbelievers and the fanatics. Numbers are larger among the minimalists and the publicists, with the center of the curve being occupied by the practicing and the devout Muslims. This relationship is illustrated in figure 2.1. Percentages are merely suggestive and could easily vary from time to time and country to country. Lebanon and Egypt are worlds apart from Yemen and Saudi Arabia. The rural areas of the Islamic world are often centuries behind their urban centers.

The intensity of religious emotions also tends to ebb and flow as Muslims attempt to reconcile their religious upbringing with the seductive allure of Western lifestyles. Make no mistake, the glitzy life portrayed in Western movies and television programs does have strong appeal to Muslims trapped in the bleak existence of the Third World. Indeed, it is not unusual for individuals to vacillate between the two extremes, exuding piety one day and laxity

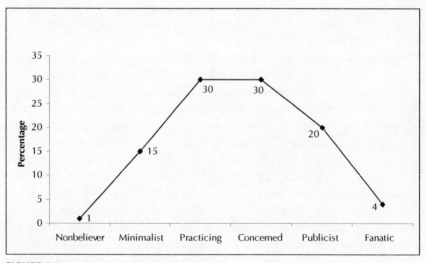

FIGURE 2.1
Six basic levels of Muslim religious beliefs

the next. Many of the perpetrators of the September 11 attacks seemed to have experienced similar psychological dilemmas.

The lines separating the different levels of religious intensity are also blurred and shifting. Minimalists merge with practicing Muslims and the latter with concerned Muslims and publicists. Social pressures to display one's faith have increased dramatically over the past few decades and tend to peak during times of crisis. Nevertheless, each of the categories outlined above has a center of gravity and influences how Muslims express their views politically.

As might be expected, support for the extremist groups tends to increase as one ascends the hierarchy of Islamic religiosity. Minimalists and practicing Muslims tend to support the secular political parties of the Islamic world but are not averse to greater religiosity in education and politics. If they support the extremist parties or groups such as the Muslim Brotherhood, it is largely to protest the ineptness of their own governments. Concerned Muslims are far less opposed to the notion of an enlightened Islamic government but have little use for the excesses of the fanatics. Many find the views of the Muslim Brotherhood reasonable and far more appealing than the tepid Islam purveyed by government preachers. All in all, concerned Muslims constitute a moderate Islamic voice in the spectrum of Islamic politics. It is they who tend to vote for the moderate Islamic parties, and it is they who are increasingly making their voice heard in the political arena of the Muslim world. Publicists, by contrast, openly proclaim their desire for an Islamic state whatever its severity. They are the activists who feel that it is their obligation to prepare the way for an Islamic government. This does not make them terrorists, but it is the publicists who constitute the main support group of the jihadists. The fanatics, in turn, provide the jihadists with their activists and die-hard supporters.

The down slope of figure 2.1 constitutes what Muslims refer to as the Islamic movement, a broad and somewhat amorphous category that incorporates the full gamut of individuals aspiring for a more Islamic government. The Islamic movement includes concerned Muslims as well as the publicists and fanatics. All in all, they constitute approximately half of the Muslim population. Few support terror against the United States, but all are deeply concerned that things are not well within the Islamic community and feel they must be changed. Members of the Islamic movement are particularly concerned that the United States has declared war on Islam.

The fit between religiosity and politics, of course, is only approximate. Even minimalists protest the oppressive and inept regimes of the Islamic world by voting for Islamic parties. Indeed, the Islamic Revolution in Iran was supported by confirmed communists who championed the Ayatollah Khomeini in a calculated effort to rid themselves of the Shah. In retrospect, this was a mistake. The clerics continue to rule, and most former leftists are either dead, exiled, or rotting in Iran's infamous jails. The converse is also true. Many Muslims with extremist views have turned to prayer rather than politics, believing that personal purity is more relevant to salvation than earthly endeavors. Others have joined Sufi groups (religious mystics) seeking greater personal communication with God. Most Sufi groups are apolitical and, as such, represent a threat to the extremists.

Separating Islamic Extremism from Anti-Americanism

Judging by the intensity of their religious behavior, the vast majority of the world's Muslims should be America's allies in its "long war" against jihadist terror. This would certainly include those Muslims falling in the minimalist and practicing categories. They fear the extremism of the zealots at least as much as the Americans, and they aspire to a quality of political and economic life personified by the United States. Most firmly believe that it is possible to blend science and Islam. Concerned Muslims should also find few complaints with American views on religion. Muslims have prospered in the United States, although some view the security measures put in place following the September 11 terrorist attacks with concern.

Unfortunately, the public opinion polls reviewed earlier indicate that hostility toward the United States is not limited to Muslim extremists. On the contrary, it includes just about all Muslims, secularists as well as religious extremists. Being anti-American does not make one a terrorist, but such anti-American attitudes do bolster the jihadists and make it difficult for both the United States and friendly Islamic governments to fight terror. This point was brought home with devastating impact as longtime allies such as Egypt and Turkey, feared a public backlash, and so declined to support the American-led invasion of Iraq.

Why, then, are Muslims so overwhelmingly opposed to American policy toward the Islamic world? Why has the United States, once a symbol of hope and friendship in the Muslim world, become the enemy? In large part, the answers to these questions are found in the massive gap that separates the way in which Americans and Muslims view the world.

Americans see themselves as a fair and reasonable people who desire nothing more than freedom, justice, and prosperity for all. As the innocent victims of criminal violence, Americans believe that they are fully justified in striking the terrorist with maximum force. In their view, their hands are free of blood.

The image of the United States that prevails in the Islamic world is radically different. Not only is the United States seen as having blood on its hands, but those hands are literally dripping in the blood of Arabs and Muslims. Five widely accepted Muslim perceptions of the United States, in particular, have soured America's relations with the Islamic world and generated support for violence against American targets. The five Muslim perceptions of the United States are provided in table 2.1. Discussion of the perceptions follows below.

Muslim Perception 1: The United States controls everything. Perhaps the most widely held of all Middle Eastern perceptions of the United States is the belief that little of importance happens in the region, if not the world, that is not the direct result of American manipulation. Some time ago, by way of illustration, we were discussing events in Baghdad with an Iraqi friend who pointed with his right hand in the direction of the American Embassy and with his left hand in the direction of the Soviet embassy. "Whenever anything happens in Iraq," he said with complete conviction, "we ask ourselves was it our friends on the left or our friends on the right?"

Our response to this perception has been to ask the following: If the United States really controls everything, why is the region slipping under the control of the extremists? Why hasn't the Arab-Israeli crisis been resolved? Why did September 11 happen? Why does bin Laden's al Qaeda network remain at large? Why are the mullahs developing nuclear weapons in Iran? There can be no doubt that America's military and economic power makes it a major player in the region, but that power has not been exercised with consummate skill. Rather than being a master chess player, the United States is more like a bull in the china shop, lurching from one crisis to another, none of which is ever fully resolved.

Perceptions of American omnipotence in the region reflect the very intrusive role of the United States in the region as well as the tremendous economic and military power that the United States does possess. Blaming

TABLE 2.1
Muslim perceptions of the United States

Muslim Perception 1	The United States controls everything.
Muslim Perception 2	America is attempting to bring the entire region under its control.
Muslim Perception 3	The United States wants to control and exploit the region, not govern it.
Muslim Perception 4	The United States is unabashedly on the side of Israel.
Muslim Perception 5	The United States has declared war on Islam.

everything on the Americans is a convenient way for the leaders and intellectuals of the region to avoid responsibility for their own ineffectiveness. In
any case, blaming the ills of the region on the United States, justified or not,
does create intense feelings of animosity toward the American government.

*Muslim Perception 2: America is attempting to bring the entire region under
its control.* This perception reflects a begrudging acknowledgment that the
United States does not, at least yet, control everything in the region. Perceptions, however, are emotional rather than rational, and apparent contradictions are part of the psychological game people play to make sense of their
world.

The belief that the United States is attempting to take over the world is far
more dangerous than the belief that it controls everything, inasmuch as it
signals a call to arms. There is still time to act! Every move that the United
States makes (or doesn't make) is interpreted as part of an evil scheme to
dominate the region and its oil resources. Allowing the Taliban to shelter bin
Laden, for example, was seen as a pretext for bombing Afghanistan and putting a regime in power that would be loyal to the United States. An even
more insidious view is that the war in Iraq was staged by the United States
to justify attacks on Iran and other Islamic regimes.

Somewhat ironically and with an obvious sense of humor, the *Al Jazeera*
TV network recently broadcast a debate on whether the United States should
be encouraged to take over the region. "At the very least," to paraphrase one
participant, "we would have democracy and human rights and would be
done with the corrupt and oppressive governments that have been the bane
of our existence."[45]

*Muslim Perception 3: The United States wants to control and exploit the
region, not govern it.* The accuracy of this perception is not a matter of much
contention. The Middle East is vital to the national interests of the United
States, and the United States has historically acted to protect that interest.
The United States has also relied heavily on friendly leaders in the region to
do its bidding, regardless of how repressive and corrupt they might have
been. As might be expected, this policy makes the people of the region feel
that their well-being is being sacrificed for the prosperity of the United States,
and this fuels long-term resentment. Ruling by proxy, however, saves both
lives and money. Occupying territory, as the Israelis well understand, is a
dangerous and costly business. The United States has learned the same lesson
in Iraq.

Muslim Perception 4: The United States is unabashedly on the side of Israel.
This, too, is a difficult perception to dispute, as a long series of American
presidents have taken office by proclaiming that "Israel has a friend in the
White House." Bill Clinton topped Ronald Reagan in his support for Israel,

and George W. Bush appears to be topping both. Israel is the largest recipient of U.S. foreign aid, and more often than not, it is a U.S. veto in the Security Council that spares Israel from yet another UN condemnation of its occupation policies. Fortunately for Israel, it is the U.S. vote that counts. Lest there be any doubt about America's sympathies, the United States has begun arming Israeli submarines with nuclear weapons and attempted to extend Israel's 2006 war in Lebanon in the vain hope of crushing Hizbullah.[46]

As might be expected, Arabs see themselves as being victimized by U.S. policy toward Israel, a view widely shared in Europe and the Islamic world. Former British prime minister Tony Blair openly criticized George W. Bush for America's one-sided role in attempting to broker a lasting peace in the region, a criticism now subscribed to by the European Union as a whole.[47]

Muslim Perception 5: The United States has declared war on Islam. This perception is fueled by the pervasiveness of America's wars on terror and Islamic extremism. No segment of Islamic society has been left untouched by the zeal of these efforts. It is also fueled by the U.S. occupation of Iraq and its increasingly belligerent policy toward Iran and Syria. It is further rooted in a history of U.S. support for oppressive Muslim regimes, not the least of which are Egypt and Saudi Arabia, the pillars of U.S. policy in the Arab world.

Of all of the above perceptions, the belief that the United States has declared war on Islam is the most lethal. It is lethal in terms of the number of people and countries involved, in terms of the intensity of the motivation inflamed, and in terms of the capacity of the jihadists to build support among Muslim populations by vilifying the United States. As the Saudi ambassador to the United Kingdom commented to a leading British magazine,

> Please don't kick the ambassador out of London for saying this, but if you go around the Muslim World, you will find the vast majority of people will support Osama bin Laden, and this is more tragic than the attack itself. Why would such a crime like this find such support, not just on the streets of Riyadh, but on the streets of Turkey, the streets of Tunis, and the streets of Britain? That comes down to the question of why people hate America.[48]

In the final analysis, it is not the accuracy of Muslim perceptions that is critical but rather the fact that they trigger deep emotional responses within the Islamic world. The United States will not be successful in countering terrorism and Islamic extremism unless it can do a better job of convincing people that America has not declared war on Islam. It would also do well to reconsider its support of oppressive regimes in the Islamic world. All fuel anti-Americanism and anti-Americanism strengthens the jihadists.

Notes

1. Heribert Busse, *Islam, Judaism and Christianity: Theological and Historical Affiliations* (Princeton, N.J.: Markus Wiener Publishers, 1998).

2. *The Koran Interpreted*, trans. A. J. Arberry (New York: Macmillan, 1955), 60–61; Sydney N. Fisher, *The Middle East: A History* (New York: Knopf, 1964).

3. Traditionally, Christians and Jews paid a tax or tribute for the right to live in peace and security among Muslim populations; Philip K. Hitti, *History of the Arabs from the Earliest Times to the Present*, 6th ed. (London: Macmillan, 1956), 204.

4. Majid Khadduri, *War and Peace in the Law of Islam* (Baltimore: Johns Hopkins Press, 1955). Islam divides the world into two, mutually hostile camps: the world of peace (Islam) and the world of war (nonbelievers). Muslims are enjoined to conquer the world of war and bring its subjects into the world of peace. Ideally, this is to be done by conversion. If conversion fails, they must be converted by force. Thus, jihad, in its meaning as a holy war, is both offensive and defensive. Jihad is used to defeat the world of war and defend the world of peace.

5. "Fatwa: What Is Jihad in Islam?" *Islam Online*, April 10, 2002, at www.islam online.net/fatwaEnglish/FatwaDisplay.asp?hFatwaID = 18243 (accessed October 21, 2002).

6. Cecil Roth, *History of the Jews* (New York: Schocken Books, 1963). Rather than focusing on a single individual such as Christ or Mohammed, the Jewish faith evolved around a series of key individuals, the foremost of whom are Abraham, the father of the Hebrew people; Moses, the prophet who, upon God's orders, led the Hebrew people to settle in Israel; and Solomon, who constructed the Holy Temple that continues to serve as one of the major symbols of the Jewish faith.

7. Yahya Armajani, *Middle East: Past and Present* (Englewood Cliffs, N.J.: Prentice-Hall, 1970), 101.

8. Henry Munson Jr., *Islam and Revolution in the Middle East* (New Haven, Conn.: Yale University Press, 1988); Farhad Ibrahim, *Confessionalism and Politics in the Arab World: The Shi'a Program in Iraq*, translated from German into Arabic by the Center for Cultural Studies and Translations (Cairo, Egypt: Library Madbouli, 1996).

9. For those interested in this topic, see James A. Bill and John Alden Williams, *Roman Catholics and Shi'i Muslims: Prayer, Passion, and Politics* (Raleigh: University of North Carolina Press, 2002).

10. Hani A. Z. Yamani, *To Be a Saudi* (London: Janus Publishing, 1998).

11. Abdullah Kemal, "The Danger of the Spread of Shi'ism in Egypt and the Sunni Countries" [in Arabic], *Rosa Al-Yousef*, October 14, 2006.

12. "Sunni and Shi'a Ulema Clarify the Views of Their Faiths on Ten Hot Questions" [in Arabic], *Al Arabiya*, November 20, 2006, at www.alarabiya.net/ (accessed November 20, 2006).

13. Vali R. Nasr, "Prepared Testimony before the Senate Committee on Foreign Relations," *Council on Foreign Relations*, January 17, 2007.

14. Related by al-Bukhaaree in Hadith 2652 in Haneef James Oliver, *The 'Wahhabi' Myth: Dispelling Prevalent Fallacies and the Fictitious Link with Bin Laden* (Online Publishing: Trafford, 2002), 1. Modern jihadists such as bin Laden are often

referred to as Salafis on the grounds that they are attempting to impose the pure Salafi interpretations of Islam on the Muslim world. This charge is heatedly denied by Saudi Arabian clerics who maintain that the Salafi is opposed to terror.

15. Hamdi Rizk, "Egyptian Muslim Brotherhood" [in Arabic], *Al-Wasat* (October 30, 1999): 31.

16. Oliver, *The 'Wahhabi' Myth.*

17. Robert Lacy, *The Kingdom: Arabia and the House of Sa'ud* (New York: Harcourt, Brace & Jovanovich, 1981), 142–43.

18. Stephanie Cronin, *The Army of the Creation of the Pahlavi State in Iran, 1910– 1926* (London: IB Tauris, 1997).

19. Andrew Mango, *Ataturk: The Biography of the Founder of Modern Turkey* (New York: Overlook Press, 2002).

20. Ahmad Moussalli, *Moderate and Radical Islamic Fundamentalism: The Quest for Modernity, Legitimacy, and the Islamic State* (Gainesville: University Press of Florida, 1999).

21. Hala Mustafa, *The Political System and the Islamic Opposition in Egypt* [in Arabic] (Cairo, Egypt: Markaz A-Mahrusa, 1995).

22. Yamani, *To Be a Saudi.*

23. Benjamin R. Barber, *Jihad VS McWorld: Terrorism's Challenge to Democracy* (New York: Ballantine Books, 2001); Monte Palmer, *Political Development: Dilemmas and Challenges*, 5th ed. (Itasca, Ill.: Peacock Publishers/Wadsworth, 2001); Gilles Kepel, *The War for Muslim Minds: Islam and the West*, trans. Pascale Ghazaleh (Cambridge, Mass.: Belknap Press of Harvard University Press, 2004).

24. Gordon Brown and Jim Wofensohn, "A New Deal for the World's Poor," *Guardian Unlimited* (London), February 16, 2004, at www.guardian.co.uk/ comment/story/0,3604,1149,00.html (accessed February 16, 2004).

25. Richard Norton-Taylor, "U.S. General Maps Out Strategic Refit for Iraq, Middle East, and Asia," *Guardian*, February 7, 2006, at www.guardian.co.uk/ (accessed February 7, 2006).

26. Tariq Modood, *Multicultural Politics: Racism, Ethnicity, and Muslims in Britain* (Minneapolis: University of Minnesota Press, 2005).

27. Hisham Sharabi, *Neopatriarchy: A Theory of Distorted Change in Arab Society* (New York: Oxford University Press, 1988).

28. F. Ajami, *The Arab Predicament*, 2nd ed. (Cambridge, UK: Cambridge University Press, 1992).

29. James A. Bill, "Resurgent Islam in the Persian Gulf," *Foreign Affairs* 63 (Fall 1984): 108–27.

30. "Over 20 Lakh Devotees Likely to Join: Biswa Ijtema Begins Today," *New Nation* 26 (January 2006).

31. Pioneering work in this area was conducted by Zeinab Radwan, *Appearance of the Hijab among University Students* (Cairo, Egypt: National Center for Social and Criminal Research, 1982). See also Andrea B. Rugh, *Reveal and Conceal* (Cairo, Egypt: American University of Cairo Press, 1987).

32. *New York Times*, October 12, 1993, A3, in Monte Palmer, *Comparative Politics* (Itasca, Ill: Peacock Publishers/Wadsworth, 2001), 434.

33. Monte Palmer, Madiha El Safty, and Earl Sullivan, "The Relationship between

Economic and Religious Attitudes in Egypt" (paper presented at the annual meeting of the Middle East Studies Association of North America, Providence, R.I., 1996).

34. Hilal Khashan and Monte Palmer, "The Social and Economic Correlates of Islamic Religiosity" (paper presented at the annual meeting of the Middle East Studies Association for North America, Chicago, December 1998).

35. "The Voice of British Muslims: Divided Loyalties on the Home Front," *Sunday Times* (London), November 4, 2001, at www.Sunday-times.co.uk/news/pages/sti/2001/11/04/siusausa01022.html (accessed November 4, 2001); "British Muslim Support for Terror," *Sunday Times* (London), November 4, 2001, at www.Sunday-times.co.uk/news/pages/sti/2001/11/04/siusausa01022.html (accessed November 4, 2001).

36. "95 Percent of Saudis Supported bin Laden's Cause," *Arabic News*, January 29, 2002, at www.arabicnews.com/ansub/Daily/Day/020129/2002012944.html (accessed February 6, 2002).

37. "95 Percent of Saudis Supported bin Laden's Cause."

38. Brian Whitaker, "Polls Apart," *Guardian*, March 4, 2002, at www.guardian.co.uk/elsewhere/journalist/story/0,7792,661807,00.html (accessed March 4, 2002); Karen De Young, "Arabs' Opinion of West: Yes and No," *International Herald Tribune*, October 8, 2002, at www.iht.com/articles/73099.html (accessed October 8, 2002).

39. Christopher Marquis, "U.S. Image Abroad Will Take Years to Repair, Official Testifies," *New York Times*, February 5, 2004. A complete transcript of Margaret Tutwiler's prepared remarks can be found at the Bureau of International Information programs, U.S. Department of State, at www.usinfo.state.gov/.

40. Surveys (n = 3617) were conducted in October, 2005, by Telhami and Zogby International and can be found at www.bsos.umd.edu/sadat/TelhamiArabSurvey .2005.htm (accessed December 5, 2005); Shibley Telhami, "America in Arab Eyes," *Survival* 49, no. 1 (Spring 2007): 107–22 (this article was prepared for a Council on Foreign Relations/International Institute of Strategic Studies [IISS] Symposium on Iraq's Impact on the Future of U.S. Foreign and Defense Policy).

41. "15-Nation Pew Global Attitudes Survey," Pew Global Attitudes Project, June 13, 2006.

42. We personally have been associated with more than twenty survey research projects in the Middle East over the course of the past thirty years. A few, such as those cited earlier, have focused directly on religiosity. Others examined attachments to traditional values and reluctance to change. Some, such as the Al Ahram survey of bureaucratic behavior, were based on random samples. Others, given the severe restrictions on survey research in the region, were based on quota samples or, in some cases, on snowball samples. We have also made extensive studies of the surveys conducted by others, synopses of which can be found in Madiha El Safty, Monte Palmer, and Mark Kennedy, *An Analytical Index of Survey Research in Egypt* (Cairo, Egypt: Cairo Papers in Social Science, 1985); Monte Palmer, Hilal Khashan, Mima Nedelcovych, and Debra Munro, *Survey Research in the Arab World: An Analytical Index* (London: Menas Press, 1982); Monte Palmer, Ali Leila, and El Sayed Yassin, *The Egyptian Bureaucracy* (Syracuse, N.Y.: Syracuse University Press, 1988); Palmer, El Safty, and Sullivan, "The Relationship between Economic and Religious Attitudes

in Egypt"; Khashan and Palmer, "The Social and Economic Correlates of Islamic Religiosity."

43. Ahmad Nizar Hamzeh and Harir Dekmejian, "A Sufi Response to Political Islamism: Al-Ahbash of Lebanon," *International Journal of Middle East Studies* 28 (1996): 217–99.

44. Rohan Gunaratna, *Inside Al-Qaeda: Global Network of Terror* (New York: Columbia University Press, 2002), 95.

45. "Contrary View," *Al Jazeera*, January 25, 2002, at www.aljazeera.net/programs/op_direction/articles/20021/1-23-1.htm (accessed January 25, 2002).

46. Oliver, *The 'Wahhabi' Myth*; Peter Beaumont and Conal Urquhart, "Israel Deploys Nuclear Arms in Submarines," *Guardian*, October 12, 2003, at www.guardian.co.uk/ (accessed October 12, 2003).

47. Kamal Ahmed and Ed Vulliamy, "Blair Fears Split with U.S. over Its Support for Israel," *Guardian*, December 16, 2001, at www.observer.co.uk/international/story/0,6903,69515,00.html (accessed December 16, 2001).

48. David Pallister, "Saudis Recall Controversial Ambassador," *Guardian*, September 19, 2002, at www.guardian.co.uk/Saudi/story/0,11599,794579.00.html (accessed September 19, 2002).

3

The Muslim Brotherhood and the Origin of the Radical Moderates

---

ISLAMIC GROUPS DEVOTED to the establishment of Islamic governments in the Muslim world tend to be of two varieties: (1) those willing to seek their goal by peaceful means and (2) those wedded to the use of violence. The former are typified by the Muslim Brotherhood, Hamas, Hizbullah, and Turkey's ruling Justice and Development Party. They, in turn, are joined by an infinite variety of Islamic parties and movements that are now reshaping the electoral map of the Islamic world. The latter are the jihadists. The Muslim Brotherhood, Hamas, Hizbullah, and the emerging Islamic political parties are often referred to as radical moderates. They are radical because they are dedicated to the establishment of religious governments in the Islamic world. They are moderate because they would prefer to achieve their goal of an Islamic government by peaceful means. They are also moderate in their vision of an enlightened Islamic state that blends religious morality with the best of modern technology. Indeed, Ayatollah Mohammed Hussein Fadlallah, the spiritual guide of Hizbullah, recently announced his support for cloning, hardly a reactionary position.[1]

One can question just how moderate the Muslim Brotherhood, Hizbullah, and other radical-moderate groups really are, but their presence as the most vibrant political force in the Islamic world is beyond dispute. By all accounts, including election results and opinion polls, they draw their support from a broad spectrum of the Muslim community. Even many less devout Muslims find their vision of an enlightened Muslim state preferable to the political decay that now pervades the Islamic world.

This suggests that the radical moderates constitute a far greater obstacle to U.S. control of the Middle East than the jihadists. While the jihadist message

38 *Chapter 3*

of violence repels Muslims and flies in the face of Islamic law, the message of the radical moderates is seductive, as is their commitment to honesty, equality, and welfare. All are rare commodities in the Muslim world. Unlike the jihadists who constitute a minute segment of the Islamic world, the radical moderates have become mainstream. They also blend their seductive message of Islam without pain with the potential for both terror and guerilla warfare. It was the latter that drove Israel from Lebanon and is now helping to drive the United States from Iraq.

For their part, the Muslim Brotherhood, Hamas, Hizbullah, and other less violent extremist groups maintain that they are not inherently anti-American. They share the West's hostility toward the jihadists, preach stability and development, and have long supported pro-American regimes in the region such as the Kingdom of Jordan and Saudi Arabia. They oppose a U.S. presence in the region but have not attacked U.S. targets for well over two decades. This is not true of Israel, a country the radical moderates accuse of occupying Muslim lands. Indeed, Hamas and Hizbullah now dominate the struggle to force an Israeli withdrawal from the lands that it occupied in the 1967 Arab-Israeli War. The Muslim Brotherhood is not far behind.

The problem, the radical moderates say, is that the United States has declared war on Islam and is unrelenting in its opposition to the establishment of Islamic governments in the Middle East and elsewhere. If the United States would cease its war against Islam and force Israel to evacuate the territories that it occupied in the June war of 1967, the radical-moderate argument continues, anti-Americanism in the region would recede and the jihadists would be brought to heel. Face reality, their argument concludes, the Islamic movement will not be defeated. It can be either the radical moderates or the jihadists. The more you attempt to suppress Islam, the more radical and violent the Islamic resistance will become.

There are, of course, no guarantees that accommodating less extremist groups such as the Muslim Brotherhood and the Hizbullah will reduce either anti-Americanism or terror—nor is there any guarantee that the radical moderates will accept the existence of Israel, whatever its boundaries. Perhaps their global persona of peace and coexistence is as seductive as their domestic persona of Islam without pain. While the European countries have established contacts with diverse radical-moderate groups, both the Israelis and the Egyptian government warn that the Muslim Brotherhood and Hizbullah are merely fronts for terror. They also warn that appeasement undermines the antiterrorist policies of America's allies in the war against terror and encourages extremism and terror.

Wherein lies the truth? If the answer were clear, American foreign policy would be far less complex than it is today. The people of the Islamic world are placing their bets—so must the United States. It must also come to a realistic assessment of what it can and cannot do to shape the affairs of the world. We'll discuss this more later. For the moment our objective is to examine the Middle East's main radical-moderate currents and their role in America's wars on terror and Islamic extremism. We begin with the Muslim Brotherhood and then move to discussions of Hamas, Hizbullah, and the Turkish Justice and Development Party. Each offers a different perspective on dealing with the radical-moderate currents in the Islamic world.

The Muslim Brotherhood

The Muslim Brotherhood spans the globe with branches in over seventy countries. The heartland of the Brotherhood is Egypt and neighboring Arab countries with large Sunni populations. Its total membership is difficult to gauge as it often operates under different names and is technically outlawed in countries such as Saudi Arabia, Syria, and Libya. Joseph Nada, the Brotherhood's commissioner for international political affairs, dodged the issue of size, but it is probable that its membership numbers in the millions, with a far larger body of dedicated sympathizers.[2] In any case, the Muslim Brotherhood is the dominant political organization in the Islamic world.

The ultimate goal of the Muslim Brotherhood is the reestablishment of Islamic rule throughout the Middle East and other predominantly Muslim areas of the world. The Brotherhood is not under any illusions that this will happen in the immediate future. Rather, it views the reestablishment of Islamic rule as a long-term process in which secular governments will gradually give way to their Islamic counterparts. As this process gains momentum, the various Islamic governments will gradually come together until a unified Islamic state of some variety emerges.[3] It is not necessary that the Brotherhood rule, merely that the leaders of the country apply Islamic law and govern in the spirit of Islam.

The Brotherhood's objective in the predominantly Christian countries of Europe and North America is to enable Muslim populations to deepen their faith by providing them with a network of mosques, religious schools, and Muslim associations. All, according to the Brotherhood, will help Muslims gain political and economic influence. This process is well underway in Europe but has lagged in the United States. In France, for example, Muslims have an official religious council that works with the French government to shape government policy toward France's large Muslim minority. Catholics, Jews, and Protestants have similar councils.

Other countries are less convinced of the Muslim Brotherhood's peaceful

intent. Russian security officials have uncovered Brotherhood cells throughout the country, accusing them of fermenting rebellion and, in some cases,
of supporting al Qaeda. The picture appears to be much the same throughout
other areas of the former Soviet Union.[4]

Is the Brotherhood a reformist organization dedicated to the peaceful evolution of an Islamic state, or is its commitment to nonviolence merely a strat-
agem? The testament of the Brotherhood is blunt and appears to leave no
doubt on the matter.

> Allah is our objective.
> The messenger [the Prophet Mohammed] is our leader.
> Quran is our law.
> Jihad is our way.
> Dying in the way of Allah is our highest hope.[5]

This, however, is not the way that they behave. For more than three decades, the Brotherhood has used persuasion rather than violence to reform
Islam from within. Moderation does not apply to the liberation of occupied
Islamic lands, the foremost of which are the Israeli-occupied West Bank and
Gaza Strip, Russian-occupied Chechnya, and Indian-occupied Kashmir. The
only way to liberate the Occupied Territories, according to the Brotherhood,
is jihad.[6] The apparent contradiction between the Brotherhood's moderate
face and its testimony glorifying jihad has caused concern that the Brotherhood's present posture is merely a strategic adjustment designed to disguise
its true intent. This is not so, says the Brotherhood:

> Jihad refers to the holy obligation to declare war upon non-believers (*kafirs*)
> who encroach upon Muslim lands. That is why we sent 10,000 troops to fight
> in Palestine in 1948, why we fought against the Soviets in Afghanistan, and why
> we were active in the predominantly Muslim regions of Central Asia long before
> the breakup of the former Soviet Union. It is also the same reason that Muslim
> Brothers play a major role in the liberation of Kashmir and offers their unequiv-
> ocal support to the Palestinian uprising (intifada). When Muslims are being
> slaughtered, what choice do we have?[7]

Aside from the holy obligation to liberate Muslim lands, the Brotherhood's
argument continues,

> God's law prohibits us from killing either innocent civilians or Muslims. The
> leaders of the Arab and Islamic World are Muslims because they have testified
> that "there is no God but Allah and that Mohammed is his Messenger." We
> cannot kill them. Make no mistake, they are sinners and will be judged harshly
> by God. That, however, is His prerogative and not ours. Our job is to lead them

back to the true path and to encourage them to apply Islamic law to the best of their ability. We summon, God judges.[8]

This argument is the key difference between the jihadists and the Muslim Brotherhood. The jihadists believe that the leaders of the Arab Islamic world have repudiated Islam through their actions and their cooperation with the United States, Israel, and other enemies of Islam. As such, they are *kafirs* and must be killed. The jihadists also fail to distinguish between military and civilian targets. All *kafirs*, in their view, are potential soldiers.

The Strategies of the Muslim Brotherhood

The Muslim Brotherhood uses three strategies to pursue its goal of reforming the secular regimes of the Islamic world: (1) teaching and preaching, (2) providing welfare to the needy, and (3) political activism. These strategies have been most thoroughly developed in Egypt but find expression in all of the seventy countries in which the Brotherhood operates. We focus on Egypt inasmuch as it remains the nerve center of Brotherhood activities.

Teaching and Preaching

The Muslim Brotherhood was founded as a youth organization designed to strengthen the religious and moral foundation of Egyptian society. Teaching and preaching remain central to its program. The Brotherhood believes it cannot achieve its objective of an Islamic state without a strong foundation of dedicated believers.

This process, according to the Muslim Brotherhood, begins by "building the Muslim individual: brother or sister with a strong body, high manners, cultured thought, ability to earn, strong faith, correct worship, conscious of time, of benefit to others, organized, and self-struggling character."[9] Strong Muslim individuals, according to the Brotherhood, build strong Muslim families, and strong Muslim families build a strong Muslim society. This accomplished, it is but a small step to the establishment of an Islamic state and the eventual reestablishment of the Islamic nation (*Umma*). Somewhat disconcertingly, the last step in the Brotherhood chain is "mastering the world with Islam."[10]

The Muslim Brotherhood's indoctrination program is carried out in a vast network of mosques, schools, and religious associations. Sermons and lectures stress the need for a moral society and urge vigilance against the enemies of Islam. The leaders of Muslim countries are seldom attacked directly, but it is not difficult to read between the lines. The United States and Israel are fair game. The Egyptian government denies that it censors Brotherhood sermons, but it watches their content very closely. The censors also pay close attention to the Brotherhood's vast media network, which, although heavily religious in content, seldom misses the opportunity to criticize the United States and Israel. This, of itself, is a major source of embarrassment for a Mubarak regime widely believed to have sold out to the United States.

Indoctrination, however, is far more than sermons. It is also the discussions with the faithful that take place before and after the sermons as well as in weekly study groups, monthly meetings of combined study groups, and various trips, camps, courses, workshops, and conferences. The Muslim Brotherhood is very much a "hands-on" organization. Much like Christian fundamentalists, it is in the business of saving souls, and Brothers spend endless hours convincing potential converts of the righteousness of their cause. The Brotherhood also attempts to integrate all dimensions of the individual's life within the Brotherhood "family." Prayer and service combine to create the sense of kinship so crucial in Middle Eastern life. Many young people in the Islamic world are bewildered, and the Brotherhood provides them with the sense of belonging and purpose that they so desperately need.

Beyond providing the moral basis for a future Islamic state, the Muslim Brotherhood's indoctrination program provides the foundation for its political and social activities. Numbers are important but so is zeal. Sympathizers vote and contribute money, but the truly zealous form the cadres of the organization. It is they who get out the vote, volunteer for service in Islamic struggles such as Kashmir and Palestine, and staff the Brotherhood's vast network of schools, welfare centers, and media outlets. The preaching role of the Muslim Brotherhood has other benefits as well. Religious organizations are allowed in most Islamic countries. Political organizations are not. Teaching and preaching provide cover for a broad range of political activities that would otherwise be banned. No one is fooled, but the Brotherhood benefits from the ambiguity.

Charity and Welfare

The Muslim Brotherhood has long maintained a network of schools and clinics for the poor. Donations from the faithful provide food and clothes, doctors serve without charge in Brotherhood clinics, and Islamic schools combine religious education with instruction in the three "Rs." For students at higher levels, Brotherhood tutors assist with preparation for exams. This is a vital service, for the poor cannot afford to be tutored by their teachers or to buy the notes of their professors. Brotherhood services compare very favorably with the services provided by the government, most of which are dismal.[11] In addition to fulfilling a religious obligation, the Brotherhood's welfare services provide yet another hands-on opportunity for recruiting members and building a positive image of the Muslim Brotherhood as a caring organization capable of meeting the needs of the masses. The governments of the Middle East fail on both counts. Whether or not recipients of Brotherhood services show their gratitude by supporting its political activities is an open question. At the very least, the Brotherhood's welfare programs ensure that poor youth will have some chance of finding jobs in the government and the military, a potential resource should the occasion arise.

Political Activism

From a political perspective, the Muslim Brotherhood is best viewed as a very large and powerful pressure group that is engaged in a relentless battle to force the secular governments of the Muslim world to rule in accordance with Islamic law. The Brotherhood's political agenda is most fully developed in Egypt, a country in which it is allowed to operate as a religious organization. The Egyptian constitution prohibits religious organizations from engaging in political activity, but that is a matter of little import. Egypt's elections are a farcical charade, and the Brotherhood merely uses one of Egypt's meaningless opposition parties to serve as a front for its activities. Many Brotherhood candidates also run for parliament as independents and, despite government opposition, scored dazzling victories in the first or primary round of Egypt's 2000 parliamentary elections. So dazzling was the Brotherhood's success, in fact, that the police openly prevented supporters of the Brotherhood from casting their ballots in the second round of the elections.

The fiasco was repeated in the 2005 elections with the Brotherhood having captured eighty-eight seats in the People's Assembly before massive police brutality and vote rigging stemmed the Brotherhood tide. In reality, the Brotherhood had not attempted to control the People's Assembly, contesting only 150 seats in the 454-seat assembly. A serious effort to control the People's Assembly would have precipitated a brutal showdown with the ruling party if not civil war, something neither side wanted. The supreme guide, himself, noted that his purpose was to embarrass the Mubarak regime and make a mockery of its claims that Egypt was a humane democracy.[12] The message, however, was clear. If you allow a free vote, the Muslim Brotherhood will do very well.

All of this is part of the Brotherhood's strategy of biding its time while it pushes a corrupt and inept Mubarak regime ever closer to disaster.[13] Egypt's only serious opposition party, the Brotherhood's eighty-eight representatives use the assembly as a pulpit for airing their views to a national audience and publicizing the obvious flaws of the Mubarak regime. The Brotherhood's representation in the assembly is also divided into some twenty-five specialized committees that help it keep an eye on the government and oppose legislation that it considers "anti-Islamic." This is a powerful stick, for few of Egypt's parliamentarians want to be branded anti-Islamic. The Brotherhood might lack the power to pass legislation, but it clearly has the power to weaken the Mubarak regime from within. For the moment, that is sufficient. Perhaps it is preferable, for the Brotherhood gains support for its democratic posture yet bears none of the responsibility for solving Egypt's vast social and economic problems. Toward this end, it has begun to cooperate with opposition groups of all stripes, including the far left.[14] Does this mean that the Brotherhood supports democracy? According to the Brotherhood (Ikhwan),

> This depends on your definition of democracy. If democracy means that people decide who leads them, then the Ikhwan accept it. If it means that people can change the laws of Allah and follow what they wish to follow, then it is not acceptable. Ikhwan only accept to participate in such systems because more benefit will be achieved if they do, and more evil will be avoided. A little help is better than no help at all. . . . Ikhwan accept personal freedom within the limits of Islam. However, if by personal freedom to you means that Muslim women can wear shorts or Muslim men can do *Haram* [forbidden] stuff, then Ikhwan do not approve of that.[15]

The electoral process is merely the tip of the Muslim Brotherhood's political agenda. By the mid-1990s, the Brotherhood was in control of sixteen of Egypt's eighteen main professional associations including those for lawyers, teachers, engineers, and reporters. As Egyptian law allows only one major association for each profession, the Mubarak regime found itself in the embarrassing position of having to negotiate on all aspects of Egypt's professional life with an illegal organization.[16] The Brotherhood used its bargaining power with the government to win unparalleled economic, medical, and personal benefits for its members, victories that have extended its popularity and demonstrated its capacity to get things done. Most members of Egypt's professional associations are not brothers or sisters, but they know a good thing when they see it.

The government often annuls Muslim Brotherhood victories in association elections but to what avail? Repression only gives credibility to the victim and serves as further testimony to the oppressive nature of the Mubarak regime. Government efforts to purge brothers and sisters from the ranks of Egyptian teachers have had the same result. The Muslim Brotherhood has responded by upping the ante. Once inviolable, the government-controlled

General Federation of Trade Unions (GFTU), the only legal trade union in Egypt, has been targeted for takeover by the Brotherhood.[17] The challenge has also been blatant and direct, with the Brotherhood running candidates for the governing council of the GFTU under its own banner rather than following its customary practice of using surrogates. There is no chance of a Brotherhood victory, but it is one more step in the Brotherhood's relentless effort to strip away the government's facade of openness (democracy is too strong of a word) and to portray itself as the champion of honesty, efficiency, and human rights.

Particularly threatening to the Mubarak regime has been the Brotherhood's direct or indirect control of Egypt's student associations. Students in the Islamic world take to the street for the slightest provocation, making them the most volatile actors in the region's politics. If student protests show signs of promise, other groups join in. It is the students, however, who get things started. Husni Mubarak's ruling National Democratic Party has increased its efforts to gain a foothold among Egypt's university and high school students but with minimal success.

Recent student elections at the American University of Cairo (AUC), a bastion of secularism and moderation, provide an interesting study in the Brotherhood's tactics for taking over student governments. The process begins by forming a student branch of the Muslim Brotherhood consisting of known Brotherhood members and sympathizers. This accomplished, Muslim students displaying religious inclinations are recruited to join the organization. Membership in the Muslim Brotherhood is not necessary. With a critical mass in place and well financed by the parent Brotherhood, the student branch of the Brotherhood approaches aspiring candidates for the student presidency with a simple proposition. The Brotherhood will support one's candidacy in exchange for a program compatible with the Brotherhood's philosophy, a matter to be discussed with a religious leader in an off-campus mosque.[18] This is a very tempting proposition, for the student presidency is a prestigious position that promises a fast track to national politics. The Brotherhood's demands, moreover, are simple. All they ask of the candidates is that they work to create a moral environment at AUC, something that the Brotherhood finds lacking. Western-style pop singers are particularly offensive to the Brotherhood and are to be discouraged, as are similar fine arts programs. Once the candidate is selected, the student branch of the Brotherhood launches a vigorous people-to-people campaign that transforms the election from a contest of personalities and issues into a morality pageant that pits Islam and virtue against secularism and evil. The Internet plays a key role in this process. The Brotherhood doesn't always win, but subtle pressure to follow the Islamic way has been increased.[19]

Control of Egypt's professional associations, student unions, community organizations, and mosque complexes gives the Brotherhood control of the "street."[20] At a moment's notice, a signal from the Brotherhood can send demonstrators careening through the streets of Cairo and Egypt's other major cities. Cairo is the nerve center of Egypt, and to disrupt Cairo is to disrupt Egypt. The Brotherhood does so frequently, usually to oppose Israeli suppression of the Palestinians or U.S. policies in Iraq.

The Muslim Brotherhood is not the only group involved in the anti-American demonstrations, many of which begin as spontaneous explosions of frustration and anger. The Brotherhood, however, has been an active participant in the demonstrations, and its ability to inflame the street represents a constant threat to the Mubarak regime.

Less visible are the Brotherhood's relentless efforts to extend its "fifth column" of religious activists within the military and the security services. All pretenses aside, Egypt remains a military regime dependent on military support for its survival. The regime knows that the Brotherhood and the jihadists enjoy broad support in the military, a fact that makes them reluctant to use the regular army against either. Rather, most anti-Brotherhood and anti-jihadist activities are carried out by special security forces in which the Mubarak regime has greater confidence. Even so, the Brotherhood's support within the military provides a measure of security from government repression.

Can the Muslim Brotherhood Be a Source of Stability?

The Muslim Brotherhood considers violence to be counterproductive, arguing that it only serves to kill innocent people and to punish Muslim populations by crippling the economy. The jihadist attacks during the 1980s and 1990s, it notes, devastated Egypt's tourist industry, leaving tens of thousands without work. The Brotherhood also condemns jihadist violence for giving the Islamic movement a bad name and for giving Islam's enemies a pretext to launch a new crusade against Islam. The Muslim Brotherhood cautions that governments are more powerful than the Islamic groups. Little, accordingly, is to be gained by fighting a war that will cripple the Islamic movement and ruin its opportunity to achieve an Islamic state by peaceful means. This said, there can be little doubt that the Brotherhood's capacity for violence remains. Although the Brotherhood denies that it possessed an armed militia, a December 2006 military demonstration by Brotherhood students at Al-Azhar University was seized upon by the Egyptian press as evidence that the Brotherhood possesses an increasingly active military wing. The students said that their demonstration was merely a skit to show support for the Palestinians.[21]

Reflecting its standoff with the Egyptian government, the Brotherhood has offered the Mubarak regime a simple deal: Allow us to promote our religious agenda in a peaceful manner, and we will allow you to rule. Government politicians will enjoy all the perks of office and the wealth that accrues to the ruling class; the Brotherhood will help Egypt become a more religious state. The alternative, the Brotherhood implies, is a return to the jihadist violence of the 1980s and 1990s. The deal is a very tempting one. Cooperation with the Brotherhood would allow the Mubarak regime to pretend that it supports Islam. It would also allay accusations that Mubarak is a puppet of the United States. More importantly, giving the Muslim Brotherhood broader scope for its activities would isolate the jihadists by providing more moderate Muslims with a legitimate outlet for their concerns. This, of course, is the rub. The Mubarak regime probably fears a broad-based Islamic party more than it fears the jihadists.

As long as its cat and mouse game with the Muslim Brotherhood stays within reasonable limits, the government turns a blind eye to most Brotherhood activities. The line between reasonable and unacceptable is fine, and much depends upon how nervous the Mubarak regime is at any given moment and how much pressure it is receiving from Washington to appear more democratic. Prior to Egypt's 2006 parliamentary elections, the United States was attempting to portray itself as the champion of democracy in the Middle East and asked the Egyptians to play along. The outpouring of support for the Brotherhood dampened the democratic zeal of both, and the United States remained silent as Egyptian security forces unleashed their clubs and rifle butts on Brotherhood supporters. Arrests of Brotherhood leaders increased apace, but the supreme guide remained unperturbed, noting that twenty thousand members of the Brotherhood have been arrested over the past decade or so without slowing its advance. He also issued a stern warning to the United States, which he condemns for giving the green light for the arrests. "Do you really think that if the supreme guide is gone the Brotherhood will be affected? . . . We are deeply rooted and these insolent security actions do not affect us. . . . The Brotherhood is a huge organization, it is not 100 or 10,000. We are present everywhere, in tens of thousands, and nothing will stop us from pursuing our goals and our plans." And when asked if the Brotherhood's goal was an Islamic state, he responded demurely, "Our objective is to bring up our children on the right path. An Islamic state can't be established in the absence of freedoms. First we demand freedom and when we have freedom the nation will choose the constitution it sees fit."[22]

Are these mind games? Perhaps, but it is a worried government that is forced to use clubs and rifle butts to prevent a fair election.

The deal that the Brotherhood is offering Mubarak was accepted by King Hussein of Jordan during the 1950s.[23] The young king, then a teenager, used the Brotherhood to counter the leftists and Palestinian radicals intent on overthrowing his shaky monarchy. The king prospered, as did the Muslim Brotherhood. The United States, however, is now putting increasing pressure on Jordan's new king, Abdullah II, to curtail the Brotherhood's support for the intifada in Palestine. This is a tall order, for approximately 70 percent of Jordan's population is of Palestinian origin, and support for the Palestinian uprising is a key element in the Brotherhood's program. The line between the Muslim Brotherhood and Hamas in Jordan is also blurred. The Palestinian resistance group, Hamas, was founded as the military wing of the Jordanian Muslim Brotherhood, and the Brotherhood has been instrumental in brokering tensions between Hamas and the king.

Strong relations were also forged between the Muslim Brotherhood and the government of Yemen during the 1990s, thanks in large part to the Brotherhood's role in easing tensions between Yemen and Saudi Arabia in the aftermath of Iraq's invasion of Kuwait.[24] Much to the irritation of the Saudis, Yemen had supported Saddam Hussein, perhaps believing that the Saudi monarchy would be the next to fall. It did not, and Yemeni workers were expelled from Saudi Arabia. Saudi Arabia also supported a rebellion that erupted in the south of Yemen a few years later. The Brotherhood's intercession eased both crises, and the Brotherhood became a legal political organization operating under the name of the Yemeni Society for Reform.[25] Rather than opposing the government, the Brotherhood became its supporter. The Yemeni government has also mended its ways and is now an ally of the United States in its struggle against the jihadists. Whether it can convince the United States that the Brotherhood is a peaceful organization remains to be seen.

Syria, by contrast, condemns the Muslim Brotherhood as a terrorist organization. The Brotherhood launched a campaign of terror in Syria during the early 1980s that showed signs of becoming a full-scale civil war. The Syrian government unleashed a military assault on the Brotherhood, slaughtering as many as thirty thousand of its members. More moderate estimates place the figure at ten thousand. In any case, the carnage was horrendous. Membership in the Brotherhood became a crime punishable by death. The leadership of the Brotherhood in Syria fled to Jordan, Germany, and Iraq, as did most of its active members.

The Brotherhood retaliated by launching terrorist strikes into Syria during the mid-1980s, but the Jordan-German branch of the Syrian Brotherhood has since fallen in line with the nonviolent position of the Cairo leadership. Indeed, it has applied to the Syrian regime for permission to return to Syria as a cooperating partner of the ruling Ba'ath party. The Syrian regime has thus far rejected the Brotherhood's offer, the key sticking point being the Brotherhood's refusal to acknowledge its responsibility for the events leading up to the 1982 massacres. In the view of the leadership of the Syrian Brotherhood, it was the government that had created the crisis by attempting to liquidate the Brotherhood.[26] In the meantime, the Brotherhood has formed an alliance with a former Syria vice president in the hopes of overthrowing the Assad regime. Does it bother the Brotherhood to join arms with a former leader that supported efforts to exterminate them? It does not bother the Brotherhood at all. The important thing is to place its members in positions of power. It can do this by working with the regime or by attempting to overthrow it. It currently appears to be doing both simultaneously. The United States, for its part, appears to be supporting the Brotherhood's efforts to overthrow an Assad regime that it accuses of sponsoring terror. Middle East politics makes strange bedfellows. One cannot predict how long the Assad regime will survive in Syria, but it is a sure bet that Brotherhood will be around to help bury it.

The same practice of making odious alliances for the sake of gaining political influence is being played out in Iraq.[27] Although hostile to the U.S. occupation, the Iraqi Islamic Party, a Brotherhood affiliate, has participated in the Iraqi government pieced together by the United States. Its position is logical. It shares the fundamentalist goals of the ruling Shi'a elite and can represent the interests of Iraq's Sunni minority better than either the former Ba'athist supporters of Saddam Hussein or the jihadists. Once again, the United States and the Brotherhood find themselves on the same side. Much the same is true throughout the Middle East including Libya and Yemen.

The Israelis are uneasy about Washington's backdoor flirtations with the Muslim Brotherhood, and well they should be. Hamas, the Palestinian branch of the Muslim Brotherhood, now represents the core of the Palestinian resistance to Israeli occupation of the West Bank and Gaza Strip. Reflecting its Brotherhood heritage, Hamas has refused to accept Israel's right to maintain a Jewish state on Islamic land. This does not necessarily mean that the two parties cannot coexist. This topic will be discussed more fully in chapter 4.

How the Muslim Brotherhood Is Organized

The far flung activities of the Brotherhood are guided by an organizational apparatus consisting of a supreme guide, a deputy supreme guide, a thirteen-to fifteen-member guidance bureau responsible for formulating policy, a larger consultative council, and some twenty-five specialized committees.[28] The Islamic jurisprudence (*fiqh*) committee consists of trusted Muslim scholars and ensures that the Brotherhood's policies are in line with the Koran and Sunna. Other committees guide the teaching, preaching, welfare, and political activities of the Brotherhood, and a large legal staff defends Brothers who run afoul of the law in the execution of their religious duties. Less visible committees presumably guide the covert activities of the Brotherhood, but these are matters of great secrecy.

Supreme guides have traditionally been elected for life, but Joseph Nada notes that this has now been changed. Incoming supreme guides will be limited to two six-year terms in office.[29] For the moment, the point is largely moot. Ma'moun El-Hodeibi was eighty-three at the time of his election to the position in 2002, having served as deputy supreme guide since 1986. He passed away fourteen months later and was succeeded on January 14, 2004, by Mohammed Mahdi Akef, age seventy-five. Both were selected by the fifteen or so members of the guidance bureau, most of whom were longtime loyalists of the same generation. Clearly, the Muslim Brotherhood is controlled by a narrow circle of very old men.

Akef, by way of background, joined the Brotherhood in 1950 at age twenty-two. Four years later, he was accused of plotting the assassination of then president Abdul Nasser and spent the next twenty years in prison. After his release, he spent time in Saudi Arabia, Germany, and the United States and was particularly active in establishing youth camps. Returning to Egypt in 1987, Akef gained a seat in parliament and was placed in charge of the Muslim Brotherhood's youth and professional organizations.[30]

The supreme guide is charismatic (divinely guided) and, according to the Brotherhood's critics, brooks no contradiction. Rather, he serves as a source of imitation and emulation. Bylaws exist, but they give the supreme guide sweeping powers to appoint "commissioners" and initiate policy as he sees fit. Joseph Nada's appointment as commissioner for international political affairs was made by the supreme guide alone, and his appointment was not well known within the ranks of the Muslim Brotherhood. IslamOnline.com, a major website sympathetic to the Brotherhood, denied that such an appointment had ever been made. Memos of Nada's appointment appeared in 2002 but were unsigned.

Also little known was Nada's peace negotiations with the Mubarak government and his efforts to mediate tensions between Iran and Saudi Arabia following the Iranian Revolution. Similar mediation was carried out between the Iraqis and the Kuwaitis during the Iraqi occupation of Kuwait. Make no mistake, the Brotherhood carries considerable clout within the Islamic world.

When an incredulous *Al Jazeera* interviewer asked, "You mean that only the supreme guide knew of the missions that you were charged with and that the rest of the Muslim Brotherhood didn't know?" Nada responded, "That is his right according to the bylaws. It is he who deals with issues as they arise and it is often essential that no one knows about it until the appropriate time or that only specific people know about it."[31]

The authoritarian leadership style of the Muslim Brotherhood is typical of secret societies, but it has a price. The dictatorship of the aged has led to accusations that the Brotherhood's leadership has lost touch with the demands of the present. Some believe that the supreme guide is too old to carry out his responsibilities effectively. The election of a new supreme guide often brings rumors of rebellion by the younger, midlevel leadership of the Brotherhood, most of whom are now well into middle age.

Generational tensions, however, are more than a matter of age. The younger midlevel leaders are those university activists who played a crucial role in reviving the Muslim Brotherhood in the post-Nasser era. Now well represented in the ranks of doctors, engineers, and other professionals, it is they who claim responsibility for the Brotherhood's recent electoral successes as well as its stunning success in seizing control of Egypt's professional associations.[32] They also feel that they are more in touch with the realities of the modern world than the old guard and that their time for power has come. Rumors of tensions within the Brotherhood are denied by all parties. Nada, clearly one of the old guard, dodged the issue in his *Al Jazeera* interviews, suggesting that tensions are part of all organizations.[33] He also suggested that the younger generation, now in its fifties and sixties, lacked the discipline of its elders.[34]

The ambiguity surrounding the Brotherhood's operations is not difficult to understand. The Brotherhood is a secret organization, and most of its activities are technically illegal. The Middle East is a volatile region, and a sudden change in the political climate could result in a brutal crackdown on the Brotherhood reminiscent of the purges of the Nasser era. Governmental surveillance of the Brotherhood is pervasive, and its lawyers are very busy people.

Some insight into the Muslim Brotherhood's finances were also provided by Nada, who, in addition to being the Brotherhood's commissioner of international political affairs, is a Swiss industrial magnate and Islamic banker accused by the United States of financing a broad array of radical Islamic groups, including the Muslim Brotherhood. When asked about accusations in *Time* and *Newsweek* that his bank was the "collection box," Nada simply replied that he did not believe that the Brotherhood had any money to deposit. When asked by *Al Jazeera* how a group such as the Brotherhood could operate without money, he replied that the organization relied on its members and did not take money from governments or outside sources: "As I told you before, each member operates independently, doing what he can, maybe spending his money or his energies and the energies of his children. Maybe he travels, organizes meetings, prints books, performs free surgery in a Muslim Brotherhood clinic or tutors students. Giving services is the same as giving money."[35]

This, of course, begged the question, for many Brotherhood members are extremely wealthy, especially those from the Gulf. Nada also failed to mention that the Muslim Brotherhood has its own businesses and that its members have great influence in the region's large, benevolent associations that do collect huge amounts of money for religious purposes. This, too, is a gray area in which information is difficult to come by.[36]

The International Muslim Brotherhood

There is only one supreme guide, and he resides in Cairo. Branches of the Brotherhood in other countries are headed by a general secretary and a local consultative council. The Brotherhood reportedly developed an international network in the 1970s, but Joseph Nada, the Muslim Brotherhood's commissioner for international political affairs, debunked suggestions that he headed such an organization and derided its very existence. The fiction of a "network," according to Nada, was fabricated by the international security services in order to link the Brotherhood to the terrorist activities of the jihadists. His six-part interview with the *Al Jazeera* television network, however, did note that regional representatives of the Brotherhood meet frequently to ensure that they are pursuing a common policy and to discuss mutual concerns, the most pressing of which are U.S. accusations that the Muslim Brotherhood is a terrorist organization. When the need arises, the country and regional representatives meet on a broader continental basis.[37] Regardless, the supreme guide and the guidance bureau shape the key elements of Brotherhood policy from their offices in Cairo, leaving it to the branches to work out the details in accordance with their particular needs and circumstances.

While Nada might debunk the fiction of an international Muslim Brotherhood network, Israelis and American security services accuse the Muslim Brotherhood of sponsoring a broad network of pan-Islamic organizations in Europe including the Islamic Society of Germany, the Union of Islamic Organizations in France, and the Union of Islamic Communities and Organizations in Italy.[38] These and their counterparts in other European countries serve as an umbrella organization for a variety of local Islamic centers.

Country networks, in turn, are linked by a variety of pan-European organizations such as the Federation of Islamic Organizations in Europe and its youth branch, the World Assembly of Muslim Youth. Islamic youth in Europe are also integrated via the more moderate Forum of European Muslim Youth and Student Organizations, which claims to represent groups in some twenty-six European countries.[39]

It is not clear that any of the above organizations are wholly owned subsidiaries of the Muslim Brotherhood, but the Brotherhood is deeply involved as is, in many cases, the Saudi government. The Saudi regime bases its legitimacy on its role as the guardian of Islam and finances Islamic organizations throughout the world, most of which have a clear Wahhabi hue. The Brotherhood is moderate by comparison.

American and Israeli sources attribute the spread of Islamic organizations in Europe, many of which serve on government councils, to the naivety of European leaders.[40] European leaders scoff at the accusation that they are naive or soft on Muslim extremism. They well understand that the Muslim community is an essential part of Europe and must be better integrated into European political life if violence and extremism are to be avoided.

Whatever the merits of the above argument, there can be little doubt that European Muslims will be increasingly organized in the years to come. They have no other option if they are to survive economically and politically. As things currently stand, the growing organization of Europe's Muslims has inclined European leaders to take a far more moderate view of the Muslim Brotherhood and other radical-moderate groups than the United States or Israel. They are also far more inclined to support the Palestinian cause than either the United States or Israel. This said, the growing organization of European Muslims has not been adequate to break the cycle of poverty and fear that besets much of the Muslim community. Indeed, the Muslim and non-Muslim communities of Europe appear to be growing farther apart.[41]

The Muslim Brotherhood's Strengths and Vulnerabilities

The "moderate" approach of the Muslim Brotherhood has enabled it to appeal to a broad range of Muslims who, while supporting a strong role for religion in political life, fear the violence and extremism of the jihadists. The moderate face of the Brotherhood also makes it less threatening to protest voters intent on registering their profound displeasure with the corruption and oppression of secular governments in the Muslim world. Protest votes are certainly part of the reason for the dazzling success of Muslim parties in recent years.

Numbers also translate into power, and governments in the region think long and hard before they challenge the Brotherhood. In all probability, serious efforts to uproot the Muslim Brotherhood in Egypt, Jordan, or the Sudan would result in an Algerian-style civil war, a prospect that chills even the boldest of Arab leaders. It certainly chills President Mubarak. Arrests were made, but most are symbolic and temporary. The Brotherhood, accordingly, enjoys considerable freedom in pursuing Islamic reform as long as it stops short of challenging the power of the regime. Perhaps justifiably, the Brotherhood and parallel organizations claim victory for the growing strength of the Islamic movement. Secular regimes still reign, but the power of moderate Islamic groups continues to reach new heights throughout the Muslim world. Patience has its rewards.

The Muslim Brotherhood also benefits from its flexibility. Unlike the jihadists, the Brotherhood is not locked into an all or nothing strategy of violence that unnecessarily provokes the animosity of secular governments. Rather, it can adapt its policies to fit the needs of the situation, biding its time while it builds a foundation for eventual victory. In much the same manner, all Muslims, including Shi'a, are welcome to join the organization as along as they are willing to work toward the establishment of an Islamic state within the framework of Brotherhood guidelines. God can deal with the sinners and sort out the sectarian conflicts once the goal of an Islamic state has been achieved.

The jihadists, for their part, are scathing in their critique of the Muslim Brotherhood. Flexibility and patience, from the jihadist perspective, are merely excuses for doing nothing. "Where is the progress toward an Islamic state?" the jihadists ask. They can find none. On the contrary, they condemn the Brotherhood's strategy of cooperation for perpetuating secular regimes by "taking the heat off" and making them appear Islamic in the eyes of the public. In the process, corruption and immorality have embedded themselves ever deeper in Islamic society.

The jihadists also scoff at the Muslim Brotherhood's claim that radical Islam is too weak to challenge the military might of the secular regimes. The Shah of Iran, they note, claimed to have the fifth-largest army in the world when his regime collapsed without a whimper in the face of the Ayatollah Khomeini. That army, moreover, was trained by the United States and armed with the latest American weaponry but to no avail. Military might, the jihadists proclaim, cannot save corrupt apostates who have lost touch with their populations. The Iranian soldiers did not fight to save the Shah, and the soldiers of the Islamic world will not fight to save their corrupt and godless masters. Most soldiers are good Muslims, and they will join the revolution.[42]

The jihadist critique of the Brotherhood also contains a number of practical elements. Flexibility, according to the jihadists, equates with a lack of focus. The Brotherhood speaks of guidelines, but the jihadists see few guidelines other than a commitment to cooperate with corrupt regimes in the vain hope of establishing an Islamic state. With everyone doing their own thing, from the jihadist perspective, the goal of an Islamic state gets lost in the shuffle.

The Brotherhood's emphasis on size, from the jihadist perspective, has had the same result. By attempting to gather the vast array of Islamic currents into a single organization, the Brotherhood finds itself in the impossible position of trying to please everyone. The result is stagnation and the defection of the most dedicated members of the organization. The Brotherhood, in the view of the jihadists, has become nothing more than a huge bureaucracy, the zeal of its members being sapped by petty concerns of status and authority.

Perhaps the most telling item in the jihadist critique is its accusation that the Muslim Brotherhood is soft on the Shi'a. By embracing the Shi'a, the jihadists charge, the Brotherhood is giving tacit approval of the Shi'a heresy. The Koran, and the Sunna, say nothing of Hidden Imams or ayatollahs. These are all embellishments that have diverted Islam from its true course and cannot conceivably be part of an Islamic state based on the Koran and the Sunna.

In addition to the jihadist critique of the Brotherhood, we would note that the Brotherhood finds itself in competition with the jihadists for the hearts and minds of a large portion of the Middle East's population. Continued moderation threatens defection to the jihadists, while increased radicalism threatens reprisals by the government. The fine line that the Brotherhood has pursued in recent decades is becoming increasingly difficult to walk as the distance between the governments of the Islamic world and their populations continues to broaden.

What is the truth? Is the Muslim Brotherhood a vast octopus that is gradually sapping the will of the secular governments to resist the Islamic movement, or is it, as the jihadists maintain, a vast moribund bureaucracy that has lost its capacity for effective action? Is the Muslim Brotherhood the militant revolutionary organization proclaimed by its credo, or does it undermine the Islamic movement with false hopes of finding a peaceful road to an Islamic state? If only we knew.

Notes

1. Clinia Nasser, "Fadlallah Condones Human Cloning: Cleric Asks 'Why Should Anyone Prohibit Something New?'" *Daily Star* (Lebanon), April 2, 2002, at www .dailystar.com.lb/04_03_02/art24.htm (accessed April 3, 2002).

2. Joseph Nada, "Interview with Joseph Nada, Commissioner of International

Political Affairs for the Muslim Brotherhood" [in Arabic], parts 1–6, by Ahmed Mansour of *Al Jazeera Online*, at www.aljazeera.net/ (accessed September 9, 2002)."

3. Muslim Brotherhood Movement Homepage, n.d., at www.ummah.net/ikhwan (accessed April 12, 2002).

4. "Russian Security Services Uncover Muslim Brotherhood Operations," *Islam Online*, October 18, 2002, at www.islamonline.com (accessed October 18, 2002); Ahmed Rashid, *Jihad: The Rise of Militant Islam in Central Asia* (New York: Penguin Books, 2002).

5. Muslim Brotherhood Movement Homepage.

6. Muslim Brotherhood Movement Homepage.

7. Paraphrased from the Muslim Brotherhood Movement Homepage.

8. Paraphrased from various Brotherhood documents.

9. Muslim Brotherhood Movement Homepage.

10. Muslim Brotherhood Movement Homepage.

11. Saad Eddin Ibrahim, *Egypt, Islam, and Democracy* (Cairo, Egypt: American University of Cairo Press, 1996).

12. Mohamed Akef, "Worried about the Future," *Al Ahram Weekly*, September 21–27, 2006, at http://weekly.ahram.org.eg/2006/813/eg5.htm (accessed September 21, 2006).

13. Kemal Habib, "The Islamists and the Political Transformation in Egypt" [in Arabic], *Al Jazeera*, October 10, 2005, at www.aljazeera.net/NR/exeres/30FF13F2-5090-4B5F-BE92 (accessed October 13, 2005).

14. Gamal Essam El-Din, "Brotherhood Changes Tack," *Al Ahram Weekly*, November 9–15, 2006, at http://weekly.ahram.org.eg/2006/819/eg5 (accessed November 10, 2006).

15. Muslim Brotherhood Movement Homepage, questions section, some punctuation modified.

16. Joel Campagna, "From Accommodation to Confrontation: The Muslim Brotherhood in the Mubarak Years," *Journal of International Affairs* 50, no. 1 (Summer 1996): 278–304.

17. "The Brotherhood in Egypt Considers Their Prohibition from Union Election Unacceptable" [in Arabic], *Al Arabiya*, November 13, 2006, at www.alarabiya.net/ (accessed November 13, 2006).

18. Karim El-Khashab, "A Mirror Image," *Al Ahram Weekly*, November 9–15, 2006, at http://weekly.ahram.org.eg/2006/819/eg5.htm (accessed November 10, 2006).

19. "The Brotherhood Penetrated the American University (of Cairo)" [in Arabic], *Rosa al Yousef*, May 20, 2006, at www.rosaonline.net/alphab/article.asp?view=1181 (accessed May 20, 2006).

20. Fysal Al-Qassem (moderator), "The Arab Street Panel Discussion" [in Arabic], *Al Jazeera*, April 16, 2002, at www.aljazeera.net/programs/op_direction/articles/2002/3/4-25-1.htm (accessed May 6, 2002); Abdullah Mahar, "Will the Islamic Street Explode after the Strike on Afghanistan?" [in Arabic], *Al Jazeera*, October 30, 2001; Interview with Abdullah Al Hamid II Sheikh Mubarak, Royal School of Islamic Jurisprudence, at www.aljazeera.net/programs/shareea/articles/2001.10/10_301.htm (accessed November 5, 2001).

21. Ismail Faraj, "The Guide of the Brotherhood Breaks His Silence and Reveals the Truth about the Militias at Al Azhar" [in Arabic], *Al Arabiya*, December 21, 2006, at www.alarabiya.net/ (accessed December 21, 2006); Gamal Essam El-Din, "Unmasked Condemnation," *Al Ahram Weekly*, December 21–27, 2006, at http://weekly.ahram.org.eg/2006/825/eg5 (accessed December 22, 2006).

22. Akef, "Worried about the Future."

23. Musa Keilani, *The Islamic Movement in Jordan* [in Arabic] (Amman, Jordan: Dar Al Bashir, 1990).

24. Joseph Nada, "Interview with Joseph Nada," part 4, August 28, 2002, at www.aljazeera.net/programs/century_witness/articles/2002/8/8-28-1.htm (accessed September 9, 2002).

25. Abdul Karim Qassem Saeed, *The Muslim Brotherhood and the Fundamentalist Movement in Yemen* (Cairo, Egypt: Madbouli, 1995).

26. Ali Sadr Eddin Al-Baiya'nooni, "The Political Future of the Muslim Brotherhood in Syria" [in Arabic], interviewed by Ahmed Mansour, *Al Jazeera*, November 29, 2001.

27. Hamid Al Majid Kawaisi, "The Program of the Muslim Brotherhood and the Reality of Relations between the Brotherhood and the [Arab] Regimes" [in Arabic], *Al Jazeera*, March 11, 2006 at www.aljazeera.net/NR/excres/16403B46-A856-4042-8564 (accessed March 11, 2006).

28. Amr El Choubaki, "Speaking in Tongues," *Al Ahram Weekly* 663 (November 6–12, 2003), at http://weekly.ahram.org.eg/print/2003/663//egl.htm (accessed November 8, 2003). For a more extensive review of the Brotherhood, see "Special File: The Muslim Brotherhood: Where Is It Headed?" [in Arabic], *Al Jazeera*, December 2, 2002, at www.aljazeera.net/in-depth/muslims_brothers/2002/12/12-2-18.htm (accessed December 5, 2002); Akef, "Worried about the Future."

29. Joseph Nada, "Responses to Testimony of Youssef Nada" [in Arabic], part 6 of six interviews by Ahmed Mansour of *Al Jazeera*, October 5, 2002, at www.aljazeera.net/programs/no_limites/articles/2002/10/10_5_1.htm (accessed October 13, 2002).

30. "Settling for Small Steps," *Al Ahram Weekly*, January 24, 2004, at http://weekly.ahram.org.eg/2004/674/eg5.htm (accessed January 24, 2004). Dates and activities vary from source to source.

31. Nada, "Responses to Testimony."

32. Amil Khan, "Brotherhood Faces Crisis," *Middle East Times*, no. 45, November 2002, at www.metimes.com/2K2/issue202-45/eg/brotherhood_faces_crisis.htm (accessed November 9, 2002).

33. Nada, "Interview with Joseph Nada," part 5, September 9, 2002, at www.aljazeera.net.programs/century_witness/articles/2002/9/9-5-1.htm (accessed September 9, 2002).

34. Nada, "Responses to Testimony."

35. Nada, "Interview with Joseph Nada," part 1, August 4, 2002, at www.aljazeera.net/prorams/century_witness/articles/2002/8/-7-1.htm (accessed September 9, 2002).

36. Abdu Zinah, "Funding the Brotherhood," *Asharq Al-Awsat*, February 3, 2007.

37. Nada, "Interview with Joseph Nada," part 1.

38. Lorenzo Vidino, "The Muslim Brotherhood's Conquest of Europe," *Middle East Quarterly* (Winter 2005), at www.meforum.org/article/687 (accessed March 7, 2006); Islamische Gemeinschaft Deutschland, Union des Organisations Islamiques de France, and Unione delle Comunita'ed Organizzazioni Islamiche; Fiammetta Venner, *OPA: l'Islam sur de Farnce, les ambitions de l'UOIF* (Paris: Calmann-Levy, 2005).

39. Vidino, "Muslim Brotherhood's Conquest."

40. Vidino, "Muslim Brotherhood's Conquest."

41. Rachid Al-Ganoush, "The Future Existence of Islam in Europe" [in Arabic], *Al Jazeera*, April 14, 2006, at www.aljazeera.net/NR/exeres/AC240E59-40EE-46FC-A997 (accessed April 14, 2006).

42. Tarig El Halim, "Views on the Transformation of the Islamic Movement in Egypt: The Muslim Brotherhood in Half a Century" [in Arabic], *Al Manar al Jadeed*, no. 15 (December 2001); Ahmed Qauwisi, "The Islamic Movement on the Doorstep of the Twenty-first Century" [in Arabic], *Al Manar al Jadeed*, no. 15 (December 2001).

4

Hamas

The Ascendance of Religious Extremism in the Arab-Israeli Conflict

H AMAS, THE LARGEST OF THE Palestinian Islamic extremist groups, began as an offshoot of the Palestinian wing of the Muslim Brotherhood. The Brotherhood had been established in Jerusalem and other major Palestinian cities by 1946, some two years before the 1948 Arab-Israeli War that culminated in the establishment of Israel. The Israelis won the war, but Jordanian and Iraqi forces occupied Jerusalem and the central regions of Palestine, an area generally referred to as the West Bank. Egypt retained the Gaza Strip, a narrow coastal plain adjacent to Egypt's Sinai Peninsula.

The emir of Transjordan annexed the West Bank in 1952 and renamed his small sheikhdom the Kingdom of Jordan. In the process, he annexed a large share of the Palestinian population. Some were the residents of the West Bank. Others were refugees. All became citizens of Jordan, and Jordan became a predominantly Palestinian country. The price of the annexation was the assassination of the Jordanian king, Abdullah I. He was followed in office by his grandson, Hussein, then a youth in his late teens. Attempted coup followed attempted coup, but the young king survived. He had three pillars of support: the British, loyal Jordanian tribes who feared a Palestinian takeover, and the Muslim Brotherhood. The king's alliance with the Brotherhood was a natural fit. Both were wedded to tradition, and both feared the leftists.

The situation changed dramatically with the crushing Arab defeat in the Arab-Israeli War of 1967, the Six Day War. The West Bank and Gaza, the remaining parcels of geographic Palestine, were now under Israeli occupation. Palestinians feared that they would be driven from their remaining lands and forced into a stateless diaspora of refugee camps and endless migration. The Arab states supported the Palestinian cause, but they did not want more Palestinian refugees.

To make matters worse, the Palestinians could no longer rely on Egypt or other Arab countries to liberate their land. If Palestine were to be liberated, it would be liberated by Palestinians. But how was this to be achieved? How were Palestinians to succeed where the Arab armies had failed? Answers to these questions are still being worked out. Suffice it to say that the Palestinians possessed two paths to their quest. The first was the Palestinian Liberation Organization (PLO), a loose confederation of leftist groups under the leadership of Yasir Arafat. The second choice was the Muslim Brotherhood.

The aftermath of the Six Day War found Arafat and the PLO in the ascendance. For much of the Arab world, the PLO was the government of the Palestinians. For Israel, the PLO was public enemy number 1. Israel feared PLO terror. It also feared that the international community would forcibly establish a PLO-led government in the Occupied Territories. The latter fear was greater than the former. Few Israelis worried much about the Muslim Brotherhood and its imitators. On the contrary, the Israelis encouraged the growth of the Brotherhood as a counterweight to Arafat and the PLO.[1] In retrospect, this was a mistake.

Hamas and the Muslim Brotherhood

The Palestinian branch of the Muslim Brotherhood feared that the ascendance of a very secular PLO would stifle the Islamic movement in Palestine, much as Nasser had stifled the Muslim Brotherhood in Egypt. Particularly disconcerting for the Palestinian Brotherhood was the PLO's military capacity. The PLO had its own militias; the Palestinian Brotherhood did not.

It was this reality that led to the emergence of Hamas as the military wing of the Palestinian Brotherhood.[2] The official date for the founding of Hamas is listed as 1987. In reality, the nucleus of Hamas was established much earlier and was simply called the military wing (*raa el askary*).[3] The original members of Hamas were all members of the Brotherhood, but with time, Hamas developed its own identity and its own membership. Membership in the Muslim Brotherhood was not a prerequisite—zeal was.

The line between the two movements has always been vague. The 1988 Covenant of the Islamic Resistance Movement, the official name of Hamas, referred to the organization as "one of the wings" of the Muslim Brotherhood in Palestine.[4] The Muslim Brotherhood, for its part, makes no bones about its support for Hamas. That support includes funding. It also includes the smuggling of weapons from Egypt into Gaza. Just how much control the Muslim Brotherhood exercises over Hamas is a matter of conjecture. At least for the moment, Hamas appears to be more concerned with liberating Palestine than its does with establishing an Islamic state in a Palestine with very secular traditions.

Hamas utilizes strategies similar to those of the Muslim Brotherhood to pursue its objectives: preaching, welfare, and politics. Teaching and preaching are the province of Hamas's mosques and schools, while its welfare services are coordinated by the Islamic Association, one of the nonmilitary branches of the organization. The Islamic Association maintains a wide variety of clinics, orphanages, and training centers, all of which are vital to the existence of a population characterized by extreme poverty.

The political agenda of Hamas traditionally focused on terrorist strikes against Israeli targets carried out by the Izz al-Din al-Qassam battalions, its military wing. Military politics has now been joined by electoral politics as Palestine moves toward statehood. The electoral wing of Hamas suggested that Hamas will transform itself from a resistance movement into a democratic political organization once a viable Palestinian state has been established. That remains a distant prospect but gives hope to those arguing that the Muslim Brotherhood and its offshoots are willing to operate within a democratic framework. The military wing of Hamas supports its political wing by promising a future of unrelenting terror if a Palestinian state is not forthcoming. It also assures that the power of Hamas will not be eclipsed by al-Fatah, the dominant group in the PLO and Hamas's major competitor for control of the Palestinian resistance.

Each of Hamas's diverse branches operates in relative independence, a strategy that provides it with maximum flexibility. Despite their relative autonomy, the line separating Hamas's diverse branches is often blurred. Hamas's welfare agencies, for example, play an active role in caring for the families of martyrs. Hamas's casualties have been heavy, and it is essential that martyrs, including suicide bombers, depart for heaven confident in the knowledge that their loved ones will be cared for. Families of martyrs, according to Israeli sources, receive an estimated one thousand dollars adjustment allowance, although the exact sum remains a matter of debate.[5] It would also be disingenuous to suggest that teaching, preaching, and welfare did not play a key role in Hamas electoral activities. Politics and religion do mix in the Middle East. It would be even more disingenuous to suggest that Hamas's electoral politics could be divorced from its military power. That might happen with time, but that time is not now.

Hamas, Al-Fatah, and the PLO

The emergence of Hamas coincided with bitter conflicts within the ranks of a PLO expelled from Lebanon and attempts to manage affairs in the Occupied Territories from its headquarters in Tunis. The core issue centered on how best to deal with Israeli occupation. While many in the PLO demanded a continuation of the PLO's commitment to the liberation of all of Palestine, Arafat and the dominant wing of his al-Fatah organization were moving toward a strategy of reconciliation that would see a Palestinian state in the West Bank and Gaza coexisting with Israel. At long last, a Palestinian state would be in place. While the radicals accused Arafat of selling out the Palestinian cause, Arafat and his supporters pleaded logic. An Israel supported by the United States was too strong to be defeated militarily. The crucial thing was to gain a foothold in Palestine. The next step would be dictated by circumstances. Saudi Arabia, Egypt, and Jordan, close allies of the United States, sided with Arafat and pushed for what would be called a two-state solution. Syria, Iraq, and Iran supported the radical elements in the PLO, and civil war loomed. Adding to the PLO's woes were mounting charges that Arafat was becoming a dictator and that his officials, most drawn from al-Fatah, had become a stifling bureaucracy as corrupt as it was ineffective.[6] Israel, for its part, was attempting to create an alternate leadership structure in the Occupied Territories consisting of mayors and local councils. The experiment proved ineffective, leaving the Palestinians with little in the way of coherent leadership.[7]

Such was the environment in mid-1987 when the West Bank and Gaza Strip erupted in violence. Called the intifada (ground rumbling), it pitted Palestinian youth wielding stones and Molotov cocktails against fully armed Israeli soldiers supported by tank battalions. The intifada was a largely spontaneous uprising by a Palestinian population pushed to despair by Israeli efforts to colonize what remained of their land. The Israelis countered that they were merely reclaiming the lands of ancient Israel and that the colonization of the territories occupied by the June War of 1967 was a "coming home."

There was no question of the Palestinians defeating the Israeli army, but neither was an increasingly demoralized Israeli army able to crush the uprising. Hamas had not started the uprising, but the intifada provided fertile ground for the newly proclaimed organization to establish itself as a major player in Palestinian politics. The more the intifada dragged on, the more powerful Hamas became. In many areas of the Occupied Territories, its health and welfare services provided the only lifeline available to a population teetering on the brink of disaster. Politics was not far behind.

The brutality of Israel's attempts to crush the Palestinian uprising dominated the international press, and world pressure for a settlement of the Palestinian problem grew apace. The peace process began in Madrid in 1991 and dragged on until 1993, when the world was stunned to learn that Yasir Arafat and Israeli prime minister Yitzhak Rabin had been conducting secret negotiations in Oslo, Norway. The negotiations were successful, and on September 13, 1993, Israel and the PLO signed a formal agreement calling for a negotiated Israeli withdrawal from large areas of the West Bank and Gaza Strip. The PLO, in return, pledged Palestinian recognition of Israel.[8] The details remained to be worked out, but the principle of exchanging land for peace had been accepted by both Israel and the PLO. It had not been accepted by either Hamas or an Israeli right intent on retaining the ancient lands of Judea and Samaria.

The world breathed a collective sigh of relief with the signing of the Oslo Accords and Rabin and Arafat were feted as heroes. It was all for naught. Rabin was assassinated by an Israeli fanatic in 1996 and replaced in office by a right-wing government headed by Binyamin Netanyahu. Netanyahu was intent on retaining as much as land in the Occupied Territories as possible and had little interest in dealing with Yasir Arafat. Netanyahu, like many Israelis, had long considered Arafat to be the mastermind of anti-Israeli terrorist activities. For most Israelis, there could be no peace with the Palestinians as long as Arafat remained in charge of the Palestinian Authority (PA).

Arafat and the PLO, for their part, were finding it difficult to make the transition from a revolutionary organization into a responsible government. Arafat, the president of the newly created PA, differed little from other Arab dictators. A corrupt PA bureaucracy, headed by members of Arafat's al-Fatah organization, served itself while providing few services to its subjects.[9] Arafat also lacked the ability to control the terrorist attacks of Hamas, the Islamic Jihad, and other resistance groups who had opposed the Oslo Accords. He also seemed unable to stop the resistance (terrorist) activities of his own al-Aqsa Brigades, the military wing of al-Fatah.

The gruesome pageant of terror, repression, and incompetence played into the hands of Hamas's leaders who cared for the needy while leading the charge against Israel. The more brutal the Israeli repression, the more the conflict between the Palestinians and Israelis was transformed from a war between the PLO and Israel into a war between Islam and Judaism. Israel would negotiate with a very secular PA that had recognized Israel's right to exist, but it swore that it would never negotiate with an Islamic extremist group intent on Israel's destruction.

Adding to the tension between the two sides was a growing realization that there would be a Palestinian state of some form or another. This realization unleashed an Israeli land grab designed to create "new realities" in the Occupied Territories. If and when the final settlement came, the lands under control of the PA would be little more than Indian reservations walled in by Jewish settlements.

By 2000, the Palestinian population could stand no more, and the Occupied Territories again erupted in anger. The al-Aqsa intifada, as the new uprising was called, no longer pitted stones and Molotov cocktails against Israeli tanks. Suicide bombers penetrated the heart of Israel wreaking a horrendous toll on Israeli civilians. Ariel Sharon, then prime minister of Israel, vowed that the Jewish state would never again be held hostage to Palestinian terror. If the Palestinians wanted war, they would have it. Israel was in a struggle for its existence, and the al-Aqsa intifada would be crushed by the full might of the Israeli military. There would be neither mercy nor negotiations until the terror stopped.

Sharon's popularity soared, but the terror did not stop. Sharon, the most brutal of Israeli generals, was also a realist and proclaimed that force alone could not solve the Palestinian problem, as the Israelis tended to refer to the intifada. By 2003, the West had also had enough of the violence. The United States and its European allies forged a "road map" that would result in a two-state solution to this most enduring of conflicts. A Palestinian state would evolve in Gaza and the West Bank, the exact boundaries of which would be determined by negotiations between Arafat and Sharon. The negotiations would begin once the terror had stopped.

Both sides agreed in principle to the road map, and the al-Aqsa intifada wound down. The terror did not stop and neither did Israeli repression. Arafat's headquarters, much of it reduced to rubble by Israeli strikes, had become a virtual prison. Each side blamed the other. Sharon called for the removal of Arafat as a condition for future negotiations. In the meantime, Sharon had embarked on the construction of a massive wall around Israel proper, most of it built on Palestinian land. He also chose New Year's Eve 2004 to proclaim that Israel would make a strategic disengagement from the Occupied Territories at a time and place of its own choosing. It would be they who determined the "final" boundaries of Israel. Israel would retain sustainable boundaries. The rest, presumably, would be ceded to the PA, but even that was not clear. Had Sharon intended to abandon the settlements in the Occupied Territories that were rapidly turning Palestinian areas into reservations? The construction of the security fence around Israel proper suggested that this was the case. What, then, would happen to the settlers? Could they remain? Would they be safe? The Americans applauded, but the Israeli right cried foul. Had Sharon, the champion of victory by force, capitulated to terror?

Hope for a negotiated settlement revived with the passing of Yasir Arafat in November of 2004. The longtime protagonist of Israel had outlived virtually every leader of his era. Mahmoud Abass, an Arafat lieutenant and leader of the moderate wing of al-Fatah, was duly elected president of the PA. Hamas had emerged as the equal of al-Fatah during the al-Aqsa intifada but chose not to field a candidate for the presidential elections in the name of national unity. While al-Fatah was in decline, Hamas was on the rise.

The world rejoiced with the election of a moderate Palestinian committed to a peaceful resolution of the Palestinian conflict. Israel had been recognized and terror disavowed. All that remained was negotiating the details, all of which had been passed over during previous fits of optimism. Not the least of these was determining the final borders of the new Palestinian state as well as the limits of its sovereignty. Would Israel withdraw to the borders prior to the June War of 1967? Would the new Palestinian state be allowed to develop a viable army or make alliances with Israel's enemies? Would Palestinians forced into exile by previous wars be allowed to return to Israel? Who would control water rights in this most parched of regions? Other questions also abounded. Would the new Abass government be able to meet the needs of a population that the United Nations declared to be a humanitarian crisis? Would it act in a responsible and democratic manner? Could it reel in Hamas and stop the terror? Indeed, could it reel in its own al-Aqsa Brigades? Would Israel exercise patience and allow Palestinians to return to their jobs in Israel?

The answer to all of the above questions was a resounding no. The more Israel and Abass's al-Fatah government fumbled the ball, the stronger Hamas became. Just how strong Hamas had become was evidenced by its dazzling victory in the parliamentary elections of 2005. Palestine, not yet a state, now had two voices. Abass and al-Fatah controlled the presidency, and Hamas controlled the government (prime minister and cabinet). But who was in charge? Who had the most power? No one was quite sure, and the rules were being made up as the situation evolved.

The Hamas Victory and Its Consequences

The Hamas victory was yet another victory for a surging Islamic movement that threatens to sweep all before it. But it was more than that. It was a defeat for those in Israel and the United States who hoped that the establishment of a symbolic Palestinian state was capable of quelling the violence that had reined for more than five decades. While the al-Fatah (PLO) organization had recognized Israel and sought an accommodation with the Jewish state, Hamas refused to do so. The gauntlet had been thrown down. The struggle

for the Holy Lands was no longer a struggle between the Israelis and a displaced Palestinian population. It was a test match between Islam and the
West that would determine the fate of the region.

Hamas's victory provided Israel and the United States with a critical
choice. They could either work with Hamas, in the hope of encouraging it
along the path of moderation, or they could attempt to crush it.

Shlomo Ben-Ami, a former Israeli foreign minister, argued that Israel
should allow Hamas to rule and enable it to be effective.[10] Hamas, he flatly
stated, is not al Qaeda. Rather, he viewed Hamas as a national independence
movement that had used terror to achieve well-defined national goals. Israeli
moderation, in his view, would encourage Hamas to engage in a meaningful
dialogue with Israel and bring an end to the madness of mutual destruction.
Recognition of Israel and the renouncement of terror would come through
negotiations. Democracy would be served, and if it took Hamas to bring
peace to Israel, so be it. Al-Fatah talked of peace, but it was all talk. If Hamas
failed, people would soon grow frustrated with Islamic rule. Hamas would
bear the blame and not Israel. Israel would also have reestablished itself as a
peaceful nation and gotten the world off of its back. Finally, Ben-Ami noted
that nothing else had worked and that Israel had no one else to negotiate
with. Israel could either work with Hamas or attempt to force the reinstate-
ment of an al-Fatah government that could neither stop terror nor enforce
its agreements.

The advantages of enabling Hamas were countered by an impressive list of
disadvantages. Many Israelis found it difficult to empower an organization
that remained dedicated to terror and the destruction of Israel. Indeed, the
Israeli ambassador to the United Nations viewed Hamas as part of a new
"axis of terror" that was sowing the seeds of the next world war.[11] Only
slightly less worrisome were Hamas's ties with the Muslim Brotherhood and
Hizbullah, both of which viewed Israel as a usurpation of Muslim lands.
While Hamas was not accused of links to al Qaeda, the point was moot. Terror is terror. Even if Hamas were willing to recognize Israel and renounce
terror, it would demand a return to the 1967 borders with minor adjustments. That price was too high for those Israelis intent on maintaining Jerusalem and large segments of the West Bank. Worrisome, too, was Israel's
ability to control a Hamas-dominated state. Israel had accepted the principle
of a Palestinian state, but it didn't want that state to pose a risk to Israeli
security.

The United States and Israel chose to crush Hamas. While the Israelis
bombed and attempted to starve the Palestinians into submission, the Americans froze Palestinian assets and imposed an economic blockade on the Pal-

estinian-controlled areas of the Gaza Strip, an area smaller than most of America's national parks.

President Abass and his al-Fatah organization joined the fray by attempting to sabotage Hamas at every turn. Particularly contentious was the struggle for control of the security forces. When President Abass refused to cede control of the security forces to the Hamas prime minister, the latter responded by creating his own security forces, some five thousand strong. Neither side possessed the money to pay government officials, including the members of the two security forces. While government officials filled the streets demanding payment of their salaries, the two security forces squared off for combat. The Palestinian press decried what were referred to as "unfortunate events" and President Abass threatened to dissolve the Hamas parliament and call for new elections. He backed down on both threats. To do so would have ignited a civil war. In the end, the Palestinians created a national unity government in which Hamas and al-Fatah shared power. The unity government refused to recognize Israel's right to exist and immediately faced the wrath of Israel. The United States, to Israel's dismay, equivocated on the issue. It wouldn't deal with Hamas, but discussions were held with less objectionable members of the coalition government. Many European countries welcomed the new government as a step in the right direction. Hamas had won, or so it seemed.

Tragically, it was all for naught. Tensions between Hamas and al-Fatah exploded into a virtual civil war as Hamas forces drove al-Fatah from the Gaza Strip. The latter consolidated its position in the West Bank, and Palestine had two governments. Israel and the United States imposed an economic boycott on Gaza designed to starve Hamas out of office. Simultaneously, they poured money into the West Bank in an effort to make al-Fatah appear effective. President Abass became the hero of Israel and the United States. But, was he the hero of the Palestinians? To date, there is little indication that al-Fatah can either rule the West Bank effectively or stop the terror even if Hamas is crushed. Hamas will not disappear, and Abass cannot rule without its support. Ironically, some Israeli security officials worry that al-Fatah will collapse and leave Hamas as the only game in town.

Hamas Looks to the Future:
Strengths, Weaknesses, and Strategies

So dire has the Palestinian situation become that few people are willing to look beyond the immediate future.[12]

Strengths

The core of Hamas's strength is a tight and secretive organizational structure patterned on that of the Muslim Brotherhood. Leaders are assassinated and arrested, but others rise to fill the gaps. That leadership, moreover, is young, dynamic, and battle tested. It is also supported by a large body of dedicated cadres fired by a powerful blend of Islamic zeal and Palestinian nationalism.

The same blend of Islamic zeal and Palestinian nationalism has enabled Hamas to develop a strong base of support within the Palestinian community. Even those Palestinians of moderate religious views applaud its welfare programs and reputation for dedication and honesty. Many also share its hard-line stance on peace with Israel. Hamas has signaled a willingness to negotiate a two-state solution with Israel, but it has also stressed that it will not be a one-sided peace dictated by Israel and the United States. If there is peace, it will be peace with dignity that provides a viable future for the Palestinians. It will also be a peace that stops short of recognizing Israel's right to exist. Hamas hints that this could change with time.

Hamas's strength is also based on a powerful network of external support that includes the Muslim Brotherhood, Hizbullah, Syria, Iran, and Jordan. The Jordanian monarchy has close ties with the United States and Israel, but both Hamas and the Muslim Brotherhood possess powerful Jordanian branches. One way or another, weapons and money pour into Gaza. Israel admits that it can't stop the smuggling. Weapons are also being developed within Gaza.[13]

Weaknesses and Vulnerabilities

The question is, can Hamas stay the course until the United States and Israel relent on their efforts to bring it to heel? The jury is still out on this question. For openers, Hamas has found it difficult to make the transition from a resistance organization to a ruling party. Criticizing a corrupt and inept al-Fatah government is far easier than solving the enormous problems of facing a Palestinian entity lacking either sovereignty or fixed boundaries. Part of the problem is a lack of personnel experienced in the art of governance. Hamas must also fight corruption and vengeance in its ranks. The temptations of power are far greater than those of opposition, and Hamas cadres who have sacrificed so much for so long are demanding the spoils of victory.

Added to the mix are the divisions within the Hamas leadership. A local political leadership is focused on finding pragmatic solutions to the urgent problems of a population teetering on the brink of disaster, while the supreme leadership located in Damascus is more concerned with grand strategy. Assassinations and exile disrupt operations and confuse authority patterns. They also exacerbate power struggles, patronage networks, and jurisdictional disputes, all of which have a rich tradition in Arab politics. Debates rage over the desirability of a truce with Israel, and it is not clear that local leadership has full control over its military wing.[14]

Blockades and bombings have also taken a horrendous toll among Palestinians, and it is not clear that the Palestinian population has the patience to wait for Hamas to force an Israeli capitation to its demands, not the least of which is Israel's evacuation of all of the West Bank and Gaza Strip.

The international situation is also a mixed bag. Israeli public opinion has hardened in the aftermath of its defeat in the 2006 Hizbullah war, and Israeli leaders have shown little inclination to make a deal with Hamas that is likely to be viewed as yet another defeat. Saudi Arabia and Egypt have also been critical of a Hamas movement that they find sympathetic to Iran and Hizbullah. The United States wants peace in Palestine but is reluctant to pressure Israel to do anything.

Finally, Hamas must decide whether it is a religious movement or a national resistance organization. Who is the main enemy, secularism or Israel? If Hamas is primarily a national resistance organization, what are the limits of its religious agenda? Does it aspire toward a more moral society, or does it aspire toward the creation of an Islamic state? How Hamas answers these questions will have a great deal to say about its ability to mobilize the Palestinian population that is deeply divided between religious and secular camps. Hamas cannot claim to speak for all Palestinians if it retains its religious persona.

Strategic Choices for Hamas

It is the above blend of strengths and vulnerabilities that will shape Hamas's choices during the next few years. Hamas's preferred strategy was to strengthen its domestic position and gain international acceptance by governing effectively in accordance with the Palestinian constitution. This accomplished, it would then have been in a position to push for a more Islamic government as circumstances dictated. This is the presumed strategy of the Muslim Brotherhood, and it is clearly the strategy of Turkey's ruling Justice and Development Party, a model of Islamic rule to be discussed in chapter 7. The civil war with al-Fatah might have ended this dream for now, but things change rapidly in the Middle East.

Faced with these realities, Hamas possesses a number of strategic choices, the first of which is staying the course in the face of almost insurmountable pressure from Israel, the United States, and al-Fatah. This choice has the benefit of demonstrating Hamas's resolve and bravery and is presumably supported by Hamas cadres reluctant to cede positions of power and influence. Hamas is also reluctant to lose face by backing down. Who knows when the chance to rule will come again?

The Muslim Brotherhood, Iran, Syria, and Hizbullah are also reluctant see Hamas accept defeat at the hands of the United States and Israel. In their view, the outcome of Hamas's struggle has profound regional significance and cannot be decided on local considerations alone. Time, so the argument goes, is on the side of Hamas. The United States is taking a beating in the world press and will soon see its resolve to crush Hamas erode. If the United States has any hope of stabilizing the Middle East, in their view, it has to give way on Palestine. This, as noted earlier, was the candid if painful conclusion of Tony Blair, the former British prime minister. It was equally the conclusion of the blue ribbon committee of leading Republican and Democratic politicians convened by President Bush to discuss American's options in Iraq.[15]

But can Hamas stay the course? Reports by the United Nations repeatedly warn that the Palestinian situation is becoming a human disaster. It is not the time for partisan politics. Hamas had succeeded by offering hope, and that is still its strongest card. Clinging to power at the price of human misery runs the risk of undermining the very source of its popular support.

Notes

1. Emile Sahliyeh, *In Search of Leadership* (Washington, D.C.: Brookings Institution, 1988).

2. Hamas is an acronym for the Covenant of the Islamic Resistance Movement (in Arabic).

3. Interviews by Monte Palmer, Jordan, 2000.

4. The Covenant of the Islamic Resistance Movement (Hamas), August 18, 1988, at www.mideastweb.org/hamas.htm (accessed May 6, 2002).

5. This is according to documents seized in an Israeli raid on Palestinian headquarters relating to the payment to al-Fatah activists. Al-Fatah is the main group in the PLO. No mention is made of payments to Hamas or jihad activists. "Fuad Shoubaki's Office's Handling of the 'Al Aqsa Martyrs Brigades' Request for Financial Aid," Arab Terrorism website, n.d., at www.jpost.com/ (accessed July 16, 2003).

6. Abdullah Belqaziz, *The PLO and the Intifada: Yield and Future* [in Arabic] (Beirut, Lebanon: Center for Arab Unity Studies, 2004).

7. Sahliyeh, *In Search of Leadership*.

8. "A Potential Turning Point," editorial, *Ha'aretz*, February 11, 2007, at www.haaretz.com/ (accessed February 11, 2007).

9. Belqaziz, *The PLO and the Intifada.*

10. For more on this topic, see *Jerusalem Post*, April 10, 2006, at www.jpost.com/ (accessed April 10, 2006); Schlomo Ben-Ami, *Scars of War, Wounds of Peace* (London: Oxford University Press, 2006).

11. *Jerusalem Post*, April 10, 2006; Ben-Ami, *Scars of War.*

12. Tassir Nasrallah, "The Crisis of National Unity Government" [in Arabic], *Al Jazeera*, March 10, 2006; Faraas Jabir, "The Internal Crisis" [in Arabic], *Al Ayyam*, November 25, 2006; Juwad Al-Basheiti, "Palestinians: Present Differences and the Absence of Legitimacy" [in Arabic], *Al Ayyam*, November 25, 2006.

13. Muhib Al-Nawati, "The Al-Aqsa Brigades: Revealing the Secret of Escalation of Their Attacks before the Palestinian Elections" [in Arabic], *Al-Arabiya*, January 21, 2006, at www.alarabiya.net/Articlep.aspxZP = 20475 (accessed January 22, 2006).

14. Saleh al Naeimi, "Who Makes the Decisions in Hamas?" *Asharq Al-Awsat*, March 3, 2007.

15. Jonathan Spyer, "Israel and the Iraq Study Group Reports," *Strategic Insights* 6, no. 2 (March 2007).

5

Hizbullah

A Tale of Three Countries

H IZBULLAH (PARTY OF GOD) is the Shi'a equivalent of the Muslim Brotherhood. It is best known for its activities in Lebanon and particularly
for its defeat of Israel in the Second Lebanon War (2006). The Lebanese
branch of Hizbullah, however, is only one component of a far larger Hizbullah movement. Hizbullah parties also exist among Shi'a populations in the
Persian Gulf (Saudi Arabia, Kuwait, and Bahrain), and Hizbullah-type organizations now dominate the government of Iraq. All are supported by Iran.
Hizbullah also ranks high on the U.S. list of terrorist organizations and has
recently become a major focal point of Federal Bureau of Investigation (FBI)
work within the United States.

Iran: The Center of the Hizbullah Movement

The saga of Hizbullah begins in 1979 with the victory of the Islamic Revolution in Iran. In one fell swoop, or so it seemed, the Shah of Iran, the king of
kings and the key to American strategy in the Middle East, was swept away
by a surge of Islamic emotion fired by the Ayatollah Khomeini.[1] Iran had
become the first Islamic theocracy of the modern era.

The picture, of course, is far more complex. It was not Islamic emotion
alone that had driven the Shah from the Peacock Throne but also decades of
despotism, megalomania, subservience to the United States, and unbridled
corruption. Iranians of all persuasions, secular as well as religious, recoiled
from the excesses of the Shah and drifted into the ranks of the revolutionaries. Not all aspired to an Islamic paradise, but it was the fundamentalists who

had seized the moment.[2] Others, including nationalists and communists, played along hoping to sort things out once the Shah was gone. Most perished in despair. The mighty army of the Shah, the fifth largest in the world according to his publicists, simply melted away as conscripts returned to their villages.

Flushed with victory, the Ayatollah Khomeini was determined to export his Islamic Revolution throughout the Middle East. It was God's will, and he was the agent of divine intervention. The task would not be easy. The Iranian economy was in shambles and its political system in chaos. Saudi Arabia, Iraq, and the Gulf sheikhdoms, all fearing rebellion among their Shi'a populations, plotted their counterattack. The United States, fearing for its domination of the region at risk, blessed their efforts. There could be no compromise. Conflict was inevitable.

The Ayatollah, however, was not without resources. His defeat of the Shah had been the stuff of miracles, inspiring awe throughout the Islamic world. Many Shi'a believed him to be the embodiment of the Hidden Imam.[3] Sunni fundamentalists viewed him as a source of inspiration if not a saint. Ayatollah's Khomeini's power to sway the masses appeared mightier than the sword. His rhetoric had proven more powerful than the arms of the Shah, and his followers believed that it would be more powerful than the arms of the United States. "God will provide" became his rallying cry to action.

Exporting the Islamic Revolution, however, required more than emotion. It also required a political organization capable of channeling mass emotions into action. Emotions fuel uprisings, but it is organizations that seize power. Ayatollah Khomeini's efforts to build an organizational base for his Islamic Revolution were twofold. First, revolutionary organizations were established among Shi'a populations in Lebanon, Iraq, and various Gulf sheikhdoms. They would later become part of a broader Hizbullah movement. Second, the Ayatollah forged alliances with jihadist groups in Egypt, Algeria, and other Sunni countries and provided them with money, weapons, and technical support. He would have preferred to incorporate the Sunni jihadists within the Hizbullah network, but the abiding tensions between the Shi'a and Sunni branches of Islam made that impossible. The Sunni jihadists were willing to accept aid from Iran, but most continued to view the Shi'a as heretics.

Iranian success in inspiring the Sunni jihadists was immediate. The Holy Mosque in Mecca was seized in 1979, Egypt's President Anwar Sadat was assassinated in 1981, and the Syrian branch of the Muslim Brotherhood launched an abortive war against the Syrian regime in 1982. The Islamic Revolution in Iran had been the call to action. Organizing efforts among the Shi'a proved less successful. An abortive 1981 coup in Bahrain was crushed with relative ease, and Saddam Hussein, the newly crowned leader of Iraq, slaughtered Shi'a leaders bold enough to challenge his authority. Clerics suspected of loyalty to Iran topped his list.[4]

Ayatollah Khomeini well understood the threat that his Islamic Revolution posed to the West and feared a counterattack by the United States and its regional allies. It came with a vengeance in September 1980, as Saddam Hussein, encouraged by Saudi Arabia and Kuwait, invaded Iran. The United States, then smarting from Iran's seizure of American hostages, encouraged the venture. Contrary to expectations, the war went poorly as an Iranian army composed largely of religious zealots held the Iraqis at bay. As described by Sandra Mackey,

> The *Basij* [popular militias] operated from nine thousand mosques, enrolling boys below eighteen, men above forty-five, and women. Primarily the zealous products of poor, devout families from rural areas, they volunteered for temporary duty in God's war between school terms or in the interim dividing one season's harvest and the next season's planting. At the front, a *Basij-i* could be identified by his tattered leftover uniform and mismatched boots (often picked up on the battlefield), the bright red or yellow headband stretched across his brow declaring God's or Ayatollah Khomeini's greatness, and the large, imitation brass key, the key to paradise, that hung around his neck. The *basiji-is* gained fame as human minesweepers in the massive assaults that characterized the 1982–1984 phase of the war. Boys a young as twelve, shaped by the fanaticism of the revolution, walked across minefields to clear the way for the advancing *Pasdaran* [irregular troops], followed by the army.[5]

The war raged for eight years, devastating both countries and blunting the focus of the Islamic Revolution. Iran, alone, probably suffered a million casualties. No one knows for sure. The picture was not much better in Iraq. Rare was the Iraqi family without the loss of a loved one. The economies of both countries were shattered. In one way or another, the United States gave aid to both sides, a policy that led to accusations that it had orchestrated their mutual annihilation. This was inaccurate. The United States helped guide Iraqi air strikes on Iran. In retrospect, this was a mistake.[6]

Lebanon: The Crown Jewel of the Hizbullah Movement

In contrast to Iraq and the Gulf, Lebanon proved to be fertile ground for Hizbullah. Suffering the fourth year of a brutal civil war between rival religious groups, this most beautiful of countries had dissolved into chaos. Lebanon's civil war, however, was more than a war among Lebanese. Palestinian militia controlled southern Lebanon, the heartland of Lebanon's Shi'a community. The Syrians, who viewed Lebanon as a breakaway province, used the war as an opportunity to reassert their control over the country and intervened first on one side and then the other. Israel, too, entered the fray, driving the Palestinians from southern Lebanon and occupying Beirut in 1982.

The brutal Israeli occupation of Beirut caused an irate President Reagan to demand an immediate Israeli withdrawal from the Lebanese capital. The Israelis capitulated and retreated to a forty-kilometer "security zone" that included much of predominantly Shi'a southern Lebanon. President Reagan sent U.S. troops to Beirut to stabilize Lebanon and protect Israel from Palestinian attacks. In retrospect, this, too, was a mistake. The Shi'a, for their part, had been liberated from the Palestinians only to find themselves oppressed by the Israelis.

It was in this environment that Mohammed Hussein Fadlallah, a senior Lebanese cleric who now ranks as one of the leading Shi'a scholars in the Islamic world, founded the Lebanese branch of the Hizbullah. The Shi'a already possessed a political organization, Amal, but it had lost much of its zeal, and its leaders seemed more interested in local politics than revolution.[7] Hizbullah, by contrast, was to be a revolutionary jihadist organization intent on establishing an Iranian-type Islamic republic among Lebanese Shi'a. In 1982, Iran dispatched some 1,500 revolutionary guards (armed religious radicals) to Lebanon to provide organizational support and train Hizbullah's militia.[8] Radical Shi'a deserted Amal in droves, firing the ranks of Hizbullah with their revolutionary zeal. Little love was lost between the two organizations, vows of fraternity often dissolving into bloodshed.[9]

The confrontation between Hizbullah and the allied peacekeepers was immediate. The American Embassy in Beirut was bombed in April 1983, resulting in the loss of seventeen American lives. The bombing of the Marine barracks followed six months later, killing 241 U.S. military personnel. Both attacks were attributed to Hizbullah, as was the rampage of kidnapping that would follow. Sayyed Hassan Nasrallah, the current secretary general of Hizbullah, denies Hizbullah's role in the carnage, noting that Hizbullah was not fully developed at the time. "At the time there were hundreds of small groups, and there were guns. The PLO went out of Lebanon, while its stores of weapons remained in Lebanon, stores which contained rockets, explosives, guns, and trained young men. . . . These small groups did not belong to Hizbullah."[10] In any case, the United States withdrew its troops from Lebanon. The Islamic Revolution had scored another victory. Its leaders had also become convinced that the United States would withdraw from the region in the face of terrorist attacks. Israelis, too, found Hizbullah attacks costly and soon reduced their security zone to a more manageable twenty-four kilometers. Stability returned to Lebanon in 1991 as its diverse religious factions agreed to a political formula that divided power more or less equally between the Christians, the Sunni, and the Shi'a.[11] The diverse militias were disarmed and merged into the Lebanese army. The sole exception was Hizbullah. The Party of God was allowed to keep its militia for the time being. Syria maintained the peace by stationing some thirty thousand troops in Lebanon. Israel continued to occupy a twenty-four-kilometer security zone in southern Lebanon and had more or less agreed to Syria's peacekeeping operations in Lebanon—better Syria than the Palestinians.

The scars of the Lebanese civil war ran deep. On the issue of the Israeli invasion, however, there was little conflict. The Israeli occupation was an affront to Lebanese pride and yet another humiliation of Arab and Islamic sensitivities. The issue, however, was tricky. The Lebanese army was too weak to confront the Israelis, and the Syrians were wary of becoming involved in another losing war with their stronger neighbor. Appeals to the United Nations and the United States had proven futile.

The Lebanese answer to the Israelis was Hizbullah. It was Shi'a lands that were under Israeli occupation, and Hizbullah's militia possessed all of the hallmarks of a modern army with the exception of air power. Its fighters were also the most motivated in Lebanon, willing to die for God and their sect. For ten long years, Hizbullah militias pounded Israeli positions in southern Lebanon with relentless daring. Hizbullah strategists well understood that the main military weakness of Israel was its reluctance to suffer the loss of Jewish life. The weakness was exploited relentlessly.

Volunteers flocked to Hizbullah's ranks as it donned the mantle of "national resistance." It remained a preeminently Shi'a organization, but martyrs came from all of Lebanon's major religions, Christianity included. Syria and Iran cheered from the sidelines, relishing Israeli discomfort as it struggled to extricate itself from what Israeli commentators were calling Israel's Vietnam. Ariel Sharon, then minister of defense, was vilified for getting Israel into the mess in the first place. Israel railed against Syria and Iran for arming Hizbullah and threatened to bomb Damascus if the attacks continued. Syria and Iran pleaded innocence. Hizbullah, they said, was Lebanese.

The struggle against Israel also enabled Hizbullah to establish a new international persona. Terrorism against peaceful nations, including the United States, was renounced. Hizbullah proclaimed that it was no longer a revolutionary terrorist organization but rather a movement of national liberation. Attacks on Israeli troops, they noted, were justified by international law. Israel was an aggressor country occupying Lebanese territory. Europe long recognized this metamorphosis, but the United States remained skeptical.

Israelis are not quick to admit defeat, but by 2000, they had had enough. The security zone that Israel had occupied since 1982 was evacuated with the exception of the Sheba Farms, a small area of southern Lebanon that had been controlled by Syria at the time of its occupation by Israeli forces. Israel maintained that it would only relinquish its control of the area as a part of a broader peace agreement with Syria. The United Nations supported the Israeli position, but Lebanon did not. The wound remained open.

The moment of Hizbullah's glory was equally a moment of crisis. The cause that had propelled Hizbullah into the limelight of Middle Eastern affairs had now vanished. With Israel defeated, Lebanon's power brokers began to view Hizbullah with suspicion. A Lebanon that had stoically accepted Israeli bombing as the price of liberation now saw its resolve weaken. Lebanon's economy was on the verge of collapse, and the country needed peace, not another war. Hizbullah's success had also propelled Israel closer to the negotiating table with Syria. The price of peace with Israel would be Syria's clampdown on Hizbullah. Syria had little else to offer. Iran was also becoming problematic. An ever-deepening economic crisis had forced the Islamic Republic to cut back on its financial (not military) support for Hizbullah. Iranian liberals, moreover, had gained control of the presidency and were more interested in rapprochement with the United States than in spreading world revolution. Hard-line clerics were still dominant, but change was in the air.

Hizbullah thus faced a triple challenge: (1) it needed a cause that would fire the passion of its adherents; (2) it needed to find a role in the revamped Lebanese political system; and (3) it needed to adjust to the possibility of a Syrian betrayal. A failure in any one of the three areas would have catastrophic effects on the future of the organization, the most immediate threat being that of a peace treaty between Israel and Syria.

Always resilient, Hizbullah would make Israel's assault on the Palestinian intifada the centerpiece of its program. The liberators of Lebanon would now devote themselves to the liberation of Jerusalem. A long record of cooperation with Hamas had already been established, and the Hizbullah strategy for attacking Israeli forces had increasingly become the model adopted by the Palestinians. In many ways, Palestine became a win-win situation for Hizbullah. Palestinian victories became Hizbullah victories while Palestinian losses justified greater militancy on the part of the Party of God. Israel played into the hands of Hizbullah by continuing to occupy the Sheba Farms. The official position on the Lebanese government was that Lebanon remained under Israeli occupation until the farms were evacuated. This was all the pretext that Hizbullah needed to continue its attacks on Israeli positions in the Sheba Farms.

The Israeli evacuation of southern Lebanon created an unstable situation in which Hizbullah guerillas and Israeli troops faced each other across the

Lebanese-Israeli border. This was Hizbullah territory, and the Lebanese army was neither involved nor consulted. The main border remained relatively calm, but Hizbullah seized upon Israeli control of the Sheba Farms to continue its struggle against the Israeli invader. A dangerous game of tit for tat ensued, with the Israelis jets bombing Hizbullah positions in the south and jangling Beirut's nerves with sonic booms and the destruction of an occasional power plant. Hizbullah responded with limited rocket attacks on Israeli settlements in the border region. Abductions were common on both sides. UN observers noted the violations but were helpless to halt them. And yet, there appeared to be an unspoken set of rules to this most dangerous of games, each side stopping short of provoking an all-out conflict.

The dangerous standoff between Hizbullah and Israel was incorporated in America's global war on terror ignited by the September 11 terrorist attacks on the United States. Iraq and Iran were branded charter members of President Bush's axis of evil, with Syria and Hizbullah, staunch allies of Iran, not far behind. Hizbullah, in the minds of the administration's neoconservative strategists, was a terrorist organization and would have to be destroyed. The situation, however, was not pressing, and the administration's core objective was the destruction of al Qaeda followed by Iraq, Iran, and Syria. With Iran and Syria destroyed, Hizbullah, a minor player, could be mopped up at Israel's leisure.

The overriding concerns of the war on terror stabilized the standoff between Israel and Hizbullah and raised hopes of a new Middle East free of terror and religious extremism. Defeat of Saddam Hussein in Iraq would transform this oil-rich country into a bastion of U.S. military power in the Gulf region and serve as the launching pad for an invasion of Iran if air strikes failed to topple the mullahs. The youthful and inexperienced president of Syria would be overthrown by internal forces and replaced by a democratic regime amenable to peace with Israel. Devoid of external support, Hizbullah would be lucky to survive as a political party, regardless of its Islamic ambitions. Lebanon's Christians and Sunni would see to that. It all seemed so simple. But, then, the best dreams always do.

Five years later, this sweetest of dreams had become the most hideous of nightmares. Hamas had won the 2005 Palestinian legislative elections and the United States, hopelessly bogged down in Iraq, had merely traded Saddam Hussein for a Shi'a regime beholden to Iran. The Islamic Republic, buoyed by the U.S. debacle, accelerated its pursuit of nuclear weapons and vowed to annihilate Israel.

It was in this environment that the controlled tit-for-tat game between Israel and Hizbullah came unraveled. Hizbullah abducted two Israeli soldiers, and Israel, supported by the United States, launched a devastating air assault on Hizbullah positions in southern Lebanon, Beirut's southern suburbs, and the Bekaa Valley. Roads, bridges, and power stations were destroyed. When air attacks proved insufficient to defeat Hizbullah, the Israel Defense Forces (IDF) pushed ever deeper into southern Lebanon. Hizbullah rockets pounded Israel, and Hizbullah missiles blew up Israeli tanks. Stunned by the deadly effectiveness of Hizbullah missiles, Israel became reluctant to send supply and rescue helicopters in the battle zones. The Israeli press added to Israeli despair by painting grizzly portraits of Israeli soldiers bleeding to death for lack of medical support while others ripped canteens from dead Hizbullah fighters in search for water. Israeli politics degenerated into a slug-fest of finger pointing and name calling, each blaming the other for the disas-ter. Key generals resigned, while the prime minister and minister of defense resisted overwhelming pressure to do so. Reports on what went wrong emerged from every quarter, and the United States and Israel exchanged barbed accusations over who pushed whom into the disastrous war. The United States denied culpability but could not deny its role in keeping the conflict alive long after it was obvious that the Israelis were losing.

This is not to suggest that Hizbullah emerged from the war unscathed. Hizbullah's victory was based on its ability to survive a withering Israeli attack. Israel was embarrassed and its image of invincibility further shattered, but Israel remained the stronger of the two parties. A new and improved war has been promised. The Party of God suffered heavy losses in men and mate-rial and was blamed for provoking a needless war that resulted in the destruc-tion of Lebanon's economy. Nasrallah, himself, admitted that he would not have ordered the kidnapping of the Israeli soldiers if he had anticipated the intensity of the Israeli attack.

Hizbullah's strategic position was weakened by the war. The Lebanese army assumed control over the border areas, and international observers strengthened their presence in the border region. Both were called on to dis-arm Hizbullah, but neither did so. The threat, however, remains. The war also pushed Lebanon to the brink of a civil war that could find Hizbullah squeezed between Israel on one side and a variety of Christian, Druz, and Sunni militias on the other. Such militias don't formally exist, but all major groups contain "reserve" militias. No one wants a civil war, but the topic has become the preoccupation of Lebanon's talk shows.

Finally, it could be argued that the Hizbullah was a victim of its own suc-cess. Israel acknowledged that it had severely underestimated the military capacity of Hizbullah. It will not do so a second time. Hizbullah's success also set off alarm bells in the United States, Egypt, Saudi Arabia, and Jordan, all of whom had hoped for an Israeli victory. All fear growing Shi'a and Ira-nian influence in the region, and there can be no doubt that their hostility will continue. Efforts to overthrow Syria's minority Shi'a government continue, and it is possible that the Syrian regime will attempt to save its own skin by selling out Hizbullah. The prospect of a war with Iran also looms. What will Hizbullah do then?

Whatever its problems, there can be no question that Hizbullah delivered the Israelis a stinging defeat and that it emerged from the war stronger than it entered it.[12] Those who hoped that Hizbullah would be disarmed were severely disappointed. It was not. Nor were its supply lines from Syria and Iran severed. Indeed, during the summer of 2007, one year after the war, Nasrallah proclaimed that Hizbullah possessed rockets that could reach all areas of Israel.[13] As a result of its strengthened position, Hizbullah has demanded some one-third of the seats in the cabinet, a position that would give it virtual veto power over the decisions of the Lebanese government, regardless of its composition. Nasrallah's international stature also soared with a columnist in Egypt's semiofficial newspaper, *Al Ahram*, calling him the dominant moral force in the region.[14] There can be no doubt that Hizbullah serves as the model for its Iraqi clones, a topic to be discussed next, as well as for Hamas and other Sunni extremist groups.

The United States and its allies, for their part, must now decide whether to coax Hizbullah toward moderation or continue their effort to destroy it. With these thoughts in mind we turn to an examination of Hizbullah's goals, organizational structure, strategies for achieving its goals, strengths, and weaknesses.

What Is Hizbullah and How Does It Operate?

First and foremost, Hizbullah is a Shi'a religious organization dedicated to the defense and propagation of Islam. Its ultimate goal is the establishment of Islamic governments in the Middle East and broader reaches of the Islamic world. Hizbullah is also a political party representing the interests of Lebanon's Shi'a community, a welfare agency providing a broad array of health and welfare services to Lebanon's poor, and a vast military machine that has proven its mettle by forcing the Israeli evacuation of southern Lebanon in 2000 and defeating the IDF in their brief war of 2006. Israel and the United States note that Hizbullah is also a base for terrorist groups attacking Israel. Hizbullah does not deny these charges, maintaining that liberation is not terrorism.

Hizbullah, moreover, is a business conglomerate replete with gas stations, construction companies, electric utilities, supermarkets, banks, and a television network. It is also probable that Hizbullah's commercial activities include drugs, counterfeiting, money laundering, and gunrunning, although such charges are heatedly denied by the Hizbullah leadership.[15] Finally, Hizbullah is a satellite of Iran's Islamic Revolution and an agent of Iranian foreign policy. Far from denying its links with Iran, the home page of Sayyed Hassan Nasrallah, the secretary general of Hizbullah (Lebanon), proclaims that he is "the representative of the Imam Khamenei, the Supreme Guide of Iran, in Lebanon."[16] It could not be otherwise, for Iran remains Hizbullah's chief supplier of money, weapons, and international support.

In reality, Hizbullah is all of the above and more. It is a state within a state that controls territory, defends its territory, and conducts foreign policy independently of the Lebanese government. More to the point, the Lebanese government finds it difficult to conduct its foreign policy without the agreement of Hizbullah. Hizbullah is also widely believed to have established an international network that extends from Europe to North and South America. Hizbullah denies the existence of such a network.

Much like the Muslim Brotherhood and Hamas, then, Hizbullah's activities cover the waterfront. They teach and preach, they provide a vast array of welfare services including hospitals and schools, and they are deeply involved in both domestic and regional politics. All contribute to Hizbullah's power base. The military wing is the foundation of the organization's power in Lebanon, while its schools, mosques, and media outlets fire the zeal of the faithful and provide a ready avenue of recruitment. Hizbullah's welfare agencies highlight both the compassion of the organization and the efficiency of its operations. The Lebanese government fails on both counts. They also provide opportunities for recruitment, although we could find few signs that gratitude led to increased membership in the organization. Hizbullah's commercial activities provide much-needed cash as well as employment for its cadres.

Estimates of Hizbullah's strength are difficult to come by, with estimates of its hard-core fighters ranging from a few hundred to thousands. In a recent interview with *Al Jazeera*, Hassan Nasrallah brushed aside the commentator's suggestion that Hizbullah had four thousand fighters willing to die for their cause, responding, "God is willing, we have a great number . . . with a martyrdom wish . . . and do not need to mention that number."[17] While the estimates of the organization's strength vary, it was sufficient to drive the Israelis from southern Lebanon. It also has some two hundred thousand dedicated members, all of whom have been thoroughly screened by the Hizbullah security services.[18]

This vast array of activities is guided by a religious elite headed by Sheik (religious scholar) Hassan Nasrallah, the secretary general of Hizbullah. Nasrallah is assisted by a guidance bureau (*shura* or council) including a judicial council that runs Hizbullah's legal system in the areas under its control, a jihad council devoted to the defense of Islam, a parliamentary council that manages Lebanese politics, and an executive council whose members oversee the day-to-day activities of its social, education, labor, finance, health, and information (propaganda) units. A separate Military and Security Apparatus reports directly to the secretary general. It, in turn, is divided into a security unit and an Islamic resistance unit. Each of the three regions of Lebanon in which Hizbullah operates also has a director. The regions, in turn, are divided into branches and groups. A very detailed discussion of Hizbullah's organizational structure is to be found in Ahmad Nizar Hamzeh's *In the Path of Hizbullah* (2004).

Most senior officials, in common with the Iranian political system, are clerics. Ayatollah Hussein Fadlallah, the founder and spiritual guide of Hizbullah, is one of the leading religious figures of the Shi'a world. For his followers, and they include Iraqis as well as Lebanese, his pronouncements are much like the pronouncements of the pope if not more so. Alas, he is no longer involved in running the organization.[19] This is because Nasrallah shifted his loyalty from Fadlallah to Ali Khamenei, the Spiritual Guide of Iran.[20] Fadlallah far surpasses Khamenei in Islamic jurisprudence, but not in politics. Indeed, Khamenei is so pleased with Nasrallah's performance that he has twice extended his three-year term of office and will undoubtedly do so in the future.[21] Let there be no mistake, it is Iran that has the final word on Hizbullah affairs.

This said, Iran is usually content with shaping the broad contours of Hizbullah activities. Hassan Nasrallah acknowledged the "guidance" role of Iran in a *Time* magazine interview:

> Khamenei is supreme spiritual leaders (*vali-e-faqih*), religious model. As is the duty of this model he does advise Hizballah as well as other Muslims, not just in private meetings but in public speeches. . . . What he told Hizballah is what he always says in his speeches: that the only route to freeing the occupied lands is jihad, that people must awaken and resist, and that the people of Palestine must be helped. . . . Muslims must follow these prescriptions, and we have such a religious belief.[22]

All of this takes money, huge amounts of money. Hizbullah's militia absorbs vast amounts of money, as do its welfare and service programs. Activists also have to be paid and the families of martyrs cared for. Traditionally, Iran supplied Hizbullah with weapons and footed the bill for its social service network. Iran's economic problems have now become so severe that it can no longer play that role. Arms continue to arrive, but Hizbullah has been increasingly forced to rely on its own resources for the remainder of its operations. Some years ago, *Al-Watan Al-Arabi*, an Arabic news journal, contained a remarkable article detailing an emergency meeting of the Hizbullah politburo in which new funding strategies were studied. An expansion of business activities was discussed, as was greater reliance on drugs, gunrunning, and counterfeiting.[23] For its part, the U.S. Drug Enforcement Agency has accused Hizbullah of having ties with a U.S. drug ring.[24] The United States also accuses Hizbullah of being financed by diamond smugglers in Sierra Leone, many of whom are Shi'a of Lebanese origin.[25]

Hizbullah: Strengths and Vulnerabilities

The success of Hizbullah over the course of the past two decades can be attributed to a variety of factors, not the least of which is the dynamism of the Hizbullah leadership and the zeal of its members. Lebanese of all faiths grudgingly acknowledge that the Hizbullah leadership is outstanding. Hizbullah students at the American University of Beirut are among the most serious in the student body. This is a well-trained, well-organized, and very sophisticated organization. All things considered, it is clearly the most efficient organization in Lebanon. It is also a high-tech organization adept at utilizing the latest weapons and communications technologies as well as an organization that combines flexibility and specialization with a secret mode of operation. All of this has made it extremely difficult for foreign intelligence agencies to penetrate Hizbullah operations. This is particularly true of Hizbullah's security and military units, the members of which are deployed in small autonomous groups. The capture of a single individual or unit, as the Israelis have found to their dismay, does not threaten the organization as a whole.

The strength of Hizbullah also finds its roots in a Shi'a culture that lends itself to militancy and sacrifice.[26] Martyrdom is the ultimate sacrifice and assures entry into heaven. Adding to the spirit of sacrifice within Shi'a culture is the tremendous veneration of devout Shi'a for their religious leaders. Hassan Nasrallah studied in both Najaf and Qum, the two major centers of Islamic learning. Nasrallah's official biography glories in suffering and sacrifice, noting, "With high spirits, Sayyed Hassan Nasrallah dealt with the martyrdom of his eldest son, Hadi, who was martyred during a clash with the 'Israelis,' as a father who was happy for the martyrdom of his son, for (it is) obtaining the blessing of the martyrdom that opens the gates of the garden [of heaven] for a believer."[27] As a young religious student, Nasrallah is also said to have received the personal blessing of the Ayatollah Khomeini, an Islamic saint if not the reincarnation of the Hidden Imam.[28]

Having listened to countless hours of Nasrallah's sermons, we can testify to their power and charisma. U.S. evangelists pale by comparison. The Arabic language is the language of the Koran and lends itself to emotion but none more so than in Nasrallah's speeches. Nasrallah's charisma builds upon the emotionalism of Shi'a culture. It also builds upon the sense of crisis or victimhood that finds its roots in historical oppression of Lebanon's Shi'a population. Nasrallah's speeches not only promise paradise in the hereafter. They also promise the victory of the dispossessed on earth.

Hizbullah, for all of its Iranian ties, is part and parcel of Lebanon. Shi'a constitute at least one-third of Lebanon's population, far more by some estimates. Hizbullah's members are everywhere and do everything. Even Shi'a who are not members of Hizbullah support the organization with services, contributions, and information. Iran provides much of Hizbullah's funding, but the faithful also do their share, many contributing as much as one-fifth of their income.

Hizbullah takes little for granted, and the zeal of its members is continually reinforced by Hizbullah mosques, media, schools, and welfare agencies. Particularly important are the services that Hizbullah provides to the families of its fallen martyrs. These services include monthly food allowances, education, health care, resources, and, permitting, housing.[29] All enable Hizbullah fighters to serve their God with the confidence that their families will be provided for. Pictures of fallen martyrs adorn billboards and buildings in the predominantly Shi'a areas of Lebanon, assuring that Hizbullah martyrs will be honored by the living and serve as heroes for future generations of Shi'a fighters. Honor, too, is a key element of Arab and Islamic culture.

Hizbullah also thrives because the Lebanese government is too weak and too fragmented by religious bickering to take effective action against this most powerful of organizations. So fragile is the Lebanese political system, in fact, that recent parliamentary elections were contended by some eighteen different religious and ethnic groups, each being assured of seats in the National Assembly in some semblance to their size and power. The same principle applies to the allocation of positions in the bureaucracy and military, although the command structure of the military inclines toward the Maronite Christians. Even the leadership of the country is a three-way tug of war between Lebanon's three presidents: the president of the country is a Christian Maronite; the president of the government (prime minister) is a Sunni Muslim; and the president (speaker) of the National Assembly is a Shi'a Muslim. None can accomplish anything without the support of the others. Each of Lebanon's main religious sects, moreover, can hold the government hostage until its interests have been accommodated. This, then, is the Lebanese government that the United States is pressuring to rein in Hizbullah, an ironic position seeing that Hizbullah has a stranglehold on what the Lebanese government can and cannot do.

In much the same manner, Hizbullah thrives from an international order that is confused and in disarray. Europe resents American leadership of the international order and seems far more concerned with al Qaeda than it does Hizbullah. Russia, Japan, and China are even more open in their cooperation with Iran, the guardian angel of Hizbullah. The United States, for its part, is bogged down in Iraq, Afghanistan, and just about every place else. Many pundits suggest that there has been weak leadership all around. The Israeli press has been particularly hard on its leaders.

It was this formidable combination of assets that enabled Hizbullah to withstand the Israeli pounding of its positions in the 2006 war while forcing the Israelis to suffer unacceptable losses. The hoped-for uprising of Sunni and Christian Lebanese failed to materialize, and American and Israeli efforts to force the disarmament of Hizbullah went for naught. The Lebanese army, supported by international observers, did replace Hizbullah guerrillas on the Israeli border, but Hizbullah didn't seem to mind. It used the cover to rebuild its arsenal, U.S. threats to Syria and Iranian suppliers not withstanding.

Does this mean that Hizbullah is invincible? No, it does not, quite the contrary. Hizbullah is probably the most vulnerable of the major Islamic groups. There are many problems, not the least of which is the hostility of Lebanon's Christians, Sunni, and other sects toward Hizbullah. Hizbullah adventurism is blamed for provoking the Israeli war of 2006, and they rightly fear that future Hizbullah adventurism could bring another round of devastation. Many also believe that Hizbullah places the interests of Iran and Syria above the interests of Lebanon. Few Lebanese want to suffer for the sake of either— neither are they enamored with the thought of a Shi'a state in all or part of Lebanon. Nasrallah has accused elements of the Lebanese military of conspiring with the Israelis during the 2006 war much as he now accuses his adversaries of conspiring with Israel and the United States to disarm Hizbullah.

The struggle between Hizbullah and Amal, the rival Shi'a organization, once showed signs of serving as a check on Hizbullah, but that is currently less the case. Hizbullah has surpassed its once larger rival in recent elections, and the leaders of the two movements have become allies in promoting the cause of Lebanon's Shi'a.[30] This could change should Hizbullah falter.

The charismatic leadership style of Nasrallah is also problematic. His decisions go unchallenged within Hizbullah, and many Shi'a believe him to be divinely guided. That, however, remains to be seen. Nasrallah's popularity, like that of all demagogues, has soared during times of victory. It can just as easily collapse in time of sustained disaster. Thus far he has guessed right, but that too could change. He admitted to misjudging Israeli intentions in the 2006 war and could well do so again in the future. Next time he might not be so lucky. His Lebanese opponents will be prepared to pounce.

The assassination of Nasrallah, an avowed goal of the Israelis and others, could well sew confusion within Hizbullah. This threat should not be over-rated. His security is tight, and even he quips that he is not sure where his next location will be. Replacements will also be found, and Nasrallah will become a martyr. Dead martyrs can be more dangerous than live dema-gogues.

A far more immediate threat to Hizbullah is the very real possibility of a peace treaty between Syria and Israel, a key feature of which would be the dismantling of Hizbullah's military wing. Hizbullah is mindful of this threat, and as early as 2000, rumors were circulating that Hizbullah had established shipping facilities in Cyprus as an alternative transit route for Iranian arms should Syrian cooperation prove unreliable. The U.S. strike on Iraq also had an unnerving effect on Syria, with the Assad regime going out of its way to convince Washington that it does not support terror. For the moment, Wash-ington remains unconvinced, but that too could change.

Hizbullah's ties with Iran are also a two-way street. Hizbullah's presumed subservience to Iran has become a cause of concern among Lebanon's neigh-bors. It is not Hizbullah, per se, that they fear but rather Hizbullah as the agent of Iran. These concerns are particularly strong among the Israelis, the Jordanians, and the Saudi Arabians. Indeed, the latter reportedly worked a deal with the United States to denounce Hizbullah for its role in the 2006 war in return for U.S. efforts to rein in Israel in the Occupied Territories. The Americans didn't carry out their part of the deal, and the Saudis were embarrassed.[31]

In any case, Israel and the United States have vowed Hizbullah's destruc-tion, and it is probable that Israel will be better prepared for its next war with the Party of God. Saudi Arabia might have been embarrassed by the United States' perfidiousness but remains locked in a cold war with Iran and, ipso facto, Hizbullah. It is Saudi Arabia, more than any other country, that would be the target of a Shi'a Crescent, however fanciful.

There is also the threat that Iran's Islamic revolution will dissolve in a nuclear holocaust. This, too, could be fanciful. Both the United States and Israel have denied rumors of planned nuclear attacks on Iran. This, of itself, means the topic is being discussed.

Future Strategies

How then does Hizbullah use its strengths to keep its enemies at bay? Hizbul-lah's strategies begin with the psychological game. Hizbullah attempts do deflect international criticism by claiming that it is a peaceful Lebanese movement that has been forced to take up arms by Israeli aggression.[32] America is criticized for its support of Israel and its hostility to Islam, but attacks on the United States and its interests are avoided. Once the Israeli threat to Lebanon has passed, according to Hizbullah propagandists, it will transform itself into a political party dedicated to a just and moral society. Ties to Iran are pooh-poohed, and Hizbullah disavows any interest in transforming all or part of Lebanon into an Islamic republic.

Offers of peaceful coexistence are balanced by threats of civil war if efforts are made to disarm or otherwise destroy Hizbullah. Lebanon and the world can take their pick. They can negotiate with Hizbullah or suffer the consequences.

Hizbullah's psychological strategy, in turn, sets the stage for its negotiation strategy. Given this choice between negotiations and conflict, all of the major players with the exception of Israel and the United States have chosen negotiations. Hizbullah is a key component of Lebanon's government, and it also negotiates independently with Saudi Arabia, Syria, and other key countries in the Middle East. For that matter, it also negotiates with the United States and Israel. Hizbullah negotiators are adept at making alliances within Lebanon and count both Christian and Sunni groups among their temporary allies. They are equally skilled at the international level by making their cooperation a key element in any hope for peace in the region. While it is unlikely that Hizbullah would sell out Iran, it is possible that it would sacrifice Syria if the price were right. Presumably, it would also be a willing ally in the war against al Qaeda and other Sunni jihadist groups that denounce the Shi'a as heretics.

Both the psychological and political strategies are underscored by Hizbullah's three-pronged military strategy. Hizbullah has the capacity to conduct terrorist operations of all varieties, the 2006 kidnapping of Israeli soldiers being a case in point. Its militia also makes it a potent guerrilla force capable of repelling Israeli attacks and cowing its domestic opponents. More recently, Hizbullah has developed an assault wing based on rockets and unmanned drones. Hizbullah rockets proved their mettle during the 2006 war with Israel and give every indication of increasing in power, range, and guidance sophistication. The present, from the Israeli perspective, is dangerous enough. But what if Hizbullah rockets and unmanned drones were equipped with small-scale nuclear warheads? Iran is rushing its nuclear program, and old Soviet tactical nuclear weapons are presumably for sale on the black market. Chemical and biologic weapons are also coming on line—very scary, indeed.

Ironically, Hizbullah owes much of its success to Israel. Hizbullah uses the struggle against Israel as the foundation of its Islamic and nationalistic legitimacy. Israel is also the justification for its militia, and the charisma of both Hizbullah and its Nasrallah have soared with its 2000 and 2006 defeat of Israel. On the broader regional scale, Hizbullah, along with Iran, has emerged as the leading champion of the Palestinians. This, in turn, has also allowed Hizbullah to make alliances with a broad range of Sunni Muslim extremist groups that would otherwise be rendered difficult by the deep hostility between the two Muslims sects.

Notes

1. James A. Bill, *The Eagle and the Lion: The Tragedy of American-Iranian Relations* (New Haven, Conn.: Yale University Press, 1988); Sandra Mackey, *The Iranians: Persia, Islam and the Soul of a Nation* (New York: Dutton, 1996); Said Amir Arjomand, *The Shadow of God and the Hidden Imam* (Chicago: University of Chicago Press, 1984).

2. Marvin Zonis, *Majestic Failure: The Fall of the Shah* (Chicago: University of Chicago Press, 1991).

3. Marvin Zonis and Cyrus Amir Mokri, "The Islamic Republic of Iran," in *Politics and Government in the Middle East and North Africa*, ed. Tareq Y. Ismael and Jacqueline S. Ismael (Miami: Florida International University Press, 1991), 114–50.

4. Farhad Ibrahim, *Confessionalism and Politics in the Arab World: The Shi'a Program in Iraq* [in Arabic], translated from German by the Center for Cultural Studies and Translations (Cairo, Egypt: Library Madbouli, 1996).

5. Mackey, *The Iranians*, 323.

6. Gay Cavender, Nancy C. Jurik, and Albert K. Cohen, "The Baffling Case of the Smoking Gun: The Social Ecology of the Political Accounts in the Iran-Contra Affair," *Social Problems* 40, no. 2 (1993): 152–65.

7. Augustus R. Norton, *Amal and the Shi'a: Struggle for the Soul of Lebanon* (Austin: University of Texas Press, 1987).

8. Eyal Zisser, "Hizballah in Lebanon: At the Crossroads," *MERIA* 1, no. 3 (September 1997), at http://meria.idc.ac.il/journal/1997/issue3/jv1n3a1.html (accessed May 9, 2002).

9. Michael Young, "Hizballah Outside and In," *MERIA*, October 26, 2002, at www.meria.org/pins/pin37.html (accessed May 9, 2002); "Army Comes between Rival Resistance Groups: Dispute over Soccer Field Leads to Several Injuries," *Daily Star-Lebanon*, February 2, 2002, at www.dailystar.com.lb/02_02_02/art17.htm (accessed February 2, 2002).

10. "Interview with the Secretary General of Hizbullah Sayyed Hassan Nasrallah," *Al Jazeera*, February 14, 2002, 7–8, at www.nasrallah.net/English/Hassan/khitabat/khitabat033.htm (accessed April 16, 2004).

11. Farid El Khazen, *The Breakdown of the State of Lebanon, 1967–1976* (London: IB Tauris, 2000).

12. Alastair Crooke and Mark Perry, "How Hezbollah Defeated Israel: Part 2: Winning the Ground War," *Asia Times*, October 13, 2006, at www.asiatimes.com/

(accessed October 13, 2006); Alastair Crooke and Mark Perry, "How Hezbollah Defeated Israel: Part 3: The Political War," *Asia Times,* October 14, 2006, at www .asiatimes.com/ (accessed October 14, 2006); Anshel Pfeffer, "Analysis: Israel's Numerous War Wounds," *Jerusalem Post,* January 9, 2007, at www.jpost.com/ (accessed January 9, 2007).

13. Barak Ravid and Jonathan Lis, "Police Chief: 90% of Smuggled Drugs Slip through Our Net," *Ha'aretz,* July 23, 2007, at www.haaretz.com/ (accessed July 23, 2007).

14. Amr Elchoubaki, "More than Resistance," *Al Ahram Weekly,* August 8, 2006, at http://weekly.ahram.orgc.eg/2006/808/op2.htm (accessed August 9, 2006).

15. Jihad Salem, "Important Emergency Meeting in the Majlis as Shoura (Hezbullah Lebanon) to Discuss the Disaster of the Decrease in Iranian Support"[in Arabic], *Al-Watan Al-Arabi,* April 9, 2003; Sayeed Al-Qisi, "Secret Report Accuses Hizbullah of Engaging in the Marketing of Drugs" [in Arabic], *Al-Watan Al-Arabi,* June 3, 2005, 16–18.

16. "Citation of the Biography of His Eminence Sayyed Hassan Nasrallah," Nasrallah home page, n.d., at www.nasrallah.net/main/moharamf/cnasrashorac.html (accessed April 16, 2003).

17. Interview with the secretary general of Hizbullah Sayyed Hassan Nasrallah by *Al Jazeera,* February 14, 2002, at www.nasrallah.net/English/Hassan/khitabat/ khitabat033.htm (accessed April 16, 2003).

18. Ahmad Nizar Hamzeh, *In the Path of Hizbulluh* (Syracuse, N.Y.: Syracuse University Press, 2004).

19. "Hizbullah—the Party of God: Hizbullah—Social Radicals," Hizbullah home page, n.d., at http://almashriq.hiof.no/clebanon/300/320/324/c324.2/hizballah (accessed April 9, 2002).

20. Hamzeh, *In the Path of Hizbullah.*

21. Hamzeh, *In the Path of Hizbullah.*

22. "Interview with Hizballah Secretary-General Sheik Hassan Nasrallah," *Time* (Europe), November 1, 2000, at www.time.com/time/Europe/webonly/mideast/ 2000/11/Nasrallah.html (accessed May 9, 2002).

23. Salem, "Important Emergency Meeting," 32–33.

24. Sayeed Al-Qisi, "Secret Report Accuses Hizbullah of Engaging in the Marketing of Drugs," *Al-Watan Al-Arabi,* June 3, 2005, 16–18.

25. "Hezbollah Extorting Funds from West Africa's Diamond Trade," *Ha'aretz,* June 30, 2004, at www.haaretz.com/hasen/spages/445455.html (accessed June 30, 2004).

26. Manocheht Dorraj, "Symbolic and Utilitarian Political Value of a Tradition: Martyrdom in the Iranian Political Culture," *The Review of Politics* 29, no. 3 (1977): 489–521.

27. Nasrallah home page, n.d., at www.nasrallah.net/cmain/moharamf/nasra shora.html (accessed April 16, 2003).

28. Najh Mohammed Ali, "The Iranian Source Reveals That the Imam Khomeini Designated Nasrallah as His Agent" [in Arabic], *Al-Arabiya,* August 18, 2006, at www.alarabiya.net/ (accessed August 18, 2006).

29. Jacob Qasir, "Report about the Advance and the Help of Emdad Committee

for Islamic Charity until Date of 31/3/1997," Hizbullah home page, May 9, 1988, at http://almashriq.hiof.no/lebanon/300/c320/324/324.2/hizballah/emdad/index/html (accessed April 15, 2003).

30. Rodger Shanahan, "Hizballah Rising: The Political Battle for the Loyalty of the Shi'a of Lebanon," *The Middle East Review of International Affairs* 9, no. 2 (March 2005).

31. Nawaf Obaid, interview, Saudi-U.S. Relations Information Service, August 22, 2006, at www.saudiusrelations.org/articles/2006/interviews/060822 (accessed August 22, 2006).

32. Naim Qassem, *Hizbullah: The Story from Within* (London: Saqi Books, 2005).

6

Iraqi Hizbullah

I RAQ CURRENTLY POSSESSES three Hizbullah-type organizations: the
Supreme Council for the Islamic Revolution in Iraq (SCIRI),[1] the Dawa
(Call) Party, and the Sadrists. All advocate an Islamic state in Iraq. All
demand Shi'a control of Iraq. All are dedicated to the protection of the
Islamic faith and the expansion of Shi'a Islam. All have organizations patterned on the Hizbullah model reviewed in chapter 5. All have deep roots in
the Iraqi Shi'a community. All fire mass emotions by exploiting the poverty
and suffering of Iraq's Shi'a. All nominally acknowledge Ayatollah Sistani, an
Iranian, as the reigning paramount ayatollah of Iraq. This does not mean that
they accept his spiritual guidance. All have pledged to support Iran in case of
a conflict with the United States. All are willing to have the United States
cleanse Iraq of Saddam's forces and Sunni jihadists. And, all have come
together to form the ruling Unified Iraqi Coalition (United Alliance), which
is blessed by the United States.[2] This might sound strange given Washington's
hostility toward Hizbullah, but the Middle East is a confusing place.

All three groups also possess a military capacity, although the website of
the Dawa Party claims that it no longer possesses a standing militia. Weapons
pour in from group members who have infiltrated the security services, the
leadership of which is firmly in the hands of the ruling Shi'a coalition. It
could not be otherwise, for the future of Iraq is uncertain and the survival of
all three groups will rest heavily on their military capacity. U.S. protests have
brought symbolic attempts to stem the flow of arms to the militias, but little
more. Smuggling, corruption, ransom, extortion, and the contributions of
the faithful, often in the 20 percent range, provide the funding for political
and welfare activities, including the salaries of the fighters. In 2007, for example, Iraq's deputy prime minister acknowledged that armed groups had
infiltrated the Ministry of Oil and were stealing "hundreds of millions of

dollars" per year to finance their operations. The refineries of Baiji alone, he noted, are being robbed of 1.5 billion dollars per annum. The Baiji refineries are Iraq's largest and are located in an area controlled by the United States. When asked if he expected improvements, the deputy prime minister replied in the negative saying, "We have a regime and an administration that encourages corruption."[3] These are tough accusations from a deputy prime minister whose presumed obligation is to make things seem better than they are. But, then, maybe he was.

The United States, for its part, blames Iran for providing both arms and money to the Shi'a militias. This is probably true but not determinant. What passes for Iranian aid could well be the brisk smuggling trade that permeates the long border between the two countries. The smuggling existed during the reign of Saddam Hussein but has mushroomed as Iraq has slid into civil war. The United States avoids the words "civil war," but few Iraqi do. Iyad Allawi, a former prime minister, minced few words on the topic in a 2007 interview with *Asharq al-Awsat.* "The situation is . . . bad, but it will certainly get worse for clear reasons: the absence of the state, the adoption of a sectarian and factional policy in running the affairs of what is left of the state in Iraq, and the negative regional interferences in Iraqi affairs. . . . There is civil war."[4]

Baring the emergence of a new Saddam Hussein, it is Shi'a clerics organized along the lines of Hizbullah who will rule Iraq, or at least, most of it. The Kurds already have a de facto state in the north of the country replete with its own constitution and flag. The critical question, accordingly, is which of the three Hizbullah-style organizations will reign supreme? For the moment they have joined forces to consolidate Shi'a clerical control of Iraq, but it is not clear how long their alliance can be maintained.

For all of their similarities, no less than four key issues divide the three groups. The first issue is the struggle for dominance and the power, glory, and patronage that go with it. In the Iraqi case, that dominance is symbolized by control of the illustrious seminary (Hausa) in Najaf, the burial site of Ali, the fourth caliph and patron saint of the Shi'a. The ayatollah who controls the illustrious seminary is generally avowed to be Iraq's Grand (or paramount) Ayatollah and, as such, is the spiritual and political guide of most Iraqi Shi'a. This is a powerful position, indeed.

Second, the struggle between the three groups is also a struggle between the powerful religious clans who have traditionally competed for control of the seminary and the position of Grand Ayatollah. These include the Sadrs, the al-Hakims, the al-Koueis, and others, all of whom have played key roles in the saga of Iraqi politics in the post-Saddam era.

The third element is the struggle between Arabs and Iranians for control of Shi'a politics, the core of which is control of Iraq's holy cities. SCIRI, like Hizbullah, is an Iranian creation and swears fidelity to Ali Khamenei, the supreme guide of Iran. The Sadrists, by contrast, are staunch Arab nationalists and oppose Iranian domination of Iraq or its Shi'a community. In their view, the center of Islamic thought must remain in Iraq's illustrious seminary rather than the Shi'a seminary in the Iranian city of Qum. Dawa falls between the two extremes.

The fourth element in the equation is the difference of opinions concerning the proper role of Shi'a clergy in the realm of secular politics. Most ayatollahs had traditionally eschewed secular politics as a dirty business that affronted their dignity. All three of the Hizbullah-style organizations are heavily politicized, but even that is a matter of degree. SCIRI accepts Iran's position that the clergy, under the leadership of the paramount ayatollah in the Shi'a world, should rule (*viliat of fiqih*). In their view, that position is now occupied by Ali Khamenei, the supreme guide and dominant political figure in Iran. An Iraq governed by SCIRI would probably bear a strong resemblance to the political system of Iran. Dawa, by contrast, calls for democratic religious rule based upon the views of the believers (*Umma*). It would be a religious state to be sure but one in which moderate voices within the Islamic community could make their presence felt. The Sadrists stress rule by the Iraqi clergy blended with a strong dose of welfare, technological advancement, and Iraqi nationalism.

As might be expected given the above differences, there is little agreement on how an Islamic Iraq is best achieved. SCIRI favors the fragmentation of Iraq along sectarian and ethnic lines, with the predominantly Shi'a areas from Baghdad south forming a Shi'a theocracy closely aligned with neighboring Iran with whom it shares a long and porous border. Such a state would be a key element in the Shi'a Crescent and provide Iran with a direct link to Shi'a communities in Kuwait and Saudi Arabia. The Sadrists, in contrast, have blended religious zeal with Iraqi nationalism in an effort to mobilize popular hostility toward both the United States and Iran. The Sadrists oppose the fragmentation of Iraq into semi-independent Shi'a, Sunni, and Kurdish regions and, more than their competitors, have attempted to build bridges with cooperative Sunni groups. Dawa has placed its bets on pursuing a moderate position that can bridge the gap between the Sadrists and SCIRI. It has cooperated with the American forces in the hope of strengthening its position in Iraq and has named the past two Iraqi prime ministers, Ibrahim al-Jaffary and Nouri al-Maliki. Neither has produced much in the way of development or security.

How Did This All Come About?

Before assessing the ability of the three groups to achieve their diverse visions of Iraq's future, it is necessary to put their evolution into perspective. At the onset, it should be noted that Iraq was ruled by the Turks for several hundred years before being occupied by the British in World War I. The Turks were Sunni and relied on Sunni Arabs in governing the three Turkish provinces that would eventually become Iraq. Sunni Arabs were also incorporated into the Turkish army, and it was they who would play a key role in governing independent Iraq. Much as in Lebanon, the Shi'a were the dispossessed of Iraq. The Sunni generals used their power to build vast plantations and passed laws reducing the *fellah* (peasants) to surfs. Shi'a power, such as it was, rested in the hands of equally rapacious tribal sheikhs.

Oppression and poverty forced poor Shi'a to migrate to Baghdad in hope of finding work and a better way of life. They found only greater despair in the sprawling slums that would soon engulf this most storied of cities. Exposure to education and westernization only served to intensify their sense of desperation.

As the British ambassador of the time predicted, despair brought revolution.[5] The late 1950s and early 1960s saw Iraq subjected to a bewildering array of coups and countercoups. For a brief period, the communists seemed on the verge of seizing power, much of their support being drawn from the Shi'a slums of Baghdad. Anger and revenge took their toll as Shi'a groups masquerading under communist slogans such as "partisans of peace" wrecked havoc in Sunni areas. Others revolted against Shi'a sheikhs cum landowners.

Retribution was swift as Sunni nationalists and Ba'athists (a leading leftist party) seized control of the government and slaughtered Shi'a communists with a vengeance. The period was too complex for easy recounting, but in the mid-1970s Saddam Hussein, a Ba'athist, emerged as a major power broker in the politics of Iraq. He became the supreme leader in 1979, the same year as the Ayatollah Khomeini's Islamic Revolution in Iran. The Shi'a clergy, following the quietest, nonpolitical tradition, had remained aloof to the events swirling around them and did little to alleviate the suffering of the Shi'a masses. They paid the price for their aloofness as younger and more politicized Shi'a joined the ranks of the communists and Ba'athists in the hope of advancement, equality, and an improved quality of life.

Not all of the Shi'a clergy, however, remained passive. In 1957, a group of clerics and prominent Shi'a formed the Islamic Call Party (Dawa) to fight the erosion of Islamic values by communism and other secular ideologies. The driving force in the creation of the Dawa Party was Ayatollah Sayid Mohammed Baqir as-Sadr, one of the few politicized ayatollahs of the era and the first to call for a religious government based on the voice of the people (*Umma*). He was assisted by Ayatollah Sayed Mohammad Baqir al-Hakim, the son of a former grand ayatollah. In a curious irony, the three main competitors for Shi'a power in Iraq today—Dawa, SCIRI, and the Sadrists—all trace their origins to the Islamic Call Party (Dawa) established by Baqir as-Sadr and Baqir al-Hakim in the late 1950s.

A deep split thus emerged within the Shi'a clergy between those who advocated political activism and those who remained faithful to Shi'it tradition of remaining aloof from politics. Needless to say, nonpolitical ayatollahs found favor among Iraq's secular leaders, not the least of whom was Saddam Hussein. This was all the more the case with the outbreak of war between Iraq and Iran in 1980. Saddam Hussein, aware that Iran's much-vaunted army had melted away with the fall of the Shah in 1979, chose that moment to pounce. With the defeat of Iran, it would be he, Saddam Hussein, who would control the Gulf and its oil. The United States and the Saudis supported this most misguided of ventures in the vain hope of being done with the Ayatollah Khomeini and his Islamic Revolution once and for all. The mullahs, to their dismay, proved remarkably resilient, and Saddam Hussein, fearing an uprising among Iraqi Shi'a, assassinated key Shi'a clerics suspected of political activity. Others were arrested by the score, and Iranians were forcibly evicted from Iraq's holy cities.

The members of the Dawa Party were among some million Iraqis who fled to Iran. The Iranian clerics used the Iraqi exiles to form the SCIRI, a Hizbullah-type organization replete with TV stations, welfare agencies, and a powerful militia, the Badr Corps. The Dawa Party retained its independent identity but was groomed for service in a liberated Iraq. The Sadr religious clan, being of Iraqi origins, made its peace with Saddam Hussein and remained in Iraq.

We pick up the story in 1992 with the death of the Grand Ayatollah Khoui, a profound intellectual whose ascetic views had dampened the appeal of Iraq's more radical ayatollahs. Saddam Hussein was anxious to continue this trend and promoted the fortunes of Mohammed Sadiq as-Sadr as a successor to Khoui. Sadiq as-Sadr was a relative of the founder of Dawa and an Iraqi ayatollah renowned for his ascetic, nonpolitical views.[6] Rumors of a deal between Hussein and as-Sadr swept the Shi'a community, and as-Sadr's opponents began referring to him as the "regime ayatollah."[7] Whether or not there was a deal, Saddam Hussein embraced as-Sadr and allowed him to broadcast his sermons over Iraqi radio and television, a privilege denied to his competitors. As-Sadr was also allowed a freedom of movement denied to his competitors and given control of foreign students studying in Najaf.[8]

Tensions further escalated when rumors circulated that Saddam Hussein had ordered the assassination of all non-Iraqi ayatollahs.[9]

In reality, very little is nonpolitical in Iraq. As-Sadr's sermons struck a responsive chord among the Iraqi Shi'a, and intentionally or not, he emerged as a competitor of Saddam Hussein. This danger increased in the early months of 1998 when as-Sadr's sermons grew increasingly critical of the regime, and he urged his followers to attend Friday prayers in person rather than watching them on television.[10] Attendance at Friday prayers increased apace, reportedly attracting more than one hundred thousand worshippers crowded into the Grand Mosque of Najaf and its surrounding courtyards to hear as-Sadr speak.

As-Sadr and his two sons were murdered by unknown assailants on February 18, 1999. Saddam Hussein was accused of the assassinations, but Hussein was not the only party with a motive for eliminating as-Sadr. As-Sadr's supremacy posed a dire threat to the aspirations of his rivals. Lest there be any doubt on the matter, as-Sadr had ordered Iraqi Shi'a to give their religious contributions directly to the poor and needy rather than going through the clergy. Not only had as-Sadr reduced his rivals to secondary status, but also he had deprived them of the main source of their income.

Iran's displeasure with as-Sadr was also intense. It could not be otherwise, for as-Sadr's ascendancy had dampened Iranian influence among Iraq's much-fragmented Shi'a community and strengthened the Iraqi city of Najaf as a competitor to the Iranian city of Qum as the spiritual center of Shi'a faith. These were not minor issues, for Iranian dominance of the Shi'a communities in Iraq and Lebanon had become a cardinal principle of Iranian foreign policy. To paraphrase al Qisi in reference to the four ayatollahs who were assassinated in Iraq during 1998, it is possible to make two lists of the assassinated ayatollahs: those assassinated by Saddam Hussein and those assassinated by Iran and its agents.[11] The puzzle remains a topic of active debate today, with some theories tracing a deal between Saddam Hussein, America, and Israel to bring an end to Shi'a extremism.[12]

The 2003 Iraqi war ended the saga of Saddam Hussein. His much-vaunted army was crushed, and his supporters, secular Shi'a as well as Sunni, were purged from the army and the bureaucracy. Indeed, Arab Sunni of all backgrounds had become suspect. How could Saddam Hussein have ruled without their support? It was better to be safe than face revolution.

While this made sense in the heat of the battle, it left a resurgent Shi'a clergy the most organized force in Iraq. The Ayatollah Mohammed Baqir al-Hakim, the leader of SCIRI, returned to Iraq in May 2003, protected by guards from the Badr Corps under an agreement worked out with Washington. He vowed moderation but was accompanied by a Hizbullah-style apparatus replete with its political organization, media outlets, welfare agencies, and most importantly, the Badr Corps, a militia some thirteen thousand strong.[13] Al-Hakim was the son of the cofounder of the Dawa Party in the late 1950s, a relationship that enhanced his status in the eyes of the Shi'a community. Al-Hakim was assassinated shortly after his return to Iraq.

Dawa also hit the ground running with the fall of Saddam Hussein and soon had offices in all of Iraq's major Shi'a cities. Regardless of the family links between the Dawa Party and SCIRI, it is not entirely clear whether Dawa is a competitor or ally of SCIRI. Press reports suggest that Dawa, itself, might be divided between those guided by Ayatollah Ali Khamenei, the supreme guide of Iran, and those who follow Ayatollah Mohammed Hussein Fadlallah, the founder of the Lebanese Hizbullah.[14] Dawa now appears to be far more moderate than SCIRI, but appearances are deceiving.

The most immediate challenge to both SCIRI and the United States is the Sadr movement. The Sadr movement consists of supporters of Ayatollah as-Sadr, who was assassinated in 1999, and is headed by his son, Muqtada as-Sadr. The son, presumably in his thirties, lacks the experience and religious credentials of the father and has attempted to compensate for both by whipping anti-American sentiment into a frenzy. In the fall of 2003 the young as-Sadr boasted a militia of some ten thousand strong and proclaimed his own government of Iraq. That didn't work out, but as-Sadr and his followers are now part of the ruling Shi'a coalition. His militia, the Mehdi army, controls Baghdad, the center of his power, as well as large areas of southern Iraq. For the moment, the younger as-Sadr has seized the momentum within Iraqi's Shi'a community. Should he be killed, a probable event given the challenge that he poses to the United States, SCIRI, Iran, and the Shi'a establishment, a raft of equally radical youth are waiting in the wings. The trouble is, they lack his pedigree.

Alarmed by the probable emergence of a Hizbullah clone in Iraq, a somewhat confused occupation leadership stole a page from Saddam Hussein's book and attempted to find an ascetic (nonpolitical) Shi'a cleric of Arabic origin to assist the United States in governing Iraq. No sooner had the United States taken control of Iraq than the very moderate Sheikh al-Khoei, head of the charitable al-Khoei Foundation in London and son of a former grand ayatollah, was flown to Iraq on a U.S. military aircraft and accompanied by U.S. special forces to the holy city of Najaf. He was assassinated almost immediately, with fingers pointing at the Sadrist movement. Ayatollah Sistani, a student of the elder al-Khoei who had been tabbed by al-Khoei to replace him as Grand Ayatollah at the time of his death in 1992, was also placed under house arrest by the Sadr movement and threatened with assassination if he did not return to Iran.

Even though Sistani was an Iranian national, the United States came to his rescue. Sistani had supported the 1991 U.S. call for revolution against Saddam Hussein, and much like the elder al-Khoei, his mentor, he preached that politics was best left to the politicians. This, of itself, represented a sharp break with the Iranian doctrine of *viliat of fiqih*, or rule by the clergy.[15] He had also remained in Iraq during the Saddam years, most of his time being spent in seclusion or house arrest.

Sistani's popularity among the Shi'a masses was based upon reverence for his learning and his position as the paramount Ayatollah of the illustrious seminary in Najaf. Religious authority was bolstered by his opposition to Saddam Hussein and by his call for a moderate religious democracy based on the will of the people. It was this message of moderation and democracy that was spread by the clerics who manned Sistani's growing network of offices that permeated Iraq's Shi'a areas including the holy cities and Baghdad.[16] These, in turn, were bolstered by an expanding network of mosques, religious schools, and medical services.

It was Sistani's moderation and his ability to lead the masses that made him so important to the Americans. It was also his support among the masses that enabled him to forge a ruling coalition with Sadrists, SCIRI, and Dawa. It was a marriage of convenience and expediency, a temporary alliance between traditional religious authority and Hizbullah-type political activism. Some authors argue that Sistani could be the last of the old-line nonpolitical or "quiet" ayatollahs.[17]

It is not clear, however, that Sistani was really a nonpolitical ayatollah. The mere fact of being made America's ayatollah forced Sistani to abandon his ascetic role and become involved in Iraqi politics. His agenda was clear. Iraq's Shi'a had to dominate the political process. Only this could avoid the twin scourge of Sunni dominance and secularism. Only Shi'a dominance could bring about a moderate Islamic state based upon the rule of the believers (*Umma*) guided by the clergy. He also made voting a religious obligation of all Iraqi Shi'a, women as well as men.[18] His own views were closest to those of Dawa, which represented a middle ground between fanatical Sadrists and the pro-Iranian SCIRI.

Sistani succeeded in welding the Shi'a into a successful electoral alliance but could not quell the tensions between SCIRI, Dawa, and Sadrists, nor could his emissaries convince the United States to restrain its devastation of Iraq. He, himself, refused to talk directly to the United States. In September 2006, Sistani threw in the towel. He lamented his inability to save Iraq from civil war and announced his withdrawal from politics. He remained Iraq's grand ayatollah but limited his role to religious issues.[19] But, could he withdraw from politics? Wasn't his withdrawal from politics, itself, a political act that threw America's hopes for controlling Iraq into chaos? It is also less than clear that he has, in fact, withdrawn from politics. This, like so much of in Iraq, could well be an illusion.

Differing Visions of Iraq's Future: The Strengths and Weaknesses of SCIRI, Dawa, and the Sadrists

Which of the three groups, then, is likely to emerge dominant in the struggle to control a post-U.S. Iraq? Will it be SCIRI's vision of a Shi'a state in southern Iraq allied with Iran, the Sadrist vision of a unified Iraq independent of Iran, or Dawa's vision a federated Iraq in which each of the countries three major groups would manage its own affairs?

Speculation on this question is obviously premature. Iraqi politics are in turmoil, the U.S. occupation is winding down, and the next target of the assassin's bullet remains unknown. What we can do, however, is to examine the strengths and weakness of each group. At the very least, this will provide a guide for judging events as they unfold.

The Supreme Council for the Islamic Revolution in Iraq (SCIRI)

The strength of SCIRI rests on a well-developed Hizbullah-style organization developed by Iraqi exiles in Iran during the long years of Saddam Hussein's rule. Much like Hizbullah, it contains political, welfare, and military wings, all of which are firmly established in the Shi'a areas of Iraq. Its support base appears to be particularly strong among Iraqis with ties to Iran. It is also strong among all Iraqi Shi'a who accept Ali Khamenei, Iran's supreme guide, as their source of spiritual leadership. While there is little data on this topic, SCIRI did very well in the 2005 parliamentary elections.

The core of SCIRI power in Iraq is its military wing, the Badr divisions. The Badr divisions fought on the side of Iran during the Iran-Iraq War (1980–1989) and conducted guerilla operations against the Iraqi regime following the end of the war. Currently estimated to be between thirteen and twenty thousand strong, they are battle tested and, by all indications, well trained, well armed, and well disciplined. In some ways, they appear to be an extension of Iran's Revolutionary Guard. In any case, they will play a key role in consolidating the creation of a Shi'a state in southern Iraq should the country splinter into ethnic-religious enclaves. This is a distinct possibility.

SCIRI is the major recipient of Iranian aid that includes money, arms, training, and organizational support, all of which are facilitated by the long border between the two countries. As part of the ruling coalition, SCIRI also enjoys vast opportunities for corruption and patronage. One way or another, it is very well supplied.

SCIRI's Iranian backing is equally a source of weakness. Many Iraqi Shi'a are hostile to Iran and especially SCIRI's support for Iran during the Iran-Iraq War. There is no question that Abdul Aziz al-Hakim, the leader of SCIRI, is Iran's man in Iraq. SCIRI's strong links to Iran and efforts to create an Islamic republic in southern Iraq clearly place it on a collision course with the United States. Both sides are holding their fire as the United States attempts to keep the ruling coalition in power and Iran attempts to barter its cooperation in Iraq for an end to boycotts and other issues. Besides, SCIRI sees little need to waste its resources fighting the United States when it is now clear that the United States will soon be gone.

Iraq's Sunni are exceptionally hostile to Iranian influence, and the Kurds, too, have their doubts. They support SCIRI's goal of fragmenting Iraq but worry about Iranian hostility to an independent Kurdistan. Rumors of Turkish-Iranian cooperation to keep the Kurds in check appear to be well founded.[20]

The Islamic Dawa (Call) Party

Dawa's strength lies in its deep roots in Iraq's Shi'a community and its ties to both the as-Sadr and al-Hakim religious clans. Dawa also finds strength in its moderation. As things currently stand, it is the standard-bearer for Shi'a who favor a democratic government. Even secular Shi'a and Sunni could find Dawa to be their best bet for political moderation.

Although a Hizbullah clone, the apparent moderation of Dawa has won it the strong support of the United States. Dawa has named Iraq's first two elected prime ministers and has benefited accordingly. Its supporters receive jobs, welfare, and a goodly share of the country's depleted resources. All of this has contributed to the building of a strong political organization as has its access to the public treasury and its ability to arm its members whether or not they are currently organized into a militia. Dawa has possessed a militia in the past and knows the drill. Its members are also well placed in Iraq's security forces, which, of itself, bear a curious resemblance to a sectarian militia.

Dawa's cooperation with the United States is equally a source of weakness. The United States is not popular in Iraq, and most Iraqis assume that the United States has been defeated and will soon be gone. That, at least, is the message they receive from Congress and the mounting toll of American casualties. This places Dawa on the losing side in a country that is already placing its bets on life without the Americans. Dawa's ties with Iran are also of concern to Iraqis who fear that the party is little more than a seductive front for Iran's mullahs. Adding fuel to such doubts is the fact that some members of the party do look to Iran's supreme guide as their source of imitation and emulation.

Moderation, moreover, is a hard sell in times of civil war. Nerves are frayed, and calls for patience and moderation seem strangely out of place. This is more the case for a party that claims not to have its own army. Who is to protect its supporters? The police that are known for corruption and death squads?

Sadrists

The strength of the Sadrists is based upon as-Sadr's lineage, charisma, organizational ability, participation in the ruling coalition, and powerful militia. The popularity and dynamism of the Sadrists builds upon the Sadr family name as well as as-Sadr's demonstrated ability to rile the emotions of his followers and the broader Shi'a community. He is the youngest son of Ayatollah Mohammed Sadiq as-Sadr, the reigning Grand Ayatollah murdered in 1999 as well as the nephew of Ayatollah Baqir as-Sadr, the founder of the Dawa Party, who was murdered by Saddam Hussein in 1980. Finally, as-Sadr has gained popularity from his vitriolic opposition to the U.S. occupation and Iran. As-Sadr's support is particularly strong among the disposed of Sadr City, formerly Saddam City, a massive Baghdad slum of two to three million souls. For them, he represents a lethal blend of hope, revenge, and religious salvation. His influence is also well established in Iraq's other major Shi'ite cities, but Baghdad is where the action is. To control Baghdad is to control Iraq, or at least the non-Kurdish areas of Iraq. For the moment, as-Sadr, with his powerful militia and strong base in Sadr City, is the most powerful force in Baghdad. Rumors also abound that as-Sadr's forces have infiltrated the U.S. "green zone" and that his troops constituted part of the force responsible for protecting the Iraqi government.[21]

As-Sadr's charisma is supported by a deeply entrenched organization that was established by his father with the cooperation of Saddam Hussein prior to his assassination. As-Sadr builds upon the memory of his father by claiming to be guided by his principles (his father is his source of imitation and emulation) as well as by working through regional networks devoted to the illumination of his father's thought. His father's religious network has subsequently been reinforced by Hizbullah-type political units, the most prominent of which are the Mehdi Army, the unit for political (parliamentary) affairs, and the unit for relations with the Sunni.

As-Sadr, too, derives a great deal of influence from his participation in the ruling coalition. He controls some thirty-two members of parliament and up to six ministries, figures that ensure his ability to shape the direction of Iraqi politics. It is doubtful that the coalition could survive without his support. The price of as-Sadr's participation in the government has been control of key security and bureaucratic agencies. Financing has followed, as has an exceptionally well-armed militia, the Mehdi Army, a name implying that it is the army of the Hidden Imam.

Some estimates suggest that the Mehdi Army have as many as seven thousand fighters in Baghdad alone, although reliable figures are hard to come by. The Mehdi Army possibly possess advanced weapons including armor-piercing rockets, the latter reportedly supplied by Hizbullah and Iran.[22] Why would Iran arm a potential opponent? The answer is simple. Iran's most immediate goal is to drive the United States from Iraq without putting the Badr Brigade at risk and without provoking further hostility from the United States. As-Sadr's Mehdi Army, for the moment, fills the bill. Iran will deal with as-Sadr when the time comes.

Ironically, the Sadrists are the most vulnerable of Iraq's three Hizbullah-style organizations. The most immediate threat to the Sadrists is America's efforts to destroy them. Adding to as-Sadr's woes are the ever-present fears of a double-cross by his coalition partners. Government security forces appear to be cooperating with U.S. efforts to crush as-Sadr's Mehdi Army, albeit not to the degree of destabilizing their fragile coalition. They want as-Sadr to go but not until the United States has weakened the Sunni militias as well as as-Sadr's Mehdi Army. The United States is doing its best to help them, which seems rather curious seeing that the Sadrists, for all of their faults, are probably American's best bet for defeating the jihadists, quelling fears of an Iranian-led Shi'a Crescent, working out a deal with the moderate Sunnis, and maintaining the unity of Iraq. It is also doubtful that the United States can defeat the Mehdi Army, the main units of which will merely fade away until the U.S. assault has passed. Then, following an all too familiar pattern, they will simple reoccupy Baghdad.

A far greater threat to the Sadrists is the lack of discipline within the Mehdi Army. Hastily assembled, it is more like a collection of petty militias and semireligious gangs than a coherent Hizbullah-style fighting force. As-Sadr has acknowledged as much, threatening rebels with damnation and firing some forty commanders.[23] What this means, in reality, is that the forty commanders and their followers are likely to go their separate ways. A lack of discipline within the Mehdi Army is also a sign of weakness and might be interpreted as such by marginal supporters swept along by the tide of emotion and betting on an as-Sadr victory. That, after all, is the very stuff of mass movements. And yet, it could be enough to keep him in power during conditions of chaos that prevail in Iraq. The question is can it keep him in power against the far more disciplined Badr Brigades that are organized along the lines of Hizbullah and that are far more likely to be favored by Iran?

Underlying the lack of discipline within the Sadrist movement are as-Sadr's weak religious credentials. He is a young man in a society that venerates age. His only claim to religious authority is his lineage. He does not possess the authority to issue *fatwas* (religious decrees) and cannot challenge the rulings of Iraq's many ayatollahs. Indeed, his inability to issue fatwas was his defense when opponents accused him of issuing a fatwa approving group sex for fighters preoccupied by the war.[24]

Finally, the threat of an assassin's bullet looms large. Without as-Sadr's charisma, the Sadrist movement would lose steam until a suitable replacement could rise to the fore. That would take time, all the more so because the poor discipline of his organization suggests that as-Sadr's passing would lead to debilitating strife and internal fighting.

Having trouble keeping things straight? So is an American government confronted with a curious blend of parliamentary politics, jihadist attacks, sectarian warfare, Shi'a intrigues, tribal conflicts, death squads, revenge killings, and mafia shoot-outs. At long last, the *2007 National Intelligence Estimate* acknowledges that Iraq is in a state of civil war, something that Washington has long denied. *The Estimate*, compiled by key government leaders and security officials, also notes that Iraqi security forces lack the capacity to control their own country.[25] The expression that comes to mind is *miskeen*, the Arabic slang for poor bastards.

Notes

1. On May 12, 2007, the SCIRI announced on Al Arabiya.net that the organization decided to drop the word "revolution" from its title. We are leaving the full title in this publication as it is what most readers will be familiar with and because it will take a while to become official. "SCIRI Drops Revolution from Its Title" [in Arabic], *Al Arabiya*, May 12, 2007, at www.alarabiya.net/ (accessed May 12, 2007).

2. Ellen Knickmeyer and Omar Fekeiki, "Iraqi Shiite Cleric Pledges to Defend Iran," *Washington Post*, January 24, 2006, at www.washingtonpost.com/ (accessed January 24, 2006).

3. Amar Abdullah, "Armed Groups Blamed for Loss of Oil Revenues" [in Arabic], *Azzaman*, January 17, 2007, at www.azzaman.com/ (accessed January 17, 2007).

4. Ma'ad Fayad, "Iyad Allawi Talks to Asharq Al-Awsat," *Asharq al-Awsat*, January 22, 2007.

5. Matthew Elliot, *Independent Iraq: The Monarchy and British Influence, 1941–58* (London: I.B. Tauris, 1996).

6. Ahmed Al Katib, "The Events in Najaf: Will They Ignite Riots or an Intifada?" [in Arabic], *Al-Wasat* (March 1–7, 1999): 14–15; Assad Hidar, "As Sadr in the Week Before" [in Arabic], *Al-Wasat* (March 1–7, 1999): 13–14.

7. Mustafa Sarour, "Assassination of Sadr Preceded by a Deadly Telephone Debate: Preemptive Strike or Provocation to Civil Strife" [in Arabic], *Al-Wasat* (March 1–7, 1999): 10–12.

8. Al Katib, "The Events in Najaf."

9. Al Katib, "The Events in Najaf."

10. Al Katib, "The Events in Najaf."

11. Saad al Qisi, "Najaf: City of Slaughter in the War of the Marjaiyat" [in Arabic], *Al-Watan Al-Arabi*, March 5, 1999, 20–21.

12. Haiyan Naiyoif, "New Details about the Assassination of Sadiq as Sadr" [in Arabic], *Al Arabiya*, January 28, 2007, at www.alarabiya.net/ (accessed January 28, 2007).

13. Safauddin Tabraian, "A Glance at the History and Inclination of the Supreme Council for the Islamic Revolution in Iraq," trans. Net Iran, *Hamshahri* 11, no. 3023 (April 15, 2003).

14. Sami Shaurash, "Muktadar Sadr Shuffles the Cards: Shi'a War against Americans or Shi'a War against Shi'a" [in Arabic], *Al-Wasat*, no. 612 (October 20, 2003): 4–6.

15. Sami Moubayed, "Coming to Terms with Sistani," *Asia Times*, February 10, 2005, at www.atimes.com/atimes/Middle_East/GB10Ak02.html (accessed February 10, 2007).

16. Babak Rahimi, "Ayatollah Ali as-Sistani and the Democratization of Post-Saddam Iraq," *The Middle East Review of International Affairs* 8, no. 4 (December 2004).

17. Mehdi Khalaji, "The Last Marja: Sistani and the End of Traditional Religious Authority in Shi'ism," Washington Institute for Near East Policy, *Policy Focus* 59 (September 2006).

18. "Response by the Office of H. E. Ayatullah Sistani," January 7, 2005, at www.sistani.org/messages/eng/ente/htm (accessed January 7, 2005).

19. Sami Moubayed, "Iraq Loses Its Voice of Reason," *Asia Times*, September 6, 2006, at www.atimes.com/atimes/Middle_East/HI06Ak01.html (accessed September 6, 2006).

20. Ray Close, "The Critical Iran-Turkey Triangle," *Gulf 2000*, February 1, 2007.

21. Ma'ad Fayad, "Iraqi Judge: Elements of Al-Mahdi Army Have Settled in Green Zone" [in Arabic], *Asharq al-Awsat*, January 10, 2007, at www.asharqalawsat.com/english/news.asp?section = c1&ideq761 (accessed January 10, 2007).

22. Michael Knights, "Scant Evidence Found of Iran-Iraq Arms Link," postings on ggs2@columbia.edu, January 27, 2007.

23. Ann Scott Tyson and Robin Wright, "For Sadr, a Fracturing Militia," *Washington Post*, March 29, 2007, at www.washingtonpost.com/ (accessed March 29, 2007); Sabrina Tavernise, "Cleric Said to Lose Reins of Parts of Iraqi Militia," *New York Times*, September 28, 2006, at www.nytimes.com/2006/09/28/world/middleeast/28sadr.html (accessed September 28, 2006); Sabrina Tavernise, "Influence Rises but Base Frays for Iraqi Cleric," *New York Times*, November 13, 2006, at www

.nytimes.com/2006/11/13/world/middleeast/13sadr.html (accessed November 13, 2006).

24. Faraj Ismail, "Sadrist Currents Deny Fatwa" [in Arabic], *Al Arabiya*, December 5, 2006, at www.alarabiya.net/ (accessed December 5, 2006).

25. *The National Intelligence Estimate 2007*, National Intelligence Council, February 2007, at www.dni.gov/reports/reports.htm (accessed May 2, 2007).

7

Turkey

A Model for Democratic Islamic Rule?

THE ISLAMIC JUSTICE and Development Party won a stunning 34 percent of the popular vote in Turkey's 2002 election, a figure sufficient to give it a majority of the seats in Turkey's parliament, the Grand National Assembly. Some observers considered this victory to be a fluke or protest vote, while others warned of an end to Turkish democracy as the Islamists, as they are called in the regional press, imposed a fundamentalist regime on this most secular of Middle Eastern states. Rumors of a possible military coup were widespread.

Five years later, the Justice and Development Party swept to an even larger victory, gaining some 46 percent of the popular vote in the 2007 parliamentary election, a margin of victory unknown since the 1950s. Clearly, the broad appeal of a moderate Islamic party was no fluke.

Fears that the Justice and Development Party would rush to pursue an Islamic agenda in Turkey proved to be unfounded. The Islamic Justice and Development Party has complied with both the letter and spirit of Turkey's constitution. The party has also championed Turkey's entry into the European Union (EU) and pursued a variety of progressive programs urged by the United States. These include the opening of Turkish markets to foreign investment and the scaling back of the state-owned industries so dear to the Turkish military. Cynics refer to this process as "Islamic capitalism."[1] Even more laudatory has been the ability of the Justice and Development Party to steer Turkey toward global capitalism without imposing added hardships on the poor. Turkey also remains an ally of the United States and Israel, although somewhat less so than during the previous decade. Joint maneuvers are held with both, but Turkey's Islamic leadership has made a point of urging Israel to solve the Palestinian problem by trading land for peace. Tensions with the United States peaked during the Iraq war but had less to do with Islam than heavy-handed U.S. efforts to force Turkish participation in an unpopular war.

Turkey's very secular generals warn that the moderation of the Justice and Development Party is merely a ruse to buy time while it erodes the secular foundations of Turkey's political system. Pro-Israeli sources also worry over investments being made in Turkey by the Saudis and other Gulf Arabs with reputedly Islamic leanings. It is this so-called green money, they claim, that has helped the Justice and Development Party provide welfare while reducing taxes.[2]

The warnings noted, the fact remains that Turkey stands as a model of democratic Islamic rule. The existence of a moderate Islamic party also appears to have deflated the appeal of jihadist groups such as the Turkish Hizbullah.[3] Have restrictions on religious freedom been eased? Yes. Is that bad?

The success of the Turkish experience with moderate Islamic rule poses two basic questions for our study of Islamic extremism and the strategic choices facing the United States. First, why has moderate Islamic rule worked in Turkey? Second, can the Turkish model be exported to other countries in the region? Both will be addressed in turn, but first it is necessary to place these most speculative of tasks in historical perspective.

Historical Perspective

The Islamic invasions that swept through the Middle East in the seventh and eight centuries engulfed much of Asian Turkey but were stymied in their northern expansion by the power of the Byzantium Empire that ruled Eastern Christendom from Constantinople, the modern Turkish city of Istanbul. A Muslim siege of Constantinople failed in 717, and Europe remained the bastion of Christianity. The world might have been different had the Muslims succeeded.[4] The zeal of the Muslims, however, was not to be denied, and Constantinople fell to the Ottoman Turks in 1453.

Ottoman power peaked at the end of the seventeenth century and then began a gradual decline. By the mid-eighteenth century, that decline had become a rush. The once dominant power of the region had become the "sick man of Europe." The empire survived until the end of World War I, largely because the European powers were unable to decide on a suitable burial. Britain, France, and Russia all coveted parts of the empire, and each feared that the empire's demise would tip the fragile balance of European power in favor of its adversaries.

The Turkey that emerged from the ashes of World War I consisted of the Turkish heartland. Even that would not have survived if General Mustafa Kemal had not rallied what remained of the Ottoman forces and resisted the dismemberment of the country. Kemal was a Turkish nationalist, but his vision of the new Turkey had little in common with the Ottoman Empire of old. Turkey, in his view, could only regain its power by becoming part of the West. This meant industrialization. It also meant secularization. If the Ottoman Empire had led the Islamic invasion of the Christian West, the new Turkey would become a beacon for the westernization of the Islamic world.

Kemal blamed Islam for Turkey's backwardness and launched a vicious attack on Islamic institutions and traditions. Turkey, according to Kemal, would be secular in both form and attitude. The attack on Islam began in earnest in 1925 with the abolition of dervish (Sufi) orders and the closing of their schools, shrines, and mausoleums. Symbols of Islam such as the fez were outlawed. Veils were discouraged and later outlawed in schools and public buildings. In 1926, the Swiss legal code replaced the Ottoman legal code, depriving Islamic law of its preeminent role in the affairs of business and government. The Gregorian calendar similarly replaced the Islamic calendar. In later years polygamy was abolished (not many men could afford it) and the constitution amended to delete references to Turkey as an Islamic state. Religious instruction was also removed from both public and private schools, and Sunday replaced Friday, the Muslim holy day, as the official day of rest.[5] From 1928 onward, the Turkish language was written in the Latin alphabet rather than the Arabic. This was a practical reform inasmuch as the Arabic alphabet did not lend itself to the expression of Turkish, but it also represented another break with Turkey's Islamic past.

Turkish nationalism replaced Islam as Turkey's official ideology, and nationalistic myths were used to instill pride and self-volition in a Turkish population still in the grips of Islamic fatalism. Kemal wanted a "can-do" culture, and the myths developed to achieve this end often became flights of fancy. One Turkish historical thesis claimed that Turks were white Aryans of Central Asian origins who had been "forced by drought and hunger to migrate to other areas such as China, Europe, and the Near East. In so doing they created the world's great civilizations."[6] Attila the Hun and Genghis Khan became national heroes and were portrayed as great civilizers. These and similar myths were taught in public schools until the 1940s.

Kemal was also a populist intent on welding a strong bond between the government and its people, something that was sadly lacking in the past. Tax burdens were eased, people were made equal before the law, and illiteracy, then around 80 percent, was attacked with a vengeance. All villages were required to have at least elementary schools. High schools, teachers' colleges, and universities proliferated in the major cities. People were also required to have a family name. The Grand National Assembly conferred the name of Ataturk, "father of the Turks," on Kemal.

A new economic strategy, referred to as "statism," was adopted to transform Turkey from an overwhelming agrarian country into an industrial power. As capitalists and private entrepreneurs were reluctant to invest in long-range projects, it was the Turkish government that played the role of investment banker and entrepreneur. The government planned and financed new industries. When the going got tough, it was the state that provided the money to keep them afloat. Some industries were sold to the private sector, but most remained under government control.

How well did it succeed? This remains something of a debate. The face of Turkey was changed. This is beyond question. Islam was separated from the affairs of government, industrial development took root, railroads spanned the country, a rudimentary electricity grid was established, education flourished, women were emancipated, and Turkish independence was secured. Outside observers were impressed, and Western scholars recommended "Kemalism" as a formula for modernizing less developed countries.

And yet, the process of westernization in Turkey has produced mixed results. The Turkish constitution states that Turkey is a secular state, but its current prime minister and president are members of a moderate Islamic party that advocates greater Islamic influence in the affairs of government. The wearing of religious dress (head scarves) is forbidden in public schools and government buildings but is very much in evidence among the more religious segment of the Turkish population. A plebiscite on the issue is being discussed.

In reality, Turkey continues to be a melange of East and West, each part struggling for the country's soul. Islam could not be defeated, but secularism had taken root. Perhaps a majority of Turks prefer this balance of Islam and secularism, each being moderated by the other. An alternate hypothesis is that there are two incompatible Turkeys: one modern and secular and the other traditional and religious. In this view, the current balance between Islam and secularism is merely a temporary stalemate that must inevitably give way to one or the other. This, however, remains to be seen. Our present objective is to examine why this balance between Islamic rule and secularism has managed to function as well as it has. This accomplished, we will be in a position to judge its relevance to the remainder of the Islamic world.

Why Does the Turkish Model of Islamic Democracy Work?

One answer to this question is that the Turkish military is dedicated to the preservation of secularism in Turkey and constitutes a powerful counterweight to the Justice and Development Party. The military overthrew an earlier Islamic regime and periodically fires shots over the bow of the present one. A coup d'état is unlikely but remains an option should the country's secular traditions be placed at risk. The Turkish constitution recognizes the military as the protector of secularism, and the military goes to great length to prevent infiltration into its ranks by pro-Islamic groups. This, of itself, assures that the balance between the military and the Islamists will remain a constant feature of Turkish politics for some time to come. The Islamic currents are too powerful to crush, and the military is too powerful to defy.

This said, the military has bent to reality and has allowed a moderate Islamic party to rule. Democracy has been served, and Turkey's Islamic traditions have been given their due. At least on the surface, this compromise appears to satisfy most Turks, and support for more extreme Islamic groups is minimal.

The Justice and Development Party, for its part, has been willing to go slow. It has pushed its Islamic agenda whenever possible but avoided a direct confrontation with the military. The Islamic agenda of the Justice and Development Party has also been restrained and involves little more than lifting the ban on head scarves in state institutions and giving Islamic schools equal status with secular schools. Supporters have been placed in important positions, but that's politics.

Politics or not, the Turkish president had had enough in 2006 and warned, "Religious fundamentalism has reached alarming proportions."[7] Perhaps the Justice and Development Party's real crime was consolidating its position as a major force in Turkish politics by demonstrating that an Islamic party could rule at least as effectively as its secular counterparts, perhaps more so. The party's emphasis on capitalism also threatened entrenched economic interests with ties to the military.

Some seventy years of forced secularism were not sufficient to eliminate Turkey's Islamic roots, but they did create a society with stronger secular traditions than other countries in the Islamic world. Millions of Turks have also worked in Germany and well understand the power and benefits of Western society. Not all succumbed to the lure of westernization, but many did. One way or another, few Turks seem interested in an Iranian-style Islamic Republic.

The lure of membership in the EU has also been a strong force for religious moderation in Turkey. Membership in the EU, although unlikely in the immediate future, offers the promise of far greater prosperity, democracy, and religious freedom than Turkey currently enjoys. Membership in the EU is of obvious appeal to secular Turks but no less so to the Justice and Development Party. Membership in the EU would curb the powers of the Turkish military while enabling the Justice and Development Party to broaden its religious agenda under the EU's human rights and social charters.

Before membership in the EU can become a reality, however, the Justice and Development Party must convince Europeans that it is a moderate political party closer to the model of Europe's Christian Democratic parties than it is to the Muslim Brotherhood or Hizbullah. The Turkish military must also do its part by convincing the Europeans that it has returned to the barracks for good. The EU has made it clear that there can be no more coups or heavy-handed military intervention in the democratic process.

Islamic Democracy in Crisis

Everything was going well until the presidential elections of 2007. As in many countries, the Turkish president is elected by the parliament—thus, the crisis. The next president of Turkey, the preserve of the military, would be selected by a parliament dominated by a very Islamic Justice and Development Party. What would happen if the Justice and Development Party used its majority in the Grand National Assembly to elect a president with Islamic leanings rather than following the established custom of deferring to the military? That would give the Islamists control of both the parliament and the presidency. As the president names the senior judges and is commander in chief of the military, no branch of the Turkish government would be free of Islamic influence. Could Turkey's Islamic democracy survive?

The answer to that question is now being played out in Ankara. In the spring of 2007, Turkey's Islamic prime minister suggested that he might have himself elected president. This was within his grasp because his party controlled just about two-thirds of the assembly, depending upon how one counted. Mass demonstrations, variously estimated as between a million and several hundred thousand, rocked Istanbul and other cities. In the end, the prime minister didn't nominate himself for the presidency. Instead, he nominated the foreign minister as the party's candidate for president. He was the only candidate. This was not a compromise because the foreign minister was no less Islamic than the prime minister.

The election was held and the foreign minister won. The Republican People's Party boycotted the vote and subsequently claimed the absence of a quorum. The issue was sent to the Constitutional Court whose eleven members had been appointed by a very secular and promilitary president. The election was thrown out by a nine-to-two vote. A quorum, according to the Constitutional Court, required 367 votes. [8] Gul, the foreign minister, had only 366 votes because of the boycott of the opposition party.[9] The military weighed in with a warning that it was prepared to act in its constitutional role as "absolute defender of secularism" in Turkey.[10] The prime minister lashed out at the military by reminding them that "the military chief of staff is responsible to the prime minister . . . and that it is inconceivable in a democratic state based on the rule of law for the general staff, which is under the orders of the prime minister, to speak out."[11] The prime minister then called for a snap parliamentary election in the likelihood of gaining the necessary two-thirds majority in parliament. He also vowed to amend the constitution to provide for a lower quorum as well as for a popularly elected president. This, too, was a threat to the power of the military elite that used its control of the presidency to influence government policies.[12] Both the United States and the EU warned against military intervention as new parliamentary elections were scheduled for July 22, 2007.

As we have seen, the Justice and Development Party swept to a crushing victory in the 2007 parliamentary elections. It retained its staggering majority in the Grand National Assembly and duly elected an Islamist as president of Turkey. The military boycotted the president's swearing-in ceremony and reiterated its constitutional role as the protector of Turkish secularism. Stay tuned.

The Turkish Model for Containing Islamic Extremism: Solution or Illusion?

At least on the surface, Turkey has established a viable model of moderate Islamic rule compatible with integration in a secular world. Islam has been given its due, and extremism has been kept in check. The question is, can the Turkish model be used to contain Islamic extremism in other countries of the Islamic world?

The answer to this question is a qualified yes but only if certain conditions are met. To begin with, a moderate Islamic party must be allowed to both take office and rule if it wins democratic elections. Barring this, the chances are that radical if not violent currents will come to the fore.

Once in office, the ruling Islamic party must play by democratic rules including the conducting of free and fair elections and a willingness to cede power if it loses. If a ruling Islamic party implements a moderate Islamic agenda, so be it. That was what it was elected to do, and moderate progress toward a more Islamic society will cut the wind from the sails of the more extreme Islamic currents. It will also turn the moderates against the extremists rather than forcing them into the same camp.

To be on the safe side, the power of the Islamic party must be balanced by a powerful force capable of keeping it from going to extremes. In the case of Turkey, the military is the balancer, but it could just as well be the presence of a large non-Muslim population such as the Christians in Lebanon or the presence of a strong external force such as the Israeli army in the case of the Palestinians. It might even be a relative balance between Shi'a and Sunni if they could put aside their sectarian hatreds.

The United States must be willing to accept an Islamic party and make it effective. The goal, after all, is to fight extremism by allowing the more moderate elements in the region to succeed. Fighting fire with fire is the analogy that comes to mind.

As things currently stand, few of these conditions are being met. For those familiar with the politics of the Middle East, they seem like an ethereal dream world. Democracy in the Islamic world is largely a farce, and neither the United States nor the ruling elites of the region are willing to see a moderate Islamic party succeed. The United States and Israel fear Islam, and the ruling elites of the region fear losing the perks of power and corruption. Even the most moderate of Islamic parties contains the seeds of extremism, and balance is hard to achieve. It could also be argued that Turkey is an exception. Its secular traditions are strong, and its military remains dedicated to secularism. Unlike the military of most other Islamic countries, it has been minimally infiltrated by extremist currents. Finally, the lure of membership in the EU is a profound force for moderation in Turkey. These conditions do not exist elsewhere in the Middle East. The EU is skittish about Turkish membership and has no thought of incorporating other Islamic countries any time soon.

This said, the Turkish experience might yet provide the most effective strategy for preventing the further radicalization of the Islamic world. What the United States is doing now certainly isn't working. More to the point, it is having the adverse effect of radicalizing the Islamic world, a topic discussed in more detail in the chapters that follow. In the meantime, devout Muslims throughout the Muslim world are watching the Turkish experience with a great deal of interest. Many would like to try it.

Notes

1. Mustafa Akyol, "'Islamic Capitalism' Faces Secular Challenge in Turkey," *Turkish Daily News*, December 18, 2006, at www.turkishdailynews.com.tr/ (accessed December 18, 2006).

2. Michael Rubin, "Green Money, Islamist Politics in Turkey," *Middle East*

Quarterly 12, no. 1 (Winter 2005), at www.meforum.org/article/684 (accessed December 12, 2005).

3. The Turkish Hizbullah is not linked to Shi'ite Hizbullah organizations.

4. Sydney N. Fisher, *The Middle East: A History* (New York: Alfred A. Knopf, 1964); Erik Zurcher, *Turkey: A Modern History* (London: I.B. Tauris, 2004).

5. Fisher, *The Middle East.*

6. Zurcher, *Turkey: A Modern History*, 191.

7. For more on this topic, see *Turkish Daily News*, April 14, 2006, at www .turkishdailynews.com.tr/ (accessed April 14, 2006).

8. Gamze Cavdar, "Behind Turkey's Presidential Battle," *Middle East Report Online*, May 7, 2007, at www.merip.org/mero/mero050707.html.

9. "Government Lashes Out at the Military," *Turkish Daily News*, April 28, 2007, at www.turkishdailynews.com.tr/ (accessed April 28, 2007).

10. "PM Meets Army Chief amid Government Crisis over Role of Islam," *Turkish Daily News*, May 7, 2007, at www.turkishdailynews.comc.tr/ (accessed May 7, 2007).

11. Goksel Bozkurt and Duygu Guvenc, "Top Court Annuls First Round of Presidential Elections," *Turkish Daily News*, May 2, 2007, at www.turkishdailynews .com.tr/ (accessed May 2, 2007).

12. "Government Ready to Go to the People for Electing a President," *Turkish Daily News*, May 5, 2007, at www.turkishdailynews.com.tr/ (accessed May 5, 2007).

8

The Jihadist Movement
and How it Evolved

THE JIHADISTS ARE Muslim extremists intent on establishing an Islamic state through violence. In their view, reform is an illusion. Cooperating with secular governments, they say, merely adds to their legitimacy and makes them harder to defeat in the long run. In the meantime, the cancer of Western culture corrupts Muslim youth and undermines the pillars of the Islamic faith. Much as the Prophet Mohammed declared a jihad against the infidels in Mecca, so the jihadists believe it is their task to drive the infidels from the lands of Islam. Who is an infidel? Anyone, Muslim or otherwise, who obstructs the jihadist vision of an Islamic state. It is the jihadists who will make that determination.

Beyond this point, there are so many variations within the jihadist movement that they defy description. Groups form, splinter, and regroup under different names. Some were inspired by Egyptian jihadists. Others find their roots in Iran or Pakistan. Some are large and well organized; others are embryonic. Some network; others prefer to operate independently. Osama bin Laden's al Qaeda network is the most renowned of the jihadist groups, but it is just one of many. Egypt, alone, had some ninety jihadist groups during the 1980s. Global figures could well reach several hundred. Even al Qaeda is now splintering into a multitude of autonomous groups. How tightly they are linked to al Qaeda is a mystery. Many groups have received support from al Qaeda but do not follow its dictates. Others serve as subcontractors, carrying out specific operations for al Qaeda and then returning to their own agenda. Like most subcontractors, they pick up jobs as they come along. Still others are graduates of Afghanistan or Iraq who have branched out on their own. This does not make them part of al Qaeda, but it does make them part of the jihadist threat. Even groups distant from bin Laden are inspired by his example. Adding to the confusion is America's tendency to attribute all terrorist attacks to al Qaeda, regardless of their origin. This is misleading and suggests that the problem can be solved by the arrest of the al Qaeda leadership. Arrests are made, but the attacks continue.

The present chapter traces the evolution of the jihadist movement from its origins in groups of student radicals through the evolution of international networks capable of striking America and its allies. Each step along the way has seen the jihadists respond to adversity by extending their reach and developing new and more deadly strategies for striking their enemies. That evolution continues today.

Egypt and the Origins of Modern Jihadism

The jihadist movement seemed to emerge in Egypt as part of the broader Islamic revival spawned by the humiliating defeat of the Arab armies in the Six Day War of 1967.[1] The Egyptian Army, the vanguard of the Arab forces, collapsed in about four days. In its wake came a psychological crisis as Egyptians struggled to understand how a secular regime that had spent twenty years preaching militarization and industrialization could simply crumble in the face of an Israeli attack. The picture was much the same throughout the Arab world. Islam, always a dominant force in Arab culture, filled the psychological emotional vacuum left by the war.

In reality, the jihadist movement in Egypt had begun long before the humiliation of the Arab forces in the Six Day War. Its origins, while difficult to pin down precisely, began as a bitter debate within the Muslim Brotherhood over the use of violence as a political weapon. The strongest voice on the side of violence was that of Sayyid Qutb, a brilliant intellectual who argued that reform was pointless and only served to corrupt Muslims and strengthen the enemies of Islam.[2] Infidels were to be killed, not accommodated.

The debate was largely theoretical as long as the Nasser regime was in power. By the mid-1960s, however, mass frustrations with a failed experiment in forced socialism were approaching the breaking point. Egypt, moreover, had suffered through a long and unpopular war in Yemen.[3] Sensing mass discontent, Qutb's faction within the Brotherhood plotted the violent overthrow of the Nasser regime. The plot failed and Qutb was executed.

Perhaps Qutb's greatest mistake had been impatience. The Six Day War broke out two years later and threw the Egyptian government into chaos. Nasser resigned but recanted in the face of a mass outpouring of popular emotion. Field Marshall Abdel Hakim Amer, commander of the Egyptian forces and longtime friend of Nasser, committed suicide following accusations that he had plotted to overthrow the government. His wife suggested that he was assassinated by Nasser.[4] Nasser was terminally ill and died in 1970.

Nasser was replaced by Anwar Sadat who, fearful that he would be overthrown by the communists and other leftists, revived the Muslim Brotherhood as a counterweight to his adversaries. In the process, he also opened the door to a virtual explosion of jihadist groups.[5] They, too, were given free reign to attack leftist groups intent on opposing Sadat's rule. It was they, along with the Brotherhood, who transformed the "street" from a bastion of the left into a bastion of Islam.

With leftists crushed and Sadat secure in his presidency, the jihadists demanded that the Egyptian president, a former member of the Muslim Brotherhood, transform Egypt into an Islamic theocracy. Sadat resisted, and the battle was joined. It culminated in the 1981 assassination of Sadat by the Islamic Group, Egypt's largest jihadist organization. The word jihadist had entered the world's vocabulary. Buoyed by the assassination of Sadat, the jihadists waged a relentless war against the Egyptian government that threatened to become a civil war before tapering off toward the end of the 1990s.

Most of the ninety-some jihadist groups to emerge in Egypt during the 1970s and 1980s were formed by students from middle- and lower-middle-class backgrounds. Largely rural, their conservative traditions clashed with the urban immorality of Cairo and Alexandria. Indeed, youth was the hallmark of the jihadist movement, with the majority of its members being students or recent graduates.[6] Most were trained in technical fields like medicine and engineering rather than the mind-bending fields of politics or philosophy. Such, at least, were the results of Saad Ibrahim's interviews with jihadists imprisoned in the aftermath of Sadat's assassination.[7] Most were also frustrated by the corruption of the Sadat regime and the glaring economic inequities of Egyptian society.

The early years of the jihadist movement were a spontaneous explosion of faith, optimism, frustration, and naivety. There was no organizational network as such, but members of the diverse groups, most of which were little more than small cells, seemed to be aware of each other, and interaction between groups was not uncommon. Hala Mustafa suggests that this might have been the results of contacts developed in prison, one of the main breeding grounds of jihadist movement.[8] Mobility between groups was also common as groups splintered and reformed.

By 1992, Egypt appeared to be on the brink of civil war. As described by Ibrahim Aoude, "Until July 1992, Islamic forces controlled many villages and small towns in several governorates in Egypt. In some cases they had political power that paralleled the Egyptian state."[9]

The Islamic Jihad

Most of Egypt's smaller groups have now fallen by the wayside or merged with their larger competitors. Of these, two groups, the Egyptian Islamic Jihad and the Islamic Group (Al-Gama'a al-Islamiyya) have developed a broad international reach and are featured on the U.S. list of international terrorist organizations. The Islamic Jihad was formed in the 1970s and gained notoriety with the assassination of President Sadat. In 1998, the group splintered with Dr. Ayman al Zawahiri affiliating his wing of the Islamic Jihad with bin Laden's al Qaeda network. It formally merged with al Qaeda in 2001.

Relations between al Zawahiri and bin Laden apparently developed during the Afghan rebellion against the Soviets. Egyptian "Afghans" were trained in bin Laden's camps and, with the end of the Afghan rebellion in 1989, began to make their way back to Egypt. They were implicated in 1993 plots to assassinate Egypt's prime minister and minister of interior and in a 1995 plot to assassinate President Husni Mubarak. They were also the prime suspects in failed attempts to blow up the American and Israeli embassies in Manila in 1994 as well as the successful 1995 bombing of the Egyptian embassy in Pakistan. All of the above events occurred before the merging of the Islamic Jihad and al Qaeda, and there can be little doubt that al Zawahiri added much-needed muscle to bin Laden's al Qaeda network. Indeed, the Islamic Jihad is widely believed to be the force behind the 1998 bombings of the American embassies in Nairobi, Kenya, and Dar es Salaam, Tanzania. Al Zawahiri's stamp also appears large on the 2000 bombing of the USS *Cole* in Aden, Yemen, and the September 11 terrorist attacks on the United States, although this is a matter of speculation. One might question who poses the greatest threat to America: bin Laden or al Zawahiri? Questions remain about bin Laden's health. Al Zawahiri remains at large. He is clearly capable of exploiting the resources of the al Qaeda network. He is equally capable of reestablishing his own network.

The splintering of Islamic Jihad and the merger of its al Zawahiri branch with bin Laden has left the Islamic Jihad in disarray. It has reportedly regrouped under the leadership of Tharwat Salah Shehata (Abu Sama) who was, himself, sentenced to death in absentia for his role in the 1995 assassination attempt on President Mubarak.[10] He was part of al Zawahiri's group in Afghanistan but disagreed with the merger of the Islamic Jihad and al Qaeda.

The Islamic Group (Al-Gama'a al-Islamiyya)

The background of the Islamic Group roughly parallels that of the Islamic Jihad. It was founded in 1973 in the very traditional areas of Upper Egypt (southern Egypt) and spread rapidly to student groups in Cairo and Alexandria. It, too, was used by Sadat as a counterweight to his leftist adversaries, but the honeymoon was short lived. Hounded by Sadat's police, the group's leader, Sheikh Omar Abdel-Rahman, the "blind sheikh," fled to Saudi Arabia where he was welcomed by wealthy Saudi backers. Many of the Islamic Group's members were jailed following Sadat's assassination in 1981. Others fled to Afghanistan where they joined the jihad against the Soviets. Well trained in terrorist tactics by bin Laden and others, they later returned to Egypt to continue their struggle against the Mubarak regime.

The Islamic Group shared the Islamic Jihad's commitment to violence, but its targets differed. While the Islamic Jihad focused on the assassination of key political leaders, the Islamic Group focused on creating domestic turmoil. During the 1990s, the Islamic Group launched a vicious terrorist campaign against foreign tourists that culminated in the 1997 slaughter of sixty-two tourists in Luxor. U.S. businessmen were also warned to leave Egypt or face the consequences. This was not a minor concern, for more than ten thousand Americans lived in Egypt at the time, us among them. Indeed, Egypt was rapidly becoming an American colony. The government and business community remained, but the tourists, a mainstay of the Egyptian economy, did not. Hotel occupancy collapsed. Banks, theaters, nightclubs, bookstores, and other businesses were also attacked, which compelled the minister of interior to proclaim that Egypt was at war with the jihadists.[11]

Along with its attacks on foreign tourists, the Islamic Group began to inflame tensions between Muslims and Egypt's Coptic community. The Copts, a Christian community that dates to the earliest days of Christianity, constitutes some 10 percent of the Egyptian population and had always lived in relative harmony among Egypt's Muslim majority. Tensions, however, existed and flare-ups had become frequent as the two communities began to encroach on each other's territory. Copts would say the encroachment was one sided. A particularly violent riot erupted when a family in the upper floor of a jointly occupied apartment building hung out their wash to dry on the edge of the balcony. Water dripped on the drying laundry of the family below. We don't remember whether it was Christian water that dripped on the Muslim laundry or vice versa, but the result was a full-scale religious riot. The Islamic Group entered the fray by attacking Christian shopkeepers and calling for the forced application of Sharia law on the Copts. President Mubarak denounced the growing religious violence, but the damage had been done.

It was at this point that the tide shifted against the Islamic Group. The attack on Luxor proved to be profoundly unpopular among an Egyptian workforce heavily dependent on tourism. The Islamic Group also suffered heavy losses from government attacks, and many of its key members were either jailed or forced into exile. The Islamic Group began to rethink its strategy of violence, and key members of the jailed wing of the party called for a truce with the Egyptian government. Calls for a truce split the Islamic Group into pro- and anti-truce factions. The truce was initially supported by Sheikh Abdel-Rahman, who was incarcerated in a U.S. prison for orchestrating the 1993 bombing of the World Trade Center, but he later changed his mind. The truce is holding in Egypt, but the Islamic Group remains active throughout the world. In 1998, the radical European wing of the Islamic Group developed close ties with bin Laden's World Islamic Front for Jihad against the Jews and Crusaders but retained its independence. Most published reports find the Islamic Group in disarray and of little threat to either the Egyptian government or the United States. Strangely, the Egyptian government has accepted the truce, and most members of the Islamic Group were released from prison. This was hardly the tactic of a government on the brink of victory.

Iran and the Islamic Revolution

Paralleling the rise of the jihadist movement in Egypt was the evolution of Shi'a jihadism in Iran. Much as in Egypt, religious emotions in Iran had been inflamed by a lethal blend of westernization, poverty, corruption, oppression, and bizarre leadership. As we have seen in the earlier discussion of Hizbullah, the Ayatollah Khomeini welded this reservoir of mass frustration into an Islamic Revolution that swept the Shah of Iran from his throne. Khomeini, to be sure, was not the only source of opposition to the Shah in Iran. Leftists and nationalists of all varieties, many armed, swelled the ranks of the revolution. Most doubted the capacity of the clerics to rule, believing that it would be they who claimed power. It was Khomeini, however, who captured the imagination of the masses, and it was he who would rule Iran. Secular revolutionaries fortunate enough to escape death or imprisonment fled to the West.

Perhaps the United States would have overlooked the loss of its stellar ally in the Cold War if Khomeini had proven humble and compliant. The Shah, after all, had become a bizarre individual whose erratic policies raised eyebrows in Washington.[12] The United States, moreover, had always found Muslim clerics useful allies in its struggle against the godless Soviets. Khomeini, for all of his faults, was an avowed anticommunist.

Ayatollah Khomeini, however, was not the humble sort. His hatred of the Americans eclipsed his hatred of the Soviets. The United States, Khomeini proclaimed, was a great Satan who controlled the Islamic world by keeping Israel and the likes of the Shah and Saddam Hussein in power. It was not bin Laden who focused jihadist attentions on America but rather the Ayatollah Khomeini.

No sooner had he seized power in Iran than Khomeini proclaimed a grand Islamic Revolution, a jihad to end all jihads that would drive America and everything American from the Middle East. Israel was to go, as were the secular leaders of the region, most of whom were beholden to the United States.

Khomeini's contribution to the jihadist movement was threefold. First, he created a network of Shi'a jihadist organizations headed by Hizbullah Lebanon. It was these organizations that led the charge in his Islamic Revolution. They might or might not have mellowed, but their origins were in the most violent of jihadist traditions. Second, Khomeini's victory in Iran demonstrated that Islamic groups could smite the most powerful of leaders and humiliate the most powerful of nations. All that was required was faith. The psychological impact of this message on the jihadist movement was incalculable. Everything became possible. Third, Khomeini made sure that it did. Arms and money poured into hands of the Sunni jihadists, many of whom were invited to Iran for training in revolutionary tactics. The jihadist movement now had a national home free from attack by foreign security forces.

For all of Ayatollah Khomeini's impact on the jihadist movement, it would be a mistake to believe that the marriage between Khomeini's Islamic Revolution and the Sunni jihadists was made in heaven. Iranian support was welcomed by the Sunni jihadists but not the Shi'a doctrine of Hidden Imams and ayatollahs. Both, in the view of the Sunni jihadists, were embellishments invented by the Shi'a long after the passing of the Prophet Mohammed. Neither of these had a place in the Sunni vision of an Islamic state. Many Sunni jihadists considered the Shi'a to be heretics and feared that they were intent on exporting their apostasy to the Sunni world. Their distrust was requited by the Shi'a, long the victims of Sunni oppression. Pakistan witnessed pitched battles between rival Sunni and Shi'a groups, as did the civil war in Lebanon, hardly a propitious sign for the future. Cooperation between Iran and Sunni jihadists existed, but unity did not.

Pakistan: The Jihadist Gateway to the
Far East and Central Asia

Yet a third jihadist tradition emerged in the Indian subcontinent, a region that constitutes the countries of India, Pakistan, and Bangladesh. If Egypt nourished the Arab jihadists and Iran their Shi'a counterparts, it was Pakistan that nourished jihadism in India, Afghanistan, Central Asia, and the Far East. The key element in this process was Pakistan's vast network of religious schools. Other culprits included the governments of Pakistan and the United States.

But let us begin at the beginning. India won its independence from Britain in 1947, but rejoicing soon turned to fear as a violent civil war between Hindus and Muslims swept the subcontinent. With reconciliation beyond hope, the predominantly Muslim areas of the subcontinent were hastily patched together into the country of Pakistan. The split was messy, and the newly proclaimed country of Pakistan was less a nation than a collection of hostile ethnic groups.

Islam, it was hoped, would provide the glue that held the country together. Pakistan was to be an Islamic state, the Koran its constitution. But it was not to be. The more populous eastern provinces seceded from the union in 1971, forming the new country of Bangladesh. What remained of Pakistan was fragmented by splits between Pakistan's Sunni majority (70 percent) and its Shi'a minority (27 percent). Both, in turn, were divided among themselves. The Sunni, by and large, adhered to one of three schools of Islamic interpretation: the Barelvi, Deobandi, and Ahli Hadith. The Barelvi is both the largest and most tolerant of the three schools, often blending local customs with Islamic practice. The Deobandi, by contrast, advocate the strict application of Islamic law including the establishment of an Islamic state in Pakistan. The Deobandi doctrine was also the doctrine of the Taliban in Afghanistan, the leaders of which were trained in Deobandi schools in Pakistan. The Ahli Hadith, if anything, is more extreme in its interpretation of Islam than the Deobandi and has largely been funded by Saudi Arabia.[13] For all intents and purposes, it has embraced the Wahhabi doctrine of Saudi Arabia.

Each of the three main Sunni doctrines has its own schools and mosques and has generated its own political parties. The parties have spawned radical spin-offs, many of which have been active in jihadist violence.[14] *Jane's Intel-Web* "Terrorist and Insurgency Groups" lists no less than six Pakistani groups linked to jihadist violence.[15] Jihadist violence has been most closely associated with the Deobandi and Ahli Hadith groups, both of which have seen their influence expand since the mid-1970s. The Deobandi has been favored by the Pakistani government, the Ahli Hadith by Saudi Arabia.

Adding to the religious fervor in Pakistan has been the Tabligi Jamaat, a large Islamic missionary and benevolent society that often attracts a million or more pilgrims to its annual meeting in Rawindi, Bangladesh.[16] It also possesses branches throughout the world, including the United States, Russia, France, and most countries of Central Asia. The Tabligi Jamaat is not a terrorist organization, but the zealousness of its religious teachings has led to accusations that the organization lends itself to jihadism. The Harakat ul-Mujahideen (HuM), one of Pakistan's largest jihadist groups, recruits largely from among members of the Tabligi Jamaat.[17]

While space does not allow a full discussion of Pakistani history, suffice it to say that all of the requirements for a jihadist uprising were in place by 1970: a deeply ingrained tradition of religious teaching, incompetent and corrupt secular governments, the dazzling wealth of the few pitted against the grinding poverty of the many, and a political geography characterized by remote areas largely beyond the control of the central government.

In the early 1970s, an embattled Bhutto government wavered from the secular tradition established by earlier Pakistani rulers and curried favor among the country's Islamic groups. This process became a rush in 1977 as General Zia ul-Haq seized power in a military coup and attempted to legitimize his rule by posing as the champion of Islam. The influence of secular parties faded while the Islamic groups were given broad rein to expand their operations. The extremist Deobandi were favored and grew from a small minority to some 15 percent of the Pakistani population. The Ahli Hadith also prospered, the ul-Haq government being anxious to please its rich Saudi Arabia backers. The schools of both grew dramatically.[18] The jihadist movement grew apace, as Deobandi–Ahli Hadith violence targeted both the Shi'a and the more lax Sunni Barelvi.

Perhaps to ease the sectarian violence precipitated by the jihadists, the ul-Haq regime focused their energies on Kashmir, a predominantly Muslim region on the Pakistani border that had been awarded to India in the frantic efforts to bring the 1947 civil war in India to a close. Pakistan soon fought and lost two wars with India over Kashmir and had blamed India for the 1971 secession of Bangladesh. A third war between India and Pakistan erupted in 1972 but lasted only two weeks. The jihadist represented a new front in Pakistan's continuing war with India. While Indian casualties mounted, the Pakistani government feigned innocence. The jihadist struggle for Kashmir continues unabated, symbolic crackdowns by the Pakistani authorities notwithstanding. A fourth Indo-Pakistan war could well raise the specter of a nuclear holocaust.

The Pakistani jihadists received a further boost in the early 1980s when they were enlisted in America's jihad against the Soviets in Afghanistan. In retrospect, this was a mistake. The Pakistani jihadists emerged from Afghanistan well trained, well armed, and well connected with other jihadist groups in the region.

Two Pakistani groups, in particular, have been noted for their militancy: the HuM and the Lashkar-e-Toiba (LT). The HuM is linked to radical elements in the Deobandi school long favored by the Pakistani government and is a mainstay of jihadist violence in Kashmir and India. The LT finds its roots in the Saudi-sponsored Ahli Hadith school of thought and was recently implicated in the downing of an Indian airliner and the bombing of the Indian parliament. Neither has been in the forefront of anti-American violence, but both have been linked to bin Laden and are mainstays on the U.S. List of Designated Foreign Terrorist Organizations.

As elsewhere, jihadist groups in Pakistan splinter and change their names with great frequency. The HuM, by way of example, first emerged as a splinter group of the Harkat ul-Jihad-i-Islami, a jihadist group created in 1980 to fight the Soviets in Afghanistan. The two groups later merged and formed the Harkat ul-Mujahideen. Along the way it was suspected of establishing al-Faran, a front organization, and the Jaish-e-Mohammed (the Army of Mohammed) and other terrorist groups. The Army of Mohammed duly changed its name to Khudam-u-Islam, proclaiming that its new mission was limited to preaching and welfare. The LT, for its part, was outlawed and subsequently changed its name to Jamaat-ud-Dawa. It, too, now claims that its activities are limited to preaching and welfare. The permutations continue.

In part, this endless sequence of fragmentation and regrouping is the result of personality conflicts and ideological debates within the jihadist movement. It is also a strategic ploy designed to keep the United States at bay. Once a group appears on a U.S. antiterrorist list, it is closed down by the Pakistani government and reconstitutes itself under a different name. The transformation of the HuM to the Harkat-ul-Ansar, for example, occurred in 1993 and was brought about by the U.S. anger over the HuM's refusal to return the American weapons that it had acquired during the war against the Soviets. The United States is mollified and life goes on, as does the war in Kashmir and elsewhere.

Pakistani jihadists have also played a key role in the spread of jihadism to East Asia. As B. Raman, the former head of the counterterrorism division of India's External Intelligence Agency writes,

> Evidence available to date indicates that while the terrorists from Malaysia and possibly Singapore were trained in the headquarters of the Jaish Mohammad (JEM) in Binori madrasa complex in Karachi, those from Indonesia were trained in the Muridke complex of the LET, near Labore. The HUM traditionally trained recruits from the southern Philippines and Myanmar, in addition to those of Xinjiang, Chechnya and the Central Asian Republics. The HUJI trains those of Bangladesh. Before October 7, 2001, the training camps of the HUM and the HUJI were located in eastern Afghanistan.[19]

India, as might be expected, keeps close tabs on Pakistani jihadists. Not only are the jihadists spearheading the violence in Kashmir, but also their bombing of the Indian parliament brought the jihadist war to the very heart of India. Other attacks seem to be inevitable. Muslims constitute approximately 11 percent of India's one billion citizens, and most are hostile toward an Indian government they accuse of gross prejudice against its Muslim citizens.[20] Religious flare-ups between Hindus and Muslims are common but none more so than during the mid-1970s when Indian efforts to control its exploding population focused indiscriminately on the castration of poor Muslims. The program was soon scrapped but symbolizes the abiding tension between the two religious groups. Few Indian Muslims are jihadists, but the long history of conflict between Hindus and Muslims does help explain why some Indian Muslims are sympathetic to the jihadist cause.

The situation in Bangladesh has been largely ignored by a world media constrained by sound bites but largely parallels that of Pakistan. The Jamaat, an Islamic party, is well represented in the Bangladeshi parliament, and its youth organization is active in global organizations such as the International Islamic Federation of Student Organizations and the World Assembly of Muslim Youth. These are not jihadist organizations, but they do provide a venue for communications and recruitment among Muslim students. Bertil Litner notes that the Jamaat student group dominates the approximately ten thousand Deobandi schools in Bangladesh and maintains close ties with radical groups in Pakistan, Malaysia, Indonesia, and the Middle East.[21] Faziui Rahman, the leader of the jihadist movement in Bangladesh, a coalition of Bangladeshi jihadist groups, signed bin Laden's 1998 declaration of war against America. The government of Bangladesh denounces terror but has been less than stringent in controlling a jihadist movement that enjoys a broad base of popular support.

Afghanistan and the Making of a Muslim Hero

The role of the jihadists became even more vital to the Pakistanis with the 1979 Soviet invasion of Afghanistan, Pakistan's neighbor to the north. The Soviets were closely aligned with India, and the presence of a Soviet puppet regime in Kabul raised the very real prospect that India would be in a position to control some two-thirds of the Pakistani border, a terrifying prospect for the Pakistanis.

Iran's Islamic Revolution was also of concern to Pakistani leaders, for Ayatollah Khomeini's inflammatory rhetoric was not lost on Pakistan's Shi'a population. The Pakistanis did not want the Soviets in Afghanistan, nor did they want a Shi'a revolution on their borders. Afghanistan was a predominantly Sunni country, and Pakistan wanted to make sure that it stayed that way.

The United States shared Pakistan's concern on both counts. Khomeini's Islamic Revolution threatened to sweep the United States and its allies from the region, not the least of which was the Saudi Royal family and its control of one-fourth of the world's proven oil reserves. Soviet control of Afghanistan would have much the same result, placing it within easy striking power of the Persian Gulf. Neither the Islamic Revolution nor the Soviet invasion of Afghanistan could go unchallenged.

An obvious step toward solving both problems was a U.S.-sponsored jihad against the Soviets in Afghanistan. In one fell swoop, a Vietnam-style war would be inflicted on the Soviets, Pakistan would be bolstered in its struggle with India, and Iran's new Islamic revolution would have its hands full in neighboring Afghanistan. It was better to support indigenous freedom fighters, U.S. officials reasoned, than risk the deployment of American troops in hostile territory. In retrospect, this was a mistake.

It now appears that the American-sponsored jihad in Afghanistan was the first step in transforming the jihadist movements of Egypt, Iran, and Pakistan into an international network capable of challenging the United States. A coalescing of the jihadist movement would have occurred with or without Afghanistan, but the Afghan experience accelerated this process by years if not decades.

That, however, was not clear at the time, and it seemed natural for the United States to funnel supplies to the jihadists in Afghanistan via Pakistan. The Afghan operation was placed in the hands of the Inter-Services Intelligence (ISI), the Pakistani intelligence service.[22] The Central Intelligence Agency (CIA) footed the bill and helped with weapons and recruitment but was excluded from the management of the Muslim volunteers who had begun to trickle into Pakistan at the onset of the 1980s. India and Kashmir were of greater concern to the Pakistanis than Afghanistan, but Afghanistan was the ticket to U.S. military aid. It was the ISI who decided who went where and with what arms. The United States is technically correct when it claims that it did not train bin Laden's al Qaeda fighters. It might have been better if it had.

Why did Afghanistan, a desolate and impenetrable country bypassed by the course of history, become the crucible of the world's jihadist movement? The answer is quite simple. The Americans, Pakistanis, Saudis, Iranians, jihadists, and other interested parties could not challenge the Soviet occupation of Afghanistan without creating an elaborate infrastructure of manpower, training, intelligence, supplies, money, communications, and everything else needed to fight a sustained war against a superpower.

Because the war against the Soviets was to be a religious war, that infrastructure had to be profoundly religious in nature. Pakistan became the main point of entry for waves of holy warriors who streamed into Afghanistan from all parts of the Islamic world. Many came from the Arab countries, giving rise to the term "Afghan Arabs" whether they were Arabs or not. The term stuck, and foreign fighters linked to Afghanistan continue to be referred to as Afghan Arabs. Pakistan would give refuge to some two million Afghan refugees and host some seven jihadist groups. The Afghan Arabs were God's soldiers who feared neither death nor hardship. Indeed, they seemed to court death. Men of religion also became key links in the communication and distribution process just as mosques became convenient rendezvous points. This is not to denigrate the role of the Afghans in liberating their own country from Soviet rule. It was they who did most of the fighting. It was the Afghan Arabs, however, who transformed the Afghan rebellion into a true jihad.

The rush of men and material into Afghanistan created an urgent need for a central base to process recruits and coordinate incoming Islamic aid. The task of establishing this base fell to Dr. Abdullah Azzam, a leading figure in the Jordanian branch of the Muslim Brotherhood and subsequently a professor at the International Islamic University in Islamabad, Pakistan. His second in command was Osama bin Laden, then a young man in his twenties.[23] The choice was logical, for bin Laden had been trained in economics and engineering and possessed a strong practical background in business and construction engineering. Adding to his credentials were his contacts with the Saudi royal family and wealthy Saudi contributors. By and large, he was the Saudi's man in Afghanistan. The processing base that bin Laden helped create was simply referred to as "the base" by the Afghan Arabs. "The base" in Arabic is al Qaeda. Much to the chagrin of both the Americans and the Saudis, bin Laden's al Qaeda in Afghanistan would become the embryo for his al Qaeda terrorist network.

The jihadists emerged from the war in Afghanistan with an exhilarating sense of victory and an unshakable faith in their ability to reclaim the Islamic world in the name of Allah. They also emerged from Afghanistan with a cadre of well-trained fighters who numbered in the thousands, if not the tens of thousands. It is premature to speak of an international jihadist network at this point, but fundamental steps had been taken in that direction. Groups from the three major jihadist centers—Egypt, Pakistan, and Iran—had been brought into contact with each other. They had also been brought into contact with bin Laden and his access to rich financier "angels" in Saudi Arabia and the Gulf. The jihadists, moreover, had acquired a new sense of legitimacy. Bin Laden's pictures hung from mosques throughout Saudi Arabia and the Gulf. He was the new Saladin, slaying the invading crusaders. The Soviets had been the enemy of the moment, but jihadists saw little difference between the Soviets and the Americans. Both were godless, and both were guilty of usurping Muslim lands. The Soviets oppressed Muslims in Afghanistan and Central Asia; the Americans defiled Islam through their support of Israel and their puppet regimes in Saudi Arabia, Egypt, and elsewhere.

Afghanistan gave birth to the Afghan Arabs, that free-floating pool of jihadist fanatics vowing to die in the name of God. Some of the Afghan Arabs returned to their countries of origin where they either strengthened existing jihadist organizations or created their own.[24] Others awaited God's call from the more comfortable environs of Europe, North America, or promising locations in the Third World. The very breadth of their dispersion assured a foundation for international action. Those Afghan Arabs with prices on their heads bided their time in Afghanistan.

Bin Laden, for his part, made a triumphant return to Saudi Arabia in 1989 and was lavishly feted by a Saudi royal family anxious to bask in the glow of its illustrious Islamic hero. Not only had the royal family been at the forefront of the Afghan jihad, but it was a Saudi, albeit of Yemeni origin, who had led the charge. This was powerful stuff for a Saudi regime reeling from Khomeini's charges that it was a group of debauched hypocrites who had sold out to the Americans. According to Yossef Bodansky, "The praise and media attention made bin Laden a sought-after celebrity. He spoke at countless mosques and private gatherings. Some of his fiery speeches were recorded; well over a quarter of a million official cassettes were sold and countless illegal—and later, underground—copies were also made and distributed."[25]

Bin Laden's speeches avoided criticism of the monarchy, but it was not too difficult to read between the lines. The royal family wanted to bask in bin Laden's glory. It did not want a potential competitor. In traditional Saudi style, the royal family attempted to buy him off with lavish construction contracts, but he refused. Tensions reached the breaking point with Iraq's invasion of Kuwait in 1990. The Saudis feared that they would be next and turned instinctively to the United States for protection. Bin Laden, by contrast, urged the monarch to rely on God. The jihadists had driven the Soviets from Afghanistan. They could surely protect Saudi Arabia from Saddam Hussein.[26]

The royal family was not persuaded and remained firm in its decision to rely on the United States, the price of which was the stationing of American forces in Saudi Arabia, the heartland of Islam. Bin Laden departed for the Sudan with the blessing of the royal family. He was essentially a businessman, and the Sudan offered dazzling opportunities for those not adverse to risk. He was also a jihadist.

The Sudan: An International Terrorist
Network Takes Shape

Afghanistan had provided the basic building blocks for an international jihadist network. Even with the experience of Afghanistan, however, the jihadist movement remained a series of volcanic eruptions, powerful but uncoordinated. If the jihadist movement were to achieve its goals of establishing Islamic governments in the Muslim world, it would have to transcend the outbursts of random and uncoordinated violence that had characterized the movement's early decades. Goals had to be agreed on, targets set, strategies developed, command structures established, forces marshaled, weapons procured, recruits processed, finances arranged, intelligence networks established, and safe communications secured. In short, the war machine that the United States had helped the jihadists organize in Afghanistan had to be replicated on a global scale.

Particularly pressing was the need to coordinate the three basic components of the jihadist movement: the Egyptians, the Iranians, and the Pakistanis. This meant bridging the gap between the Shi'a and the Sunni, a task equivalent to squaring the circle. The Egyptians and Pakistanis were also divided by a vast chasm of culture, language, and tradition. The former were overwhelmingly concerned with the Arab world, the latter the Indian subcontinent. Aside from Afghanistan, contact between the diverse branches of the jihadist movement had been minimal.

The hero of the Sudan was not bin Laden but rather a Muslim cleric named Hassan Abdullah al-Turabi. Al-Turabi, a brilliant intellectual, received a master's degree in law from the University of London (1957) and a doctorate of law from the Sorbonne (1964). He did not fear the West, nor was he awed by it. Rather, al-Turabi had a sound understanding of both the strengths and weaknesses of Western modernity. He applauded the West's capacity to promote human welfare through science and law but was appalled by its hedonism and moral depravity. Like many true Islamic intellectuals before him, al-Turabi sought ways of placing the technological advances of the West at the service of Islam. His goal was to bring order and development to the Muslim world without sacrificing the religious values of Islam.

For the moment, however, there were more practical matters. American hostility toward Iran and its Islamic Revolution had demonstrated that neither the United States nor its allies would tolerate an expansion of Islamic rule. They had to be forcibly removed from the Islamic world, but how? It was not enough to attack Western puppets in the Islamic world, al-Turabi argued. The United States would not relinquish its grip on the Muslim world until it had tasted the sting of defeat. This required the creation of an international jihadist network capable of fusing the energies of the Egyptian, Pakistani, and Iranian jihadists. It also required links to the Muslim Brotherhood and other more moderate elements in the Islamic movement. All would have to be mobilized in the service of Islam.

Once the network was complete, al-Turabi's argument continued, it would attack its adversaries with a three-pronged strategy. First, secular leaders in the Islamic world, most of whom were beholden to the West, would be destabilized and, if possible, overthrown. Second, Islamic lands occupied by the West would be liberated by force. This was a direct reference to Israel, a country the jihadists viewed as a Western outpost in the heart of Islam. Third, jihadist networks would be established throughout the world, particularly in North America and Western Europe. This fifth column would enable the jihadist movement to attack the enemy from within. The West would not be safe until Islam was safe.

Al-Turabi's strategy drew heavily on the experience of the Ayatollah Khomeini's Islamic Revolution, especially in its use of Hizbullah groups to drive the United States from Lebanon. The soldiers of Islam had struck, and America had recoiled. Al-Turabi had also studied the successes of other terrorist movements, the Irish Republican Army (IRA) in particular. When London subways were bombed, the British began to think seriously about withdrawing from Northern Ireland. If the United States were bombed, the Americans would begin to think seriously about withdrawing from the Middle East. All that was missing was the capacity to bring the full resources of the jihadist movement to bear in a coherent and rational manner. This had not been done. It would be al-Turabi's contribution to the jihadist movement.

The opportunity for decisive action came in June 1989, when General Omar al-Bashir, a devout Muslim and follower of al-Turabi, seized power in the Sudan. Al-Bashir became president of the country, and al-Turabi was given free rein to transform the Sudan into an Islamic state. Islamic law became the order of the day as the Sudan proclaimed itself the world's second Islamic theocracy. Al-Turabi's main focus, however, was not the Sudan. The Sudan was merely his venue for establishing a global Islamic network capable of challenging the West.

What al-Turabi Brought to the Jihadist Movement

Al-Turabi possessed a number of attributes that were essential to the development of an international jihadist network. Al-Turabi's writings had established him as a profound intellectual who possessed the moral authority to ride herd over a much-fragmented jihadist leadership. There could be no network without a head, and it was al-Turabi, more than any other single individual, who spoke for a deeply divided Islamic movement that included the Muslim Brotherhood as well as the jihadists. All, according to al-Turabi, would play a vital role in achieving their common goal of an Islamic state. The jihadists would attack the enemies of Islam with violence and the moderates by internal subversion. In much the same manner, al-Turabi's philosophy opened the door for rapprochement with Shi'a Islam, at least at the operational level. The Iranians could deal with al-Turabi far more effectively than they could cooperate with Sunni jihadists who viewed the Shi'a as heretics.

Also of key importance to the networking process was the breadth of al-Turabi's contacts, including a multitude of wealthy benevolent associations. As he later boasted, "I know every Islamic Movement in the world, secret or public."[27] He further boasted, "I also meet Heads of State of Arab countries, Muslim countries and many non-Muslim countries."[28] Two of al-Turabi's strongest supporters among the Arab heads of state were Muammar Qadaffi and Saddam Hussein. Finally, al-Turabi provided the jihadist movement with a secure base of operations. Much like Afghanistan, the Sudan was a quagmire of conflict and intrigue, a destitute and bankrupt country torn by civil war and the machinations of its neighbors. If Afghanistan had been impenetrable, the Sudan was just the opposite, sharing common and largely unpatrolled borders with no less than nine different countries. What better environment for the establishment of a jihadist network?

Bin Laden and Iran: The Twin Pillars of al-Turabi's Network

Al-Turabi possessed the stature, the vision, and the contacts required to guide an international jihadist network. Forging such a network, however, needed more than words. There had to be base camps and training facilities, financiers, weapons, experts, document forgers, communications experts, organizers, and intelligence operatives, not to mention a hard core of dedicated soldiers. This was the work of technicians. Al-Turabi was a theologian, a philosopher, and a politician, but he was not a technician—nor was the destitute country that he controlled in the name of Islam capable of sustaining an international jihadist network. It could provide shelter for the network but little more.

Fortunately, from al-Turabi's perspective, he did not have to start from scratch. Many of the technical skills required for an international jihadist network had already been developed, at least in embryonic form, by the Ayatollah Khomeini. Others were provided by the jihadist network developed in

Afghanistan. Al-Turabi's task was to bring the existing pieces together in a fertile environment for growth.

The first of these pieces was Osama bin Laden, the hero of Afghanistan. Bin Laden's skills were well known to al-Turabi, and having exiled himself to the Sudan, he became part of al-Turabi's inner circle. The relationship between al-Turabi and bin Laden was straightforward. Al-Turabi was a religious luminary: a model to be followed and emulated. Bin Laden was a jihadist, a businessman, and a war hero, but he was not a theologian. Al-Turabi concentrated on the network's grand design; bin Laden made it work. This is not to denigrate bin Laden's role. Bin Laden brought to the network his ties to Afghan Arabs, many of whom looked to him as a leader. Bin Laden also provided access to rich Saudi and Gulf angels and designed an apparently foolproof financial network, which, by all accounts, continues to befuddle American sleuths. His companies built many of the training camps for the al-Turabi network, and his foreign offices became links between the network and Islamic groups in Europe and elsewhere. In the process, bin Laden laid the foundation for what he eventually transformed into his al Qaeda network.

Al-Turabi's relationship with Iran was far more complex. Both were dedicated to forging an international jihadist network capable of resisting America and its Western allies. Each, moreover, needed the other. The Iranians needed entry into the Sunni world. Al-Turabi needed the financing and technical expertise that the Iranians could provide, not to mention the resources of their Hizbullah networks in Lebanon and the Gulf. Indeed, visits to Tehran had convinced al-Turabi that the Iranians were light years ahead of the Sunni jihadists in terms of their revolutionary capacity. Lurking in the shadows, however, was the ever-present tension between the Sunni and Shi'a versions of Islam.

Al-Turabi was willing to work things out with the Shi'a, but this was less the case with the other Sunni jihadists who continued to view the Iranians as dangerous heretics. Also lurking in the shadows was the question of who was using whom. Al-Turabi was the head of the jihadist network. It could not be otherwise. Sunni jihadists would not take orders from a Shi'a. There can also be little doubt that al-Turabi saw himself as the future caliph of the revived Islamic *Umma* or nation. He was not, as his speeches amply demonstrated, a man of small ego. It was the Iranians, however, who footed much of their bill and provided much of the technical infrastructure. Between 1991 and 1993, Iran literally transformed the landscape of the Sudan by spending millions of dollars on construction projects, many of which were implemented by bin Laden's companies.[29] In the process, jobs were provided for the

Afghan Arabs and more recent recruits. In the words of the adage, he who pays the piper calls the tune. The Iranians were not passive bystanders.

The Network Emerges

The international jihadist network that took shape between 1991 and 1993 revolved around a variety of conferences designed to find a common ground that could unite the diverse elements of the Islamic movement and particularly its jihadist wing. The conferences, in turn, led to the establishment of various umbrella organizations designed to facilitate and coordinate the activities of its members. In April 1991, al-Turabi hosted an Islamic Arab People's Conference, the deliberations of which resulted in the formation of the Popular International Organization (PIO), an organization dedicated to revolutionizing the Sunni Islamic world. A permanent council that represented the fifty countries in which Islamic revolutionary activity took place was duly established in Khartoum, the capital of the Sudan.[30] A variety of jihadist organizations affiliated with the PIO, including groups from Pakistan, Kashmir, Afghanistan, Egypt, Algeria, and elsewhere. Later the same year, al-Turabi reportedly established a parallel body designed to coordinate relations between the jihadists and the Muslim Brotherhood.[31] Al-Turabi was the spiritual guide of the PIO and its coordinator, but he lacked the power to impose his views on the various affiliate organizations.

By and large, al-Turabi's PIO was little more than a clearinghouse for channeling support and information to various jihadist groups. Links were strengthened between the Pakistanis and Arabs, and, to a lesser degree, between Iran and the Sunni jihadists. The Egyptians and the Algerians were the particular beneficiaries of this enhanced cooperation and received training in Pakistan and Iran as well as in the Sudan.

Al-Turabi's PIO also possessed a hard-core contingent of Afghan Arabs who were unable to return to their home countries. Again, al-Turabi's control was less than absolute. Many of the Afghan Arabs looked to bin Laden for leadership. Others inclined toward Pakistan and the infamous ISI. The rift was not a minor one. Pakistan was intent on using the Afghan Arabs in Kashmir, while al-Turabi was intent on the destabilizing of sub-Saharan Africa, about half of which was predominantly Islamic in character. Islamic Africa, al-Turabi preached, was in chaos, and well-organized Islamic groups could seize power with relative ease. It was, in his view, free for the taking.[32]

No sooner had al-Turabi's network taken shape than the Muslim world exploded in violence. Algeria dissolved into civil war in 1991 as jihadists threatened to seize control of one of the largest countries in the Arab world. Egypt was not far behind. The same period saw Hamas and the Islamic Jihad challenge the Palestinian Liberation Organization (PLO) for control of the Palestinian resistance. The Palestinian struggle for independence had long been noted for its violence, but the jihadists added a new weapon to the conflict: the suicide bomber. The same period witnessed the 1993 bombing of the World Trade Towers. The war had reached America.

The Battle for Algeria

Al-Turabi and his network did not create the jihadist upheavals in Algeria, Egypt, and the Occupied Territories, but they added to their intensity. The Algerian story is of particular interest as it illustrates how rapidly an ostensibly secular state could be subverted by a determined Islamic movement. It also illustrates the dangers inherent in efforts to play the more moderate Islamic groups against the jihadists.

The story began in 1931, some three years after the founding of the Muslim Brotherhood in Egypt, when an association of Algerian *ulema* was founded to fight the French colonization of Algeria. The movement was inspired by the Muslim Brotherhood and eventually opened a liaison office in Cairo to encourage young Algerian students studying in Egypt to adhere to the teachings of the Brotherhood. Most of these students were pursuing their studies at Cairo's renowned Al-Azhar University, and it was they, in conjunction with students from other religious universities, who established Algeria's first Islamic party in 1947. The Algerian branch of the Muslim Brotherhood was established in 1953. Algeria's war for independence was launched the following year.[33]

The bulk of the fighting in Algeria's war of independence was carried out by the National Liberation Front (FLN), a secular leftist movement that advocated the rapid industrialization of Algeria under the twin banners of nationalism and socialism. Once in power, the FLN followed the Egyptian model. Government factories provided employment for urban workers, while government welfare programs attempted to create a socialist paradise. Food and rents were subsidized, and education and health care were free to all. Both were failures. State factories and farms were unproductive, while cradle-to-grave welfare schemes became a bureaucratic nightmare. Algeria was broke, and its debtors were unforgiving.

Also unforgiving was Algeria's increasingly restive population. The Muslim Brotherhood and other Islamic groups flourished. Some advocated moderation; others became jihadists. The groups involved were so many and so varied that they defy easy description. Some were small bands, others were full-fledged militias. They fought the government, and they fought each other. The more the economic situation deteriorated, the stronger the jihadists became.

In desperation, the Algerian government jettisoned its socialist dreams and turned to capitalism. Privatization became the order of the day as the massive state-owned factories were scaled down and Algeria's social safety net began to fray. Efficiency increased but so did unemployment and poverty. Students, once confident of a government job, faced the grim prospect of unemployment. According to government figures, 1990 found approximately half of the Algerian population pauperized.[34] Not reformed was a legacy of corruption that permeated all facets of government activity. Government "barons" pushed corruption to new heights as they skimmed 10 percent off sales of divested government properties and staked claim to prime real estate.[35] It was they who were the prime beneficiaries of Algeria's gradual transition to capitalism.

Mass frustrations mounted, but the regime seemed confident that it could keep them in check until capitalism had transformed Algeria into a model of prosperity. The one current of opposition that the regime could not bottle up was the radical Islamists with their clandestine networks that lurked in the shadows of Algeria's mosques.

Mass demonstrations rocked Algeria in 1988 and raised the specter of civil war. The government attempted to buy time by allowing Algerians a limited democracy. They hoped that the emergence of moderate political parties would offer a safety valve for mass frustrations and turn the tide against the jihadists. The key element in this gamble was the legalization of the Islamic Salvation Front (FIS).[36] The FIS had emerged in 1989 as an umbrella organization designed to unify Algeria's diverse Islamic groups in what appeared to be their final battle against the Algerian government. The moderates within the FIS argued for participation in elections scheduled for the coming year. The jihadists refused but found little support for violence as long as an electoral victory was in the offing.[37] Local elections were scheduled for June 12, 1990.

It seemed that the government's strategy of divide and rule had worked. The FIS had split into two factions: moderates versus the jihadists. The moderates, according to government strategy, were to be bought off with high-level government positions while the army turned the full force of its power on the jihadists. It was not to be. Cooler heads prevailed, and a senior FIS theologian worked out a compromise between the two sides. Elected members of the FIS were "empowered to give orders and be obeyed," but they were not bound by the orders of secular officials. Elected FIS deputies were also to oppose all policies that contradicted Islamic law or that threatened the establishment of an Islamic state.[38]

The FIS captured 55 percent of the vote in the 1990 municipal elections, although it is difficult to say whether the vote was an expression of support for the fundamentalists or a protest vote against a corrupt and oppressive government. Far more frightening was the prospect of an FIS victory in the parliamentary and presidential elections promised for the following year. If the FIS repeated its sweeping victory in the local elections, Algeria would become an Islamic state, and the moribund regime of generals, politicians, and bureaucrats that had ruled Algeria since its independence would be swept from office. Presumably, they would be swept into jail.

What was there to do? The answer was obvious: rig the election. A new electoral law "concocted by the Ministry of Interior" virtually assured a victory for the regime.[39] The FIS declared a general strike. Algeria's major cities were paralyzed as demonstrators jammed thoroughfares and protestors stormed government buildings.

The government responded by rekindling the split within the FIS. Jihadists were arrested, while the moderates were allowed to operate freely. The general strike was broken, and the moderates, then dominant, led the FIS into the legislative elections. This proved to be an empty victory. The moderates controlled the shell of the FIS, but its military wings (there were two, each with different leadership) remained under the control of the jihadists.

The legislative elections scheduled for November 26, 1991, followed a two-stage format. The first stage resembled primary elections in the United States, with any candidate receiving an absolute majority of the votes being declared the winner. If no candidate received a majority, a second or runoff stage was to choose between the two leading candidates. The FIS scored a resounding victory in the first round of the elections. Its ultimate victory in the second round was never in doubt. Algeria's military leaders annulled the electoral process before a second round could be held. It was their only hope of keeping Algeria out of the ranks of the Islamists.

No sooner had the election been nullified than the FIS went into "crisis mode," its code word for going underground. A secret meeting of the FIS leadership, dominated by the jihadists, declared a jihad against the government for blocking the establishment of an Islamic state. Posters declaring the jihad appeared in all of the twelve thousand registered (legal) mosques controlled by the FIS. Far more important were the thousands of "free mosques" created by the FIS without official approval. While the registered mosques exhorted the faithful to support the jihad, the free mosques became armed camps.[40] The war had begun. To date, it has claimed the lives of more than 150,000 Algerians.

The jihadists broke with the FIS in the fall of 1992, leaving it an empty shell. They also turned against each other. Actually, the gutting of the FIS resulted in the emergence of four separate jihadist armies, not to mention a multitude of urban gangs loyal only to their leader. All were violent, but none more so than the urban gangs for whom violence became an end in itself.[41] The winner in the gruesome battle, at least for a time, was le Groupe islamique armé or the GIA. This was not surprising, for the groups that had merged to form the GIA had a long history of combat in Algeria. They also had the strongest ties to al-Turabi's network. The GIA's view of the world was simple: Algeria was to become an Islamic state ruled by the strict interpretation of Islamic law. Anyone who disagreed with this position would be killed.

The power of the GIA reached it zenith in 1995 and declined sharply thereafter. That date also marked the unraveling of al-Turabi's network. The problems of the GIA, however, were largely homegrown. Leading a jihadist group is risky business, and each disappearance of a GIA emir brought a new round of consultations as sub-emirs set about the tricky task of selecting a new supreme emir to whom they would swear absolute allegiance. For those who failed to make the cut, it was a bitter pill.

It was also a dangerous one, and defections were common. The selection process was itself flawed, with young firebrands buoyed by records of violence being elected over older and more experienced competitors. Each new emir viewed his competitors with a jaundiced eye and feared treachery at every turn. Absolute allegiance was not to be gained by compromise and negotiation. There was also the problem of the other jihadist militias. They, no less than the army and police, had become the enemy. Assaults by the military and police also took their toll on the GIA much as they took an awesome toll on Algeria's citizens.

The level of violence abated after 1998, but a day rarely goes by that is unmarked by carnage of one form or another. Sometimes the targets are rural hamlets obliterated in a hit-and-run strike. Other times they are police stations, government officials, journalists, or popular singers. In the meantime, the jihadist struggle in Algeria has been exported to a North African community in France that numbers in the millions. Few are terrorists, but the majority of North African immigrants in France live in squalor and are blamed by the French authorities for France's epidemic of crime and drugs. Given these circumstances, it is not surprising that France has become fertile ground for the jihadists.

Palestinian Islamic Jihad

Much like the evolution of Hamas discussed in chapter 4, the founders of the Palestinian Islamic Jihad had joined the Muslim Brotherhood while studying in Egypt. Unlike Hamas, their zeal soon exceeded the moderation of the Brotherhood, and they formed the Palestinian Islamic Jihad. The philosophy of the Palestinian Islamic Jihad, much like the other jihadist groups emerging in Egypt during the mid-1970s, was one of revolutionary violence. Indeed, the Palestinian Islamic Jihad became so close to the Egyptian jihadists that they were implicated in the 1981 assassination of President Sadat and deported to Gaza.[42] After a brief rapprochement with the Palestinian branch of the Muslim Brotherhood, they again branched out on their own and preached a violent blend of jihadism and Palestinian nationalism. The emphasis was on the latter, for there could be no Islamic state in Palestine until the Israelis had been defeated. That, in the view of the Islamic Jihad, could only be achieved by force. This philosophy is shared by a variety of smaller groups that also operate under the Holy Jihad name. These include the Islamic Jihad-the-Temple and the Islamic Jihad Squad.

The leaders of the Islamic Jihad viewed the 1979 victory of the Ayatollah Khomeini in Iran as a sign from God that overwhelming military force could be overcome by faith and sacrifice.[43] The leader of the Islamic Jihad fled to Beirut toward the end of the 1980s, and ties between Islamic Jihad and Hizbullah increased apace—so did ties to Iran. Hizbullah's influence on both the Islamic Jihad and Hamas can be seen in the unrelenting wave of suicide bombing that began in earnest in the mid-1990s. Suicide attacks were not unknown among Sunni jihadists, but they had been perfected by Hizbullah and its Iranian sponsors.[44]

Hamas and the Islamic Jihad cooperate but not without disagreements over strategy and leadership.[45] The early months of 2004 saw increased rumors of unity discussions between the two groups. Dr. Abdul Sitar, a political scientist at Najah University on the West Bank, suggested that such speculations were premature. He acknowledged growing cooperation in field operations between the two groups but suggested that the two organizations remained far removed from ideological unity. The Islamic Jihad remains wedded to the violent imposition of an Islamic government in Palestine, while Hamas remains rooted in the more flexible ideology of the Muslim Brotherhood and in 2005 became the ruling party in what passed for a Palestinian state. As we have seen in chapter 4, that situation now remains in flux.

In the meantime, the Islamic Jihad serves as a violent alternative to Hamas should the zeal of the latter moderate as it attempts to transform itself from a revolutionary organization into a governing party. Unlike Hamas and most other Palestinian groups, the Islamic Jihad has refused to participate in a unity government or to maintain a truce with Israel.[46] This, of itself, provides Israel with provocation for its strikes against Gaza and the West Bank. The Islamic Jihad is a small player in the Israeli-Palestinian conflict, but it is a deadly one. There are also fears that it might coalesce with al Qaeda and Egyptian Jihadist groups as part of a global jihad.[47]

The Jihadist War Comes to America

On February 26, 1993, a van loaded with explosives was detonated in the underground parking garage of the World Trade Center. Six people were killed and more than one thousand wounded. The U.S. mainland had remained free from foreign attack during two world wars, but that was no longer the case. The jihadists had struck in the heart of America's largest city. The attacks had been orchestrated by Sheikh Abdel-Rahman, a blind sheikh and the spiritual guide of Egypt's Islamic Group. The Islamic Group, as noted earlier, was one of the world's dominant jihadist movements and one of the jihadist groups accused of assassinating Egyptian President Sadat in 1981. Abdel-Rahman was implicated in the assassination but released from prison on a legal technicality.

This of itself is curious, for Egyptian authorities seldom worry about technicalities. Indeed, Egypt's prisons are littered with convicts who have never had a trial, fair or otherwise. The blind sheikh, however, was not an ordinary prisoner. Egypt was on the verge of a civil war, and little was to be gained by granting Abdel-Rahman his wish of martyrdom. All things considered, a dead saint was a greater threat to the Egyptian government than a live spiritual guide. This said, the Egyptians couldn't allow the sheikh to rally his troops from prison. The only choice was exile.

Abdel-Rahman migrated to the United States by way of the Sudan. He obviously had contacts with the al-Turabi network, but al-Turabi's involvement in the attacks on the World Trade Center remains uncertain. Abdel-Rahman was not under al-Turabi's control, but they did share common goals. Al-Turabi, moreover, was in the business of facilitating attacks on the United States, whatever their origin. Why did the American authorities allow Abdel-Rahman to settle in the United States? The only reasonable explanations are laxity and a failure to take the jihadist threat seriously. The man was not an obscure individual, and his activities were well known to American officials in the region.

U.S. authorities considered the bombing of the World Trade Center to be an isolated act. Subsequent events proved them wrong. The same year found American forces in Somalia under attack by rival warlords, the dominant ones of whom was supported by the al-Turabi network. The man in charge was Osama bin Laden. In part, the jihadist attacks were the result of a simple misunderstanding. The United States believed that it was on a humanitarian mission. The jihadists believed that the U.S. relief effort was a pretext for establishing a base in the Horn of Africa. This, from al-Turabi's perspective, could not be allowed. A U.S. base in the Horn of Africa would place his plans of the control of Islamic Africa in jeopardy and enable the United States to strike jihadist bases in the region at will. Of equal importance was al-Turabi's desire to inflict a defeat on the United States. Jihadist morale would be bolstered, and America would think long and hard before challenging jihadist forces in the future.

Somalia was ideally suited for al-Turabi's venture. Somali warlords did most of the fighting, while al-Turabi's network supplied weapons and kibitzed from the sidelines. The bitterest fighting occurred in Mogadishu in 1993, where U.S. troops took heavy losses. They left Somalia a few months thereafter. Bin Laden lists Somalia as one of his major victories against the United States. The American withdrawal from Somalia reinforced the jihadist conviction that the United States would withdraw from a country rather than take casualties. It also demonstrated the effectiveness of al-Turabi's strategy of utilizing civil wars to promote jihadist causes.

This theory was put to the test the following year as al-Turabi's network supported the Muslim side in the Bosnian Civil War. By 1994, Afghan Arabs were reportedly integrated into Muslim forces in Bosnia while the Iranians, the paymasters in al-Turabi's network, provided the Bosnian Muslims with funds and weapons. This, however, did not appear to be a source of major concern to the West. In one of the curious twists of fate so common in the region, America and its European allies found themselves on the side of the Muslims. Both turned a blind eye to the operations of the al-Turabi network.

The real test of al-Turabi's belief that the United States could be bullied from the Middle East would be Saudi Arabia. With the Americans put to flight, the fragile Saudi monarchy would collapse of its own weight, and the jihadists would be poised to claim the grand prize of Middle Eastern politics. In a single blow, they would lay siege to the holiest cities in Islam and 25 percent of the world's proven oil reserves. With the Saudis gone, the region as a whole would be thrown into chaos. The battle for Saudi Arabia began in November 1995 with the bombing of a Saudi National Guard barracks in Riyadh, the capital of Saudi Arabia. Five American trainers were killed; scores were wounded. The jihadists had also sent a message that they could strike in the heart of the Saudi kingdom. The scene repeated itself a few months later as jihadists detonated the Khobar Towers, a U.S. Marine facility in the Saudi city of Dhahran, the heart of the Saudi oil fields. A total of 241 Americans were killed.

The attacks had been carried out by local jihadists, but who called the shots: bin Laden, the Iranians, or the Iraqis? There was no smoking gun, but all were linked in one way or another with al-Turabi's Sudanese network. The shadow of bin Laden loomed large, for he was in contact with the Saudi groups, and he had become obsessed with driving the United States from the sacred soil of Islam. American troops were not occupying Saudi Arabia, but for bin Laden, their very presence constituted occupation. In the final analysis, bin Laden was implicated in the first attack, while the attack on the Khobar Towers was charged to the Saudi Hizbullah and, ipso facto, Iran.

In any case, the al-Turabi network had to be destroyed. The United States branded Sudan a terrorist state and made menacing moves to overthrow the al-Bashir regime. The Saudis weighed in by outbidding Iran for the cooperation of the Sudanese leader. Along the way, they promised to use their considerable influence in Washington to ease the U.S. pressure on Khartoum. Al-Bashir, for his part, had tired of both al-Turabi and Iran. Al-Turabi acted as if he was the ruler of the Sudan, and Iran had become lax in its generosity. Al-Turabi would manage what remained of his terrorist network from jail. This was not a difficult task, for his imprisonment was intermittent and largely symbolic. Al-Bashir was not about to risk the killing of a saint to be. The Sudan also remained an Islamic state. Al-Turabi himself complained that the severity of al-Bashir's draconian laws were excessive and a contravention of democracy.[48] The man who had jailed al-Turabi could not afford to appear anti-Islamic.

From al-Turabi to bin Laden

With al-Turabi's Islamic network in remission, the leadership of the jihadist movement shifted from al-Turabi to bin Laden. Its focus shifted from the Sudan to Afghanistan. It was in the wilds of Afghanistan, the scene of his earliest triumphs, that bin Laden established the base for his jihad against America.

The defeat of the Soviets in the late 1980s had thrown Afghanistan into chaos as rival warlords plundered what they could and destroyed much of what remained. Perhaps in desperation, a group of religious students, the Taliban, seized control of the city of Kandahar. Order was restored and Islamic rule was imposed.[49] At least for the moment, they were the good guys. The Afghan Arabs who remained after the defeat of the Soviets gravitated to the Taliban, adding to the firepower of their hosts. Bin Laden and al-Turabi provided financial support to the Taliban, as did wealthy donors from Saudi Arabia and the Gulf. The lifeline of the Taliban, however, was the Pakistani ISI.

Kabul, the capital, was seized in 1996, with much of the country following suit. War continued to rage in the largely Shi'a north, but for all intents and purposes, Afghanistan had become the world's third Islamic theocracy. It was also the strictest. Women were completely veiled and only allowed to leave their domiciles in the company of a male relative, preferably a father, brother, or husband. Western music was banned, and morality police clubbed doubters into submission. All in all, the Taliban managed to make Iran and Saudi Arabia appear as bastions of liberalism, although such images tax the imagination. The supreme guide of the Taliban was Mullah Omar, the leader of the attack on Kandahar. He had been elected to that position by his fellow students based on "his piety and his unswerving belief in Islam."[50] Some of the students also believed that he had been chosen by God.

It was to Taliban-controlled Afghanistan that bin Laden fled following his expulsion from the Sudan in 1996. It was a logical refuge, for he retained a strong base of support among the Afghan Arabs and had strong bonds with Mullah Omar, the leader of the Taliban. Whether he actually married one of Omar's daughters is a matter of some dispute.[51] Marriage is a common technique for strengthening power alliances in the Middle East, and both had a strong motive for maintaining the alliance forged during the Afghan rebellion. Bin Laden needed a refuge and a base for his terrorist network. Omar needed support in his war against the northern warlords, at least some of whom were supported by Iran. The region's legendary hospitality might also have played a role, as did their shared fanaticism. In any case, the bond between bin Laden and Omar was strong enough to survive the 2001 U.S. bombing of Afghanistan.

The bin Laden who returned to Afghanistan in 1996 was a far different individual than the bin Laden who had left the country some eight years earlier. He had gained tremendous experience by helping al-Turabi build his international network, and he was well aware of its weakness. Bin Laden had also forged contacts with jihadist groups worldwide, and he now held the keys to al-Turabi's financial network. It could not be otherwise, for bin Laden had established that network. Finally, Somalia had cast bin Laden in command of a key al-Turabi operation, a role that he relished and that provided him with direct experience in confronting the United States.

Al-Turabi, however, was but one of several forces that shaped bin Laden's view of the world. The zeal that had propelled him to Afghanistan in the early 1980s had been instilled by the intensity of his Wahhabi indoctrination. Whether this was augmented by messianic personality traits is difficult to ascertain given the limited information available. Such traits are not uncommon in the Middle East, a region renowned for its saints and holy men. Bin Laden's revolutionary views were later shaped by Dr. Abdullah Azzam, the head of the support organization created to coordinate Islamic aid to the

Afghan jihad. Bin Laden became both his deputy and his student. The original plans for al Qaeda were sketched by Azzam in 1987 and 1988 as something akin to an Islamic rapid deployment force. Bin Laden urged the immediate deployment of al Qaeda as part of a global jihad. Azzam insisted that al Qaeda remained focused on Afghanistan. Assam was assassinated in 1989. Bin Laden was implicated in his murder.[52] Bin Laden's views were also shaped by al Zawahiri, the leader of Egypt's Islamic Jihad as well as by a variety of other Muslim intellectuals. One of bin Laden's greatest strengths was his ability to surround himself with great intellects and draw on their skills.

Arabs are quick to note that the United States also played a role in honing bin Laden's revolutionary zeal. In their view, bin Laden was a devout businessman who had gone to the Sudan to avoid open conflict with the Saudi regime. His goal was to demonstrate that Muslim businesses could develop the Islamic world without dependence on the West. In the best Islamic traditions, Muslims would help Muslims. The Sudan would prosper as would bin Laden's companies. Branded a terrorist by the United States and deprived of his Saudi citizenship, bin Laden was forced from the Sudan. It was this turn of events, in the Arab view, that transformed bin Laden into a full-fledged terrorist.[53] In any case, bin Laden's bitterness toward the United States and Saudi Arabia deepened over the course of the 1990s, and his avocation as a terrorist became his vocation. His break with the Saudi regime had been slow and torturous but once made was categorical. He had urged reform on the royal family without success. They had now become *kafirs*. It was for America, however, that bin Laden reserved his greatest hatred. Much like the Ayatollah Khomeini before him, bin Laden viewed America as the "great Satan." He hated America for attacking Islam, and he hated America for blocking the success of the jihadists in Egypt and Algeria. Both were on the verge of succumbing to the jihadists, only to be stabilized by Western support. In bin Laden's view, little was to be gained from Muslims killing Muslims when the real culprit was America. The battle had to be taken to the United States. There was no other alternative. These thoughts had been the stock and trade of the al-Turabi network, but it would be bin Laden who brought them to fruition.

It was in the security of Taliban-controlled Afghanistan that bin Laden put together an international terrorist network that built on the strengths of the al-Turabi network while avoiding its flaws. The al-Turabi network had suffered from a lack of focus and was torn by internal dissension. There were too many chiefs, each with the power to counter the other. This, in bin Laden's view, was the result of al-Turabi's effort to weld the entire Islamic movement into a unified force: moderates as well as jihadists, Sunnis as well as Shi'a. First and foremost, bin Laden's network had a single head capable of issuing and enforcing his orders. Toward this end, he adopted the title of sheikh, a religious title that implied great religious learning and the right to issue religious decrees. He lacked the religious credentials to justify the title of sheikh and its prerogatives, but this was of little concern to his followers. Bin Laden's exploits in Afghanistan, Somalia, and the Sudan spoke for themselves. Unlike al-Turabi, bin Laden was not a philosopher bogged down in the fine points of Islamic jurisprudence. His philosophy was his faith, and that faith required jihad.

Also avoided was al-Turabi's error of attempting to integrate the entirety of the Islamic movement within the confines of a single organization. Bin Laden's network was a jihadist network. Unlike the Muslim Brotherhood and Hizbullah, it had little interest in cooperating with secular regimes or their foreign masters. Bin Laden's organization was also a Sunni organization. Cooperation with Shi'a Iran and its Hizbullah network was welcome, but that would be a strategic decision decided on a case-by-case basis. Much the same was true of the Pakistanis, although they required more finesse. Afghanistan was home territory for the Pakistanis, and it was Pakistan that became bin Laden's main supply route. Their interests had to be placated.

This said, bin Laden's network was an extension and modification of the al-Turabi network. Plans for attacks on American targets had already been drafted, although it is not clear precisely who their author had been. Cells in the United States and Europe had also been established with America and Britain proving to be fertile ground for jihadist operatives fleeing the Middle East. Viewed in this light, al Qaeda was yet another stage in the evolution of a jihadist movement that had found its origins in the student activists of the 1970s. Far more than al-Turabi's network, bin Laden's al Qaeda network became an international entity free from dependence on a single country. Al Qaeda, the Arabic word for base, became precisely that: a base for training, supplying, financing, and coordinating attacks on the United States and its key allies. Al-Turabi's network could not survive the diplomatic and economic pressure placed on the Sudan by the United States and Saudi Arabia. Bin Laden's al Qaeda network survived the bombing of Afghanistan as well as an international manhunt of unparalleled proportions.

The success of bin Laden's network speaks for itself.[54] The 1998 bombing of the American embassies in Kenya and Tanzania, the 2000 bombing of the USS *Cole*, and the September 11 bombing of the World Trade Center, the Pentagon, and the attempted bombing of the White House all bore bin Laden's stamp. Post–September 11 terrorist attacks leave little doubt that the jihadist movement is alive and well. March 2002 witnessed forty people killed when grenades were thrown into the diplomatic chapel in Islamabad, Pakistan. In May of the same year, fourteen people were killed when a car bomb exploded outside of the Sheraton Hotel in Karachi, Pakistan. Eleven people were killed and forty wounded the following month when bombs exploded in the vicinity of the U.S. Consulate and Marriott Hotel in Karachi. In October 2002, the scene shifted to Bali with the killing of 202 people in the bombing of a popular resort. Three hundred more were wounded. Most of the victims were Australians, but American tourists had been anticipated. May 2003 saw suicide attacks strike the U.S. compound in Riyadh, Saudi Arabia. In 2004, nearly 200 people were killed in an attack on Madrid rail stations, with more than one thousand wounded. The beat continued in 2005 with the bombing of a London bus and three of its subway trains. Fifty-six people were killed and more than seven hundred injured. Follow-up attacks on the bus system failed when the bombs refused to detonate. These attacks were merely the most spectacular in a long list of attacks attributed to al Qaeda.

The list of failed attacks now coming to light is even more chilling. In February 2002, Italian police arrested four Moroccans possessing maps of Rome's water system and entrances to the American Embassy. In May of the same year, an al Qaeda member was arrested for planning to detonate a radioactive bomb in the United States. In 2003, Italian police arrested five Moroccan men for plotting attacks on Italian churches, North Atlantic Treaty Organisation (NATO) bases in Italy, and various sites in London. Other 2003 plots included the discovery of British labs for producing ricin, as well as planned attacks on the Washington, D.C., subway system and the Brooklyn Bridge. In 2004, an escalation in hijacking threats made the cancellation of commercial flights between the United States and Europe commonplace, the French broke up a major chemical attack, and ricin-laced letters were mailed to the U.S. Senate Office Building, to mention but a few.

Abortive attacks continued in 2005 with Australian security authorities breaking up a Jihadist cell that was stockpiling explosives in the vicinity of a nuclear plant. In the following years Canadian authorities arrested a jihadist cell that had amassed more than enough explosives to destroy key government buildings in the heart of Ontario. British authorities also scuttled an attempt to bomb ten jetliners bound for the United States. The saga continued in 2007 as British police diffused a Mercedes packed with gas canisters and nails in London's theater district. Both the British and German officials warn of more to come.

The above list only recounts attacks on America and its Western allies. Not listed is the continuing bloodshed in Algeria, Afghanistan, Chechnya, India, Indonesia, Israel, Iraq, Kashmir, Pakistan, the Philippines, and Somalia to mention but a few. America and its allies live under various levels of alert with both U.S. and British officials warning that a major jihadist attack against a Western country is imminent.

By and large, the evolution of the jihadist movement traced above falls into five fairly well-defined stages: (1) the stage of gestation that took place during the 1970s, (2) the stage of consolidation associated with the emergence of al Qaeda in the 1980s, (3) the stage of expansion and preparation for war (on the West) that occurred during the 1990s, (4) the stage of all-out war symbolized by the September 11, 2001, terrorist attacks on the United States, and (5) the stage of restructuring and resurgence that has paralleled the war in Iraq. The war in Iraq didn't bring about the restructuring of the jihadist movement, a process that was the inevitable outcome of an upsurge in antiterrorist activity, but it had a great deal to say about its resurgence, a topic examined in greater detail in chapter 14.

Unfortunately, the stage of restructuring and resurgence could prove to be the deadliest of all. Rather than a handful of groups to keep track of, there now might be thousands. Early assessments have suggested that al Qaeda had graduated some ten to one hundred thousand recruits from its training camps prior to the September 11 terrorist attacks on the United States. Of these many have returned to their home countries to establish their own cells. Independent cells have also been established by individuals with no ties to al Qaeda. Some are directly linked to al Qaeda, but most are clones inspired by bin Laden and his al Qaeda network. It has been these people who have been largely responsible for the jihadist attacks in the post–September 11 era. Other cells spring up spontaneously and seek the financial and technological support from al Qaeda, the most famous U.S. example of which was the haphazard U.S. cell that had planned to blow up the Sears Tower in Chicago.[55] The British alone are keeping tabs on some 1,600 individuals suspected of terrorist activities, and these are the ones known to the police.[56] The picture is much the same throughout Europe.[57]

Does this mean that the jihadists are winning? Not at all. In contrast to the more moderate Islamic extremists who are winning the battle for their home turf, jihadist dreams of global victory have been put on hold. They can strike, but as the September 11 and subsequent attacks have demonstrated, they cannot conquer.

So why do the jihadists continue to evolve? Why do they think that they can win? There are probably infinite answers to these questions, but a few are prominent. First, the jihadists believe they have been entrusted with a holy mission. Second, they believe that God will support their mission by working miracles much as he did by defeating the Soviets in Afghanistan, by guiding the Ayatollah Khomeini's victory in Iran, and by orchestrating the U.S. defeat in Iraq. Whether or not the United States has been defeated in Iraq is debated in the United States, but the jihadists have long ago claimed victory. Third, they believe that the growing refinement and mobility of weapons of mass destruction will provide them with the means to destroy the United States and its allies. In their view, to take a page from Karl Marx, the technology of the West contains the seeds of its own destruction. All that is required is time. Fourth, the jihadists believe that time is on their side. The United States has been unable to defeat them, and the forces fueling Islamic extremism discussed in chapter 2 are increasing. Viewed in this light, a stalemate might be the path to victory.

It is these factors that have shaped an evolving jihadist war plan, a topic to which we turn next.

Notes

1. F. Ajami, *The Arab Predicament*, 2nd ed. (Cambridge, UK: Cambridge University Press, 1992); Sadiq Jallal Al Azm, *Self-Criticism after the Defeat* [in Arabic] (Beirut, Lebanon: Dar Al-Taliah, 1969); Adeed Dawish, "Requiem for Arab Nationalism," *The Middle East Quarterly* 10 (Winter 2003), at www.meforum.org/article/518 (accessed November 3, 2003).

2. Ahmad Moussalli, *Moderate and Radical Islamic Fundamentalism: The Quest for Modernity, Legitimacy, and the Islamic State* (Gainesville: University Press of Florida, 1999).

3. Abdel Majid Farid, *Nasser: The Final Years* (Reading, UK: Ithaca Press, 1994); Salah Addin A.-Hadidi, *Witness to the Yemen War* [in Arabic] (Cairo, Egypt: Madbouli, 1984).

4. Berlinti Abdul Al Hamid, *The Marshall and I* [in Arabic] (Cairo, Egypt: Madbouli, 1992).

5. Mohammed H. Heikal, *Autumn of Fury: The Assassination of Sadat* (London: Andre Deutsch, 1983).

6. Kemal Khalid, *They Killed Sadat: Secrets of the Legal Proceedings in the Case of the Jihad Organization* [in Arabic] (Cairo, Egypt: Preservation House, Dar I'tisam, 1988).

7. Saad Eddin Ibrahim, "Anatomy of Egypt's Militant Islamic Groups: Methodological Note and Preliminary Findings," *International Journal of Middle East Studies* 12, no. 4 (1980): 423–53.

8. Hala Mustafa, *The Political System and the Islamic Opposition in Egypt* [in Arabic] (Cairo, Egypt: Markaz Al-Mahrusa, 1995).

9. Ibrahim G. Aoude, "From National Bourgeois Development to Infitah: Cairo 1952–1992," *Arab Studies Quarterly* 16, no. 1 (1994): 19.

10. Charlene Gubash, "Egyptian Militant Group in Disarray: New Boss to Resume Mission: Bringing Down the Government," *MSNBC News*, June 2, 2003, at http://msnbc.com/news/692862.asp (accessed June 2, 2003).

11. New York Times.com, November 28, 1993, 8N, cited in Monte Palmer, *Comparative Politics* (Itasca, Ill.: Peacock Publishers/Wadsworth, 2001), 434.

12. Marvin Zonis, *Majestic Failure: The Fall of the Shah* (Chicago: University of

Chicago Press, 1991); James A. Bill, *The Eagle and the Lion: The Tragedy of American-Iranian Relations* (New Haven, Conn.: Yale University Press, 1988).

13. Mandavi Mehta and Ambassador Teresita C. Schaffer, "Islam in Pakistan: Unity and Contradictions" (a report from the CSIS Project Pakistan's Future and U.S. Policy Options, October 7, 2002).

14. "Terrorist Organization Profiles," *Kashmir Herald* 2, no. 5 (October 2002), at http://kashmirherald.com/profiles/Harkat%20ul-Jihad-i-Islami.html (accessed October 5, 2002); Mehta and Schaffer, "Islam in Pakistan."

15. "Terrorist and Insurgency Groups," *Jane's IntelWeb*, November 23, 1998, at www.ict.org.il/articles/articledet.cfm?articleidc = 85 (accessed October 24, 2001).

16. B. Raman, "Islamic Jihad and the United States," SAPRA, 2000, at www .subcontinent.com/sapra/research/terrorism/terrorism20001029a.html   (accessed June 5, 2002).

17. B. Raman, "Harkut-ul-Mujahideen: An Update," ICT, March 20, 1999, at www.ict.org.il/articles/articledet.cfm?articleid = 85 (accessed February 4, 2004).

18. Mehta and Schaffer, "Islam in Pakistan."

19. B. Raman, "The Prodigal Sons Return," *Asian Times*, October 15, 2002, at www.atimes.com/atimes/Southeast_Asia/DJ15Ae03.html (accessed June 20, 2003).

20. V. S. Naipaul, *A Million Mutinies Now* (New York: Viking, 1990).

21. Bertil Litner, "Religious Extremism and Nationalism in Bangladesh" (paper presented at the international workshop on Religion and Security in South Asia, Asia Pacific Center for Security Studies, Honolulu, August 2002).

22. Rohan Gunaratna, *Inside Al-Qaeda: Global Network of Terror* (New York: Columbia, 2002), 24.

23. Gunaratna, *Inside Al-Qaeda*, 18–22.

24. Sami Haddad (moderator), panel discussion: "The Future of the Afghan Arabs after the Defeat of the Taliban" [in Arabic], *Al Jazeera*, November 25, 2001, at http://aljazeera.net/programs/opinions/articles/2001/11/11-25-1.htm (accessed December 1, 2001).

25. Yossef Bodansky, *Bin Laden: The Man Who Declared War on America* (Roseville, Calif.: Prima Publishing, 2001), 28.

26. Anonymous, *Through Our Enemies' Eyes: Osama Bin Laden, Radical Islam, and the Future of America* (Washington, D.C.: Brassey's, 2002), 114.

27. Hassan al-Turabi, "Islamic Fundamentalism in the Sunna and Shi'a Worlds," *Sudan Foundation Religious File Number 6* (London, 1997), at www.sufo.demon.co .uk/reli006.htm (accessed June 26, 2002).

28. Al-Turabi, "Islamic Fundamentalism."

29. Bodansky, *Bin Laden*.

30. Bodansky, *Bin Laden*.

31. Bodansky, *Bin Laden*.

32. Bodansky, *Bin Laden*.

33. Liess Boukra, *Algerie la terreur sacree* (Lausanne, Switzerland: Favre SA, 2002), 194.

34. Boukra, *Algerie la terreur sacree*, 74–75.

35. Boukra, *Algerie la terreur sacree*, 73.

36. Rachid Boudjedra, *FIS do la haine* (Paris: Donoel, 1992).

37. Boukra, *Algerie la terreur sacree*, 83.

38. Boukra, *Algerie la terreur sacree*, 212.

39. Boukra, *Algerie la terreur sacree*, 214.

40. Boukra, *Algerie la terreur sacree*, 106–7.

41. Boukra, *Algerie la terreur sacree*, 236.

42. Muhammed Muslih, *The Foreign Policy of Hamas* (New York: Council on Foreign Relations, 1999).

43. Beverly Milton-Edwards, *Islamic Politics in Palestine* (London: I.B. Tauris Academic Studies, 1999).

44. Meir Hatina, *Islam and Salvation in Palestine: The Islamic Jihad Movement* (New York: Syracuse University Press, 2001).

45. Hatina, *Islam and Salvation in Palestine*.

46. "Seven Factions Call for Unity Government," *Al Quds*, October 12, 2006, at www.wap.alquds.com/ (accessed October 12, 2006).

47. Gideon Alon, "Signs of Global Jihad Found in West Bank," *Ha'aretz*, June 7, 2006, at www.haaretz.com/ (accessed June 7, 2006).

48. Hisham Aldiwan, "No Comeback in the Cards for Sudan's Former Islamic Strongman," *Daily Star-Lebanon*, June 18, 2002, at www.dailystar.com.lb/18_06_02/art21asp (accessed June 18, 2002).

49. Peter L. Bergen, *Holy War, Inc.: Inside the Secret World of Osama bin Laden* (New York: Free Press, 2001).

50. Ahmad Rashid, *Taliban: Militant Islam, Oil and Fundamentalism in Central Asia* (New Haven, Conn.: Yale University Press, 2001), 23.

51. Bergen, *Holy War, Inc.*

52. Gunaratna, *Inside Al-Qaeda.*

53. Mohanned Kharishan, "First War of the Century: Organization of al Qaeda and Its Relation with the Taliban" [in Arabic], *Al Jazeera*, October 28, 2001. This view is shared by Jason Burke in his book *Al-Qaeda: Casting a Shadow of Terror* (New York: I.B. Tauris, 2003).

54. Paul Thompson, *The Terror Timeline* (New York: Regan Books, 2004).

55. John O'Neil, "Seven Are Charged with Plot to Blow Up Sears Tower," *New York Times*, June 23, 2006, at www.nytimes.com/ (accessed June 23, 2006).

56. Elaine Sciolino and Stephen Grey, "British Terror Trial Traces a Path to Militant Islam," *New York Times*, November 26, 2006, at www.nytimes.com/ (accessed November 26, 2006).

57. Kathleen Ridolfo, "Al-Qaeda at Home in Europe," *Asia Times*, July 9, 2005, at www.atimes.com/atimes/Front_Page/GG09Aa02.html (accessed July 9, 2005).

9

The Jihadist War Plan

THE FIRST STEP IN DEFEATING the jihadists is to understand their war plan for reconquering the Islamic world. The more the United States and its allies understand this plan, the easier it will be for them to thwart the jihadists' next move. At the very least, there will be fewer surprises. Speaking of a war plan might seem unduly dramatic, but it is not. The jihadists spend endless hours debating their strategy for reconquering the Islamic world. The debate is never ending. Each victory brings new opportunities; each defeat demands new adjustments. As we have seen in the preceding chapter, the jihadists have had their share of both. The jihadist war plan, like the jihadist movement, itself, is evolving.

By and large, the early jihadists viewed themselves as a historic vanguard whose role was to ignite an Islamic revolution. Moved more by zeal than experience, they assumed that a wave of violence would spark a mass revolt and topple unpopular governments.[1] This turned out to be the case in Iran but not elsewhere. The governments of the Islamic world were unexpectedly resilient, as were their Western supporters. Muslims were also frightened by jihadist violence and put off by the hellfire content of their sermons. Big on zeal, jihadists had few practical solutions for the problems besetting the Islamic world.

Jihadist planning improved dramatically during the al-Turabi era and more so with the establishment of al Qaeda. The success of the jihadist movement has increased apace. The Islamic world is threatened with chaos, the might of the Israeli army has been defied, and the U.S. mainland has suffered the most devastating attack in its history. Each day, or so it seems, brings new alerts. Nevertheless, the record of the jihadists remains a mixed bag. America took bin Laden's best shot and survived. Its stability was never in doubt. Bin Laden and al Qaeda, moreover, had no plans for capitalizing on their victory. They expected the United States to collapse like a deck of cards and, with it, the opposition to jihadist rule in the Muslim world. They were stunned when it did not. As things stand today, America and the jihadists are locked in the most deadly of stalemates.

Two questions thus come to the fore. First, what do al Qaeda and other jihadist groups have planned for the future? Second, what is their capacity to execute their plans? Wishing does not make it so. The present chapter examines the jihadist war plan. The following chapter examines their capacity to execute their plan.

The Grand Plan

Statements of what bin Laden and his lieutenants would like to do are provided in a series of videotapes and captured documents. Taken collectively, these documents portray a grand design that begins with the mobilization of the world's Muslims against the American-Zionist crusade to destroy Islam and ends with the stage of "definitive victory." Along the way, battalions will be readied for the ultimate battle, while terrorist attacks on the United States and its allies goad the "new crusaders" into declaring war on Islam. Growing U.S. attacks on Islam will inevitably result in the overthrow of pro-American regimes in the Middle East, the foremost of which are those of Saudi Arabia, Jordan, and Egypt. Control of Iraq figures large in this equation.[2] The fall of pro-American governments, in turn, will pave the way for the establishment of a caliphate (Islamic state) in the "liberated" countries of the Middle East, presumably some time in the middle of the next decade. The establishment of the caliphate will lead to total war between an Islam armed with the latest technological weapons and a demoralized West that has lost its will to fight. Victory is preordained and inevitable.

The above progression is sufficiently vague to unite the jihadist community behind a common program without creating undue demands for coordination and discipline. Anyone can play according to their inclination and abilities. All that is required at the present time is that attacks on Western targets continue and that the United States is goaded into pursuing its war against Islam. Al Qaeda will do its part by offering guidance, training, and financing as circumstances permit. The grand plan also plays a vital psychological role by making the ultimate victory of Islam tangible and doable within the lifetime of those who want to believe. Both are important tools in mobilizing and maintaining the support of the faithful. Dates are bandied about, but the important thing from the jihadist perspective is that the jihadist movement keeps moving forward toward its eventual goal of conquest. In the meantime, the United States keeps al Qaeda in the spotlight by blaming it for the American defeat in Iraq.

Modes of Jihadist Terror

What then is the current pattern of jihadist operations, and how does this operational pattern correspond to their grand plan? To date, al Qaeda and other jihadist groups have employed at least six categories of terror to seek their objectives: (1) random terror, (2) political terror, (3) economic-techno-logical terror, (4) cultural terror, (5) revolutionary terror, and (6) catastrophic terror. Each has evolved over time and continues to evolve as al Qaeda adjusts to America's long war and seeks new ways of achieving its objectives.

Random Terror

Random terror is the indiscriminate killing of civilian populations. Targets are less important than the number of casualties—the more the better. Major urban centers are preferred locations because they are politically sensitive and garner maximum media attention. The objective of random terror is to destabilize governments by sowing panic among civilian populations. Mass resolve might be strengthened in the short run, but governments that lose the capacity to protect their citizens over a sustained period of time lose their capacity to rule. Random terror brought both Algeria and Egypt to the brink of civil war, and random terror in Israel continues to confront the Jewish state with one of the greatest challenges of its modern history. Iraq is next followed by Saudi Arabia.

Even when random terror fails to destabilize a country, the costs of survival are themselves terrifying. Egypt, Algeria, and Israel have all survived by a regime of mass arrests, military trials, and collective punishments (blowing up houses and neighborhoods). In the process, innocent people are punished for crimes that they have not committed. Some blame the jihadists for their misery. Others take revenge by supporting the jihadists.

Random terror also keeps the jihadists in the public eye and exaggerates their power. Both play a critical role in maintaining the zeal of jihadists and their supporters in this most psychological of wars. Concessions from nervous governments merely increases that zeal as does the flight of nervous foreigners.

The techniques for executing random violence are virtually limitless. They range from simple pipe bombs to the suicide attacks the Israelis now refer to

as the H-bomb.[3] Suicide attacks in Iraq have doubled every year since the
U.S.-led invasion of Iraq.[4] Other items in the list would certainly include
hijacking, kidnapping, arson, car bombing, and other acts of random violence that now dominate the daily press. Instructions for most can be found
on the Internet, with one of the best manuals for random terror being that
produced by the U.S. Army for use in Latin America. It was updated for use
against the Soviets in Afghanistan and appears to have been incorporated in
al Qaeda training programs. As a specialist on ABC commented, "In fact, a
visit to the U.S. Army's website offers scores of publicly available field manuals on everything from conducting psychological operations to sniper training."[5] The U.S. Army's latest counterinsurgency manual is also online and
provides the jihadists with a clear picture of what to expect in their confrontations with U.S. forces.[6]

The advantage of random terror, from the jihadist perspective, is that it is
cheap, is easy, requires few people, needs minimal technology, and with the
exception of the suicide bombers, is relatively safe. Individuals carry out their
deadly tasks and then fade into the woodwork. Bombs detonated by cell
phones are now making random terror far less risky. Bombs can be planted
days in advance and detonated from miles away. Stolen phones are preferable. The Middle East is also one of the most heavily armed regions of the
world, making weapons and explosives readily available. Some Lebanese have
their own rocket launchers, Kalashnikovs, and hand grenades. All are
mementos from Lebanon's long and bitter civil war. Israeli settlers are probably the most heavily armed population in the world. All things considered,
random terror is virtually unstoppable if the jihadists possess a broad base of
support within the target community.

For all of its ease of operation, random terror is essentially a psychological
softening-up process. To be effective, it must be supported by an organization capable of seizing power once a government has been weakened. The
jihadists continue to lack this capacity. Random violence against innocent
civilians is also a flagrant violation of all but the most extreme interpretations
of Islamic law. So, too, is the killing of Muslims.[7] Indeed, the very heart of
the Prophet Mohammed's message was the demand that Muslims put aside
their tribal hatreds and unify for the greater good of God. Koranic injunctions against violence continue to inhibit jihadist efforts to build the base of
popular support upon which their success will ultimately depend.

Terrorizing civilian populations, moreover, is a two-way street. It might
destabilize secular governments, but it also sows fear among the Muslim
community.[8] Rather than saviors, the jihadists become the villains. Early
jihadists successes were based on quick and dirty attacks that assumed that
victory would be swift. Victory has not been swift, and tolerance of the jihad-

ist violence has worn thin. For the most part, Muslims fail to understand why the goal of an Islamic state requires the killing of Muslims. This is all the more the case because Muslims find themselves doubly cursed. They are cursed by the random violence of the jihadists, and they are cursed by the brutality of government repression. They just want the violence to stop.

Finally, it should be noted that random terror in the Middle East is losing its shock value. Jihadist attacks against Muslims are rarely reported in the world press and receive minimal coverage in the regional press. Random terror against American and European targets gets more bang for the buck.

Political Terror

Political terror focuses its wrath on the symbols of secular power.[9] Innocents are spared, but political officials of every stripe and nationality are fair game. Presidents, prime ministers, generals, judges, diplomats, bureaucrats, soldiers, rural gendarmes, and everyone in between have felt the sting of jihadist terror. Some have been felled by an assassin's bullet. Others have perished in the rubble of buildings gutted by terrorist bombs or have been the victims of hijacking.

The logic of political violence is compelling. The political regimes of the Islamic world are illegitimate and despised by their populations. Few, at least, are willing to test their popularity in free presidential elections. The assassination of a tyrant promises to throw many countries of the Islamic world into chaos. Whether it would lead to an Islamic state is an open question. The military would decide. This, from the jihadist perspective, is not without its advantages. It was a military coup in the Sudan, it will be recalled, that paved the way for the emergence of the al-Turabi network. The 1977 Zia ul-Haq coup in Pakistan had also seen the jihadist flourish.

Much the same logic applies to jihadist attacks on American political targets. The jihadists firmly believe that the United States will withdraw in the face of sustained casualties much as U.S. forces withdrew from Lebanon in 1983 and Somalia in 1993. Scholars in the Middle East refer to the American reluctance to sustain casualties as the "Vietnam complex." Those who studied in the United States are convinced that American public opinion will prevent any American government from staying the course in a prolonged conflict. America can bomb Iraq, in their view, but it cannot endure sustained terrorist attacks against U.S. troops now occupying the country. Iraq has thus become a critical test match between the United States and the jihadists. If the United States succeeds in pacifying Iraq, secular governments throughout the Islamic world will attack the jihadists with renewed vigor, as will the Israelis, the Russians, and the Indians. Potential supporters of the jihadists will also cut their losses. If the United States runs, the jihadists will have a field day. Everyone in the Islamic world is watching Iraq.

By the same token, there can be little doubt that bin Laden believed that the September 11 terrorist attacks on the World Trade Center and the Pentagon and those planned for the White House would throw the United States into chaos. This did not happen, but the jihadists were buoyed by the success of their attacks. The jihadists also relish in the shock value of political assassinations. Random violence might have become less newsworthy, but political assassinations are still front-page news.

Finally, political terror includes the use of violence to scuttle peace agreements that might threaten jihadist sanctuaries or strengthen the U.S. position in the region. Iraq and Afghanistan fit both categories.

For all of its advantages, political terror has failed to topple the secular regimes of the Islamic world. Indeed, political survival in the Middle East has become an art form. A region that epitomized instability and chaos during the 1950s and 1960s now boasts an honor roll of aging tyrants. Hafez al-Assad ruled Syria with a hand of steel from 1970 to 2000, succumbing to old age and passing the torch of power to a son. Husni Mubarak, the president of Egypt, came to power with the jihadist assassination of Anwar Sadat in 1981 and has ruled for over twenty-five years without challenge. His son, too, is now waiting in the wings.[10] Even Saddam Hussein, perhaps the most hated man in the world, survived several U.S. presidents before his ouster by American troops. Muammar Qadaffi has set the record for survival and has extended his longevity by making peace with the United States.

For one reason or another, high-profile assassinations in the Islamic world have decreased. This does not mean that political violence has become a thing of a past, but it is clearly a tool that is used with discretion. Low-level political terror, by contrast, appears to be increasing, particularly terror against foreign nationals working in the Islamic world. Killing foreigners creates an international crisis and is manifestly political. This will not place the jihadists in power, but it will make it far more difficult for the United States and its allies to work effectively in the region. The recent nervousness of Westerners in Saudi Arabia is a case in point, with many questioning the ability of the Saudi regime to survive the barrage of political terror without dramatic reforms.[11] Killing Americans electrifies the media and provides the jihadists with key psychological victories. It also sends shock waves through the American community in the region. The temporary closing of American embassies has now become routine in the Islamic world.

Economic-Technological Terror

Also lethal are jihadist attacks on the economic foundations of secular states. Attacks on tourists in Egypt, the Philippines, Indonesia, and elsewhere have crippled key tourist industries and placed inordinate pressure on the citizens of countries already wracked by poverty and unemployment. The economy of Algeria has been virtually destroyed. Throughout history, political collapse has been preceded by economic collapse.

Economic terror is not limited to the Islamic world but now threatens to engulf North America and Europe as well. High on the jihadist agenda is the oil weapon. The industrial economies of the world run on oil, and any sustained disruption in Middle Eastern oil supplies could wreck devastation in the industrial world. The mere mention of a crisis in the Middle East sends oil prices rocketing.

To date, the oil weapon has only been used once, that being in the turmoil of the Arab-Israeli War of 1973. Oil shipments to the United States and its allies were curtailed, sending the price of oil spiraling from approximately three dollars per barrel in 1973 to some forty dollars per barrel in the early 1980s. The price of industrial goods skyrocketed, and the economies of the Third World were sent into a free fall as the cost of borrowing money became insupportable.[12]

Flooded with fabulous wealth and dependent upon the United States for their survival, the Saudis and other oil producers have renounced the oil weapon, pretending that it is possible to separate politics from economics.[13] The brutality of Israeli counterterrorist measures in Palestine has met with new calls for an oil embargo but has produced little more than an embarrassed wringing of hands by the leaders of the oil states. The Saudis bitterly condemned the U.S. invasion of Iraq but privately assured Washington that oil prices would remain stable.

The jihadists, by contrast, are more than willing to use the oil weapon against the United States and its allies. Their goal is salvation rather than survival, and many feel that the Middle East might be a more religious place without the corrupting influences of oil. Oil pipelines stretch for thousands of miles and make inviting targets, as do the refineries of the region. Iraqi pipelines have become prime targets in resistance efforts to force the U.S. evacuation of Iraq. Also vulnerable are the massive jumbo tankers that transverse the narrow straits of the Persian Gulf. The jihadists signaled their ability to attack tankers with their 2000 attack on the USS *Cole*. And, in 2002, a Yemeni terrorist group called the Islamic Army of Aden-Abyan claimed responsibility for an attack on a French supertanker. This group is presumed to have been acting under contract with al Qaeda.

The oil weapon is not merely a matter of pipelines and refineries. It also manifests itself in the fabulous wealth that pours into the coffers of the oil kingdoms, at least some of which finds its way into the hands of the jihadists. It was that wealth that financed the bin Laden's jihad against the Soviets, and the United States believes that Saudi oil money helped to finance the September 11 terrorist attacks on America. The Israelis maintain that half of Hamas's revenues come from Saudi Arabia.[14]

Other economic targets also abound in Europe and North America. The security of atomic generating plants and water supplies has been called into question.[15] The economic impact of the September 11 terrorist attacks is being measured in the billions of dollars and has thrown a pall of despair over a world economic system. Indeed, the very cost of America's war on terror has imposed phenomenal strains on the United States and its allies, with Israel recently requesting an additional ten billion dollars in U.S. aid to keep the Israeli economy afloat.[16] In retrospect, the economic impact of the September 11 terrorist attacks was far greater than its political impact, a message that is unlikely to be lost on the jihadists. The jihadists are also well aware that much of America's fabled industrial plant is largely unguarded. For the moment they are focused on high-profile targets, but this could change.

Cyber-warfare, too, has entered the jihadist vocabulary as they seek ways to exploit the West's dependence on computers. The director of Britain's National Infrastructure Security Coordination Center cautions, "For terrorist groups like al-Qaida with limited resources, it would be 'a very attractive method' of attack that would cause 'huge damage.'"[17] American officials have also reportedly concluded that al Qaeda is poised to use the Internet as a lethal weapon. The Internet, they warn, could be used to unleash the floodgates of dams or to cause damaging power surges.[18] The Internet is also becoming a virtual training ground for jihadist operatives replete with e-magazines for women and how-to guides on kidnapping, bomb making, and almost everything else the aspiring terrorist needs to know. In 2001 there were only a handful of such websites. Today, there are over five thousand.[19]

The main disadvantage of economic and technological terrorism is that it punishes innocent Muslims, including supporters of the jihadists. A wedge is thus driven between the jihadists and their support base, a liability that the jihadists can ill afford if they are to be effective. This liability does not apply to economic and technological terrorism against America and its First World allies.

Cultural Terror

Cultural terror attacks the symbols of Western culture and all other cultural influences that violate the jihadist vision of Islamic purity. Girls' schools have been attacked in Afghanistan and Saudi Arabia, journalists and pop singers have been assassinated in Algeria, and Western classics have been forced from Middle Eastern libraries. A university in Pakistan, for example, recently banned Ernest Hemingway's *The Sun Also Rises* and Jonathan Swift's *Gulliver's Travels*. Both were deemed vulgar.[20] Similar bans have been imposed at the American University of Cairo. Efforts are increasing to purge vulgarity from the Internet and satellite networks, both of which now penetrate the remotest regions of the Islamic world.[21]

But, to what end are these thing done? Cultural terrorism is not going to overthrow secular governments or send shock waves through the West. To expect it do so is to miss the point. Western pop culture, in the eyes of the jihadists, is more than a testimony to bad taste. It is viewed by the jihadist as the main weapon in America's psychological war against Islam. Some jihadists fear the cultural offensive of the United States more than they fear its weapons. The latter brings salvation; the former destroys the Muslim soul from within and paves the way to hell. Lest further evidence be needed on the matter, the American government has recently launched new radio and television stations designed to flood the Islamic world with yet a larger dose of pop music. Radio Monte Carlo and Radio Sharq (East) had already filled this void in much of the region. Islamic stations counter with a steady diet of fire and brimstone mixed with strident anti-Americanisms. The end result will probably be a generation of schizophrenic Muslims.

The jihadists are under no illusion that they can change the message of Western culture. Their hope is to slow down the perversion of Islamic minds by killing the messenger. This is a thankless task but seems doomed to continue. It is too central to the jihadist war plan to be ignored.

Revolutionary Terror

Although less visible to American audiences, the jihadists have scored major victories by taking sides with ethnic and religious conflicts throughout the Islamic world. The jihadists play the leading role in the Kashmiri conflicts and the Chechnyan conflicts, and hype the Palestinian-Israeli conflict as the jihad of jihads. They are minor players in this conflict but find it to be a propaganda gold mine. The jihadists also remain very active in Kosovo, Bosnia, Afghanistan, and Somalia, and have fueled the growing wave of religious violence that is now sweeping Africa and Asia. In Indonesia, for example, the jihadists are accused of fueling religious violence that has displaced more than six hundred thousand Christians.[22] Much the same is taking place in Nigeria. The jihadist role in inciting sectarian violence in Iraq requires little elaboration. The more Muslims find themselves in conflict with other religious groups, the more the jihadists prosper.

In the process, the jihadists are making their jihad a global reality and bolstering the morale of supporters. They are also stretching the Western capacity for intervention to the breaking point. The Russians are bogged down in Chechnya with no end in sight, Israel is under siege, the United States is attempting to extricate itself from Iraq, and UN security forces continue to patrol Kosovo and Bosnia. Afghanistan is dissolving into chaos, and the Taliban are returning. Lessons learned by the jihadists in Chechnya, Kashmir, and elsewhere are now being applied in Iraq as U.S. authorities encounter a growing number of "Afghan Arabs" willing to die in the latest of jihadist causes. In a few cases, mini-Islamic republics have been established. They are eventually crushed by U.S. forces but could be a harbinger of things to come.

Catastrophic Terror

This, in turn, leads us to the final key element in the jihadist war plan: the acquisition of weapons of mass destruction (WMD). WMDs are the ultimate weapon of terror, striking fear in the hearts of millions and leveling the playing field between superpowers and the jihadists. During the 1950s and 1960s, fear of a Soviet nuclear attack prompted the slogan "better red than dead." The "green bomb,"[23] the unfortunate name attached to Pakistan's recently developed nuclear bomb, could well have the same effect, prompting Western public opinion to press for a withdrawal from the Islamic world.

Captured al Qaeda documents indicate that efforts to acquire WMDs, including nuclear weapons, are on the drawing board. According to British sources, there is evidence that bin Laden has built a crude dirty bomb that can make an area uninhabitable for ten years.[24] Nuclear scientists from Pakistan were arrested for "cooperating" with al Qaeda but later cleared, or so it seems. Far more likely is the ability of the jihadists to acquire some of the former Soviet Union's six hundred tons of weapon-grade nuclear material that has sat virtually unguarded since the collapse of the USSR in 1990. The scariest scenario is that suitcase bombs developed by the Soviets will find their way into the hands of the jihadists. A popular French spy novel, *Djihad*, by Gerard de Villiers, traces the journey of a Russian nuclear pocket bomb from Chechnya to New York.[25] In the book, the bomb was sold to Afghan Arabs in Chechnya by a Russian commander for several million dollars and was then carried to Istanbul in the dilapidated van of an Islamic charity caring for the Chechnyan wounded. The van's trips were routine as were bribes paid to the diverse border guards. From Istanbul, the bomb was shipped in a container of cheap artifacts to an art dealer in Montreal and from there was smuggled into the United States via an obscure border crossing. Fortunately, this is the stuff of fiction.

Postwar Iraq saw frequent looting of nuclear plants.[26] The North Koreans, part of the axis of evil, have now developed nuclear weapons, reportedly with assistance from Pakistan, an ally in America's war on terror. Iran is developing nuclear weapons and already possesses delivery systems capable of reaching Israel. The Iranians deny evil intent but say that their national interest forces them to counter Israel's nuclear weapons. To make matters worse, a brisk black market in nuclear materials continues to flourish.[27] Guidance is also available on the Internet.[28]

Far more accessible are chemical and biological weapons such as ricin, salmonella, cyanide, anthrax, and smallpox. Some biological and chemical attacks have been prevented, but others have not. London officials intercepted a plot to release cyanide gas in the London Underground in 2004, and the French thwarted a major chemical attack in Paris. Ricin, the deadliest of the chemical agents, has been found in Britain, France, and the United States. Captured al Qaeda computers indicate that the jihadists also have easy access to the materials required for the manufacture of botulinum, salmonella, cyanide, anthrax, and other chemical agents.[29] Genetic technology might also become available to the jihadist before too long. Progress in biotechnology is widely reported in scholarly journals and is easily replicated once procedures have been refined.[30]

The jihadist drive for WMDs is insatiable. It is those weapons, more than any other, that provide the best opportunity for the jihadists to defeat the United States and Israel. A nuclear attack on America would probably trigger a massive U.S. strike against any Muslim country plausibly associated with the jihadists. President Bush has not ruled out the use of nuclear weapons in the war on terror, nor have the Israelis.

Would the jihadists actually resort to the use of WMDs against America and its allies knowing that it would put millions of Muslims at risk? More than likely they would. Those committed to dying in the cause of God can hardly be concerned with the sacrifice of others. The question is, can they be stopped in time?

Adjusting to the War on Terror

While there can be no doubt that the war on terror has disrupted al Qaeda operations, it is equally clear that the organization has survived a decade of concerted international efforts to destroy it. Attacks on the West continue, and barring a dramatic breakthrough in antiterror technology, those attacks are likely to continue for a long time to come.

The core of the al Qaeda central command survived by going underground, scattering, and cutting traceable links to branches and affiliates.

Branch lieutenants of bin Laden were arrested or killed, but threads leading to bin Laden or al Zawahiri proved to be elusive. Losses in communication and coordination have been compensated for by the use of autonomous homegrown cells to launch high-profile attacks on the West such as the bombing of the Madrid train station and the London subway.[31] Such attacks have a high payoff in terms of publicity with minimal damage to the organization. They also build morale among cadres and supporters, spur recruitment, and stimulate the development of more homemade cells—a moment of glory on Earth followed by an eternity in heaven.

Al Qaeda has kept itself in the limelight by intensifying its propaganda war with the West. It, too, is cheap and easy and also serves to build morale and spur recruitment. A few tapes are issued, and the Western media does the rest. More than ever, al Qaeda propaganda in this most psychological of wars focuses on Israeli occupation of Palestine. This issue, more than any other, unites Muslims and plays upon Arab feelings of humiliation. Reference to the United States as the new crusader also receives star billing as does U.S. support for Israel and its brutal occupation policies. Defeat the United States and you defeat Israel. According to the jihadists, it's that simple.

In much the same manner, al Qaeda transformed the war in Iraq into a new jihad against the crusaders. Afghan Arabs flooded into a country in which al Qaeda did not possess a significant presence and blended with a melange of Sunni resistance groups to wreck havoc with the U.S. occupation. Every American death became a jihadist victory, although they were not the main force in the resistance. In the end, al Qaeda claimed victory, and its propaganda machine glorified Iraq as yet another in a long list of jihadist victories that included the defeat of the Soviets in Afghanistan and the victory of the Ayatollah Khomeini in Iran. The message was clear. The power of God is greater than the superpowers. All that is required is faith.

In the cruelest of ironies, Iraq turned out to be far more than a propaganda victory. Much as in the Afghan case, naive recruits returned home as hardened fighters and started building their own homegrown cells. Like a contagious disease, violence increased in Saudi Arabia, Jordan, and other areas of the Islamic world, so much so that the Saudi's are building a wall to seal off the Iraqi border. Some conspiracy theorists even suggest that bin Laden planted false information about his ties with Saddam Hussein as a ploy to tempt the Americans into an attack on Iraq.[32]

Finally, al Qaeda was able to survive the war on terror by refining a deadly blend of high-tech and low-level technologies. When cell phones proved vulnerable to detection, the organization shifted to the Internet to send coded messages. Chat rooms proved to be particularly effective. Economic warfare moved from direct transactions to untraceable investments on less well-known stock exchanges. Indeed, India, a key ally in the war on terror, was forced to admit that al Qaeda had used its invisible investments to fix prices on the Indian stock exchange.

For the most part, however, al Qaeda has dodged the high-tech superiority of the United States by perfecting low-level techniques for avoiding detection. Highjacking has moved toward liquid agents that can be combined to form explosives in flight. Random terror now employs explosives manufactured from standard fertilizer available at the neighborhood garden store, and a planned attack on the New York subway system called for the use of gas canisters about the size of paint cans. The movement of personnel and financial transactions have also gone low tech. Particularly effective has been the mingling of al Qaeda operatives among the millions of expatriate Muslims who visit relatives in their home countries on a frequent basis.

Preparing for the Next Stages

Far more worrisome than the present stage of muted terror is mounting evidence that al Qaeda has turned the corner in its rebuilding process and now contemplates establishing a foundation for its long-promised Islamic caliphate. All-out war with the West will follow.[33] It could not be otherwise, for in contrast to the game plan of the radical moderates, the jihadists have left no room for coexistence with secular powers. It's all or nothing. There can only be one winner, and the battle continues until one side or the other has been defeated.

This process begins with the continued softening up of its opponents in preparation for the stage of occupying territory and its transformation into a jihadist caliphate. The softening-up process includes both increasing attacks on "infidel" targets and globalizing their scope. Opponents will become demoralized, antiterrorist efforts overextended, Islam attacked, swamps (failed states) expanded, and the zeal of cadres and supporters fired to a fever pitch. In the meantime, al Qaeda will continue to prepare its forces, reassert its control over its distended network, and develop WMDs.

Three countries, in particular, are the likely targets in this coming stage: the United States, Israel, and Saudi Arabia. Attacks on the United States are vital because of their tremendous propaganda value. The United States is the great Satan, and there is no better way to build mass support and strengthen the morale of jihadist fighters than to demonstrate the weakness and vulnerability of the United States. Iraq has been a major step in this direction, but it is vital for jihadist plans to strike the United States directly. Attacks on Israel, in turn, will place the jihadists in the vanguard of the most emotional issue in the Middle East. More than ever, the United States will be forced to rush to Israel's aid. Anti-Americanism in the Muslim world will soar accordingly as will mass contempt for America's docile Arab puppets in the region. Finally, increased attacks on the Saudi monarchy will destabilize global oil markets and ipso facto, the world economy.

How Good Is the Jihadist War Plan?

It is not very good. As things currently stand, al Qaeda lacks the means for planning and coordination vital for the next stages of their plan. The leadership is scattered and reduced to vague communications via the Internet, ambitious lieutenants are stealing the limelight from bin Laden and squabbling over what to do next, and resources are being wasted, cells uncovered, front organizations dismantled, counterterrorist measured tightened, internal conflict exacerbated, and potentially supportive populations alienated by excessive violence. The word "plan," itself, is a misnomer. In reality, it is little more than a vision with as many versions as there are jihadist luminaries.[34] The current stage was, in large part, forced upon the jihadists by the war on terror that followed the 9/11 terrorist attacks on the United States.

Does this mean that al Qaeda and related jihadist groups have ceased to be a threat to America and its allies? Not at all. It just means that al Qaeda and the jihadists have their own problems, and things could be much worse for the United States. The more pressing questions for the United States are (1) does al Qaeda have the organizational capacity and support base necessary to continue their present standoff with the United States, and (2) can they make the necessary adjustments required for the next stage of their plan? It is to these topics that we turn next.

Notes

1. Hala Mustafa, *The Political System and the Islamic Opposition in Egypt* [in Arabic] (Cairo, Egypt: Markaz Al-Mahrusa, 1995); Kemal As-Said Habib, "The Experience of the Islamic Movement in Egypt," *Al-Manara*, no. 12 (2000), at www.almanara.net/issues/12/12.1.htm (accessed December 13, 2001).

2. Brian Whitaker, "Revealed: Al-Qaida Plan to Seize Control of Iraq," *Guardian*, October 13, 2005, at www.guardian.co.uk/Iraq/Story/0,2763,1590979,00html (accessed October 13, 2005).

3. Diego Gambetta, ed., *Making Sense of Suicide Missions* (Oxford: Oxford University Press, 2006); Farhad Khosrokhavar, *Quand Al-Qaida parle: Temoignages derriere les barreaux* [in French] (Paris: Bernard Grasset, 2005).

4. Mike Shuster, "Spate of Suicide Bombings Threatens Iraq 'Surge,'" *National Public Radio*, May 3, 2007, at www.npr.org/templates/story/story.php?storyId= 9966084 (accessed May 3, 2007).

5. John Pike, interview, ABC News, December 20, 2002, at www.abcnews.go .com/sections/world/Daily_News/binladenterror_000918.html (accessed December 20, 2002).

6. U.S. Department of Army, FM-3-24, MLWP 3-33.5, 2006.

7. Yousef Qaradawi, "Violence and the Islamic Groups, Part 1" [in Arabic], interviewed by Hamid Al Ansari, *Al Jazeera*, July 7, 2001, at www.aljazeera.net/ programs/shareea/articles/2001/7/7-7-1.htm (accessed August 24, 2002).

8. Kemal As-Said Habib, "The Experience of the Islamic Movement in Egypt" [in Arabic], *Al-Manara*, no. 12 (2000), at www.almanara.net/issues/12/121.htm (accessed December 13, 2001).

9. Alex P. Schmid and A. J. Jongman, *Political Terrorism : A New Guide to Actors, Authors, Concepts, Data Bases, Theories, and Literature* (New Brunswick, N.J.: Transaction Publishers, 2005).

10. After three years of persistent rumors, President Mubarak has officially stated that his son will not succeed him in office. The rumors continue to persist. Gamal Essam El-Din, "It Won't Happen Here," *Al Ahram Weekly*, January 8–14, 2004, at http://weekly.ahram.org.eg/2004/672/eg2.htm (accessed January 10, 2004).

11. Michael Scott Doran, "The Saudi Paradox," *Foreign Affairs*, January–February 2004, at www.foreignaffairs.org/ (accessed January 1, 2004); Elie Elhadj, *The Islamic Shield* (Boca Raton, Fla.: Brown Walker Press, 2007).

12. Monte Palmer, *Politics of the Middle East* (Itasca, Ill.: F.E. Peacock/Wadsworth, 2007).

13. Charlotte Denny, "Opec Pledges Flood of Oil in Event of Conflict," *Guardian*, February 18, 2003, at http://guardian.co.uk/Iraq/Story/0.2763.897781.00html (accessed February 18, 2003).

14. Dore Gold, *Hatred's Kingdom: How Saudi Arabia Supports the New Global Terrorism* (Washington, D.C.: Regnery, 2003).

15. Stephen Flynn, *The Edge of Disaster* (New York: Random House, 2007).

16. Herb Keinon, "Israel Gets Smaller Aid Package than Requested," *Jerusalem Post*, March 21, 2003, at www.jpost.com/ (accessed March 21, 2003).

17. Barton Gellman, "Cyber-Attacks by Al Qaeda Feared," *Washington Post*, June 27, 2002, at www.washingtonpost.com/ac2/wp-dyn/A50765-2002Jun26 (accessed July 4, 2003).

18. "U.S. Officials Poised to Use the Internet as a Lethal Weapon" [in Arabic], *Al Wasat* 618 (December 1, 2003): 1–2.

19. Yassin Musharbash, "The Al-Qaida Guide to Kidnapping," *Spiegel Online*, December 1, 2005, at www.spiegel.de/international/0,1518,387888,00.html (accessed December 12, 2005); Alexis Debat, "Al Qaeda's Web of Terror," ABC News, March 10, 2006, at http://abcnews.go.com/technology/print?id=1706450 (accessed March 10, 2006); Sebastian Usher, "'Jihad' Magazine for Women on Web," BBC News, August 25, 2004, at http://news.bbc.co.uk/2/hi/middle_east/3594982.stm (accessed August 25, 2004).

20. Rory McCarthy, "Professors Fight to Keep Swift on Syllabus as Pakistan's

Islamists Target 'Vulgar' Classics," *Guardian*, July 10, 2003, at www.guardian.co.uk/
Pakistan/Story/0,2763,995166,00.html (accessed July 10, 2003).

21. Berween Shoreh, "Another AUC Book Slashed by the Censor," *Middle East Times* 49 (December 7, 1998): 402; Gabrielle Menezes, "The Art of the Ban," *Cairo Times* 7, no. 42 (January 2004).

22. Jeff M. Sellers, "Bearing the Cross: Religious Cleansing," *Christianity Today*, April 15, 2003, at www.christianitytoday.com/ct/2003/004/27.98.html (accessed July 18, 2003).

23. Green refers to Islam in that the Islamic flag is green.

24. Nick Fielding and Joe Laurier, "Bin Laden 'Almost Had Uranium Bomb,'" *Times Online-London*, March 3, 2002, at www.Sunday-times.co.uk/article/0,,
178-223894,00.html (accessed March 3, 2002).

25. Gerard de Villiers, *Djihad* (Paris: Malko Productions, 2000).

26. Ian Traynor, "Nuclear Watchdog Fears Terrorist Dirty Bomb after Looting at al-Tuwaitha," *Guardian*, May 14, 2003, at www.guardian.co.uk/international/
story/0,3604,955374,00.html (accessed May 15, 2003).

27. Gordon Corera, "Salesman of Doom," *Asia Times*, December 2, 2006, at www
.atimes.com/ (accessed December 2, 2006); Lawrence Sheets and William Broad,
"Smuggler's Plot Highlights Fear over Uranium," *New York Times*, January 25, 2007,
at www.nyt.com/ (accessed January 25, 2007); George Jahn, "AP: Nuclear Black Market Is Small, Covert," *Yahoo News*, February 2, 2004, at http://story.news.yahoo
.com/news?tmpl + story&cid'514&e + 5&u'/ap/20040202/apeon_re_eu/nuclear_black_
market.html (accessed February 2, 2002).

28. William J. Broad, "U.S. Web Archive Is Said to Reveal a Nuclear Primer," *New York Times*, November 3, 2006, at www.nytimes.com/ (accessed November 3, 2006).

29. Barton Gellman, "Al Qaeda Near Biological, Chemical Arms Production,"
Washington Post, March 23, 2003, at www.washingtonpost.com/wp-dyn/articles/
A12/87-2003Mar22.html (accessed March 23, 2003).

30. *Washington Post*, July 31, 2006, at www.washingtonpost.com/ (accessed July 31, 2006).

31. Jonathan Schanzer, *Al-Qaeda's Armies: Middle East Affiliate Groups and the Next Generation of Terror* (New York: Specialist Press, 2004).

32. Richard Norton-Taylor, "Al-Qaida 'Planted Information to Encourage U.S. Invasion,'" *Guardian*, November 17, 2006, at www.guardian.co.uk/ (accessed November 17, 2006).

33. Syed Saleem Shahzad, "Al-Qaeda Refines Its New Fighting Spirit," *Asia Times*, January 4, 2007, at www.atimes.com/ (accessed January 4, 2007); Syed Saleem Shahzad, "Al-Qaeda's Resurgence, Part 1: Ready to Take on the World," *Asia Times*, March 3, 2007, at www.atimes.com/ (accessed March 3, 2007).

34. Michael Scheuer, "Al-Qaeda's Long March to War," *Asia Times*, May 31, 2006, at www.atimes.com/ (accessed May 31, 2006).

10

The Jihadist War Machine

THE FUTURE SUCCESS of the jihadists will depend to a large degree on their ability to execute their war plan in an effective manner: (1) to recruit and train soldiers; (2) to establish communication and logistic networks; (3) to maintain base camps, weapons depots, and media outlets; (4) and to plant sleeper cells in the heart of enemy territory.[1] This is the stuff of organizations.

How good, then, are the jihadist organizations? Do they have the organizational muscle to continue their war of attrition against the West and move toward the next stage of their plan for global conquest? What are their strengths and weaknesses, and how are these weaknesses best exploited?

Questions beget questions. How are the jihadists organized? What about their leadership? How skilled and dedicated are their cadres? Can they sustain a prolonged confrontation with the United States, or will they fold under the pressure of an American onslaught? The present chapter addresses these most critical questions.

Organizing the Jihadists: The Pyramid of Terror

The typical jihadist group is a unique hybrid that blends the organizational structure of a modern bureaucracy with the authority patterns of the priesthood, the opaqueness of an oriental secret society, the cell network of a communist underground, and the honor code of the Mafia. All jihadist organizations are headed by an *emir* (prince of the believers) or *sheikh* (learned religious scholar). Titles are important because they symbolize the right to religious leadership. The emir heads a consultative council consisting of sub-emirs who, in turn, head the various administrative departments required to achieve the mission of the organization. The consultative councils are often large and could have fifty or more members depending on the size of the organization. In such cases, a handful of senior sub-emirs serve as a powerful executive committee or politburo. The consultative council, as the name suggests, is not an exercise in democracy. Opinions are aired and suggestions made, but there are no votes. The voices of powerful sub-emirs, those with a large following within the organization, carry more weight than sub-emirs of lesser stature. The wise emir listens carefully to the views of his sub-emirs and spends a great deal of time assessing the mood of the council. It would be foolhardy to fly in the face of broad opposition, but that is his prerogative.[2] A rough sketch of our view of the typical jihadist organization is provided in figure 10.1.

While the organizational chart of jihadist organizations might resemble that of a modern bureaucracy, the functions of its units reflect their deadly mission and the shadowy environment in which they operate. The religious

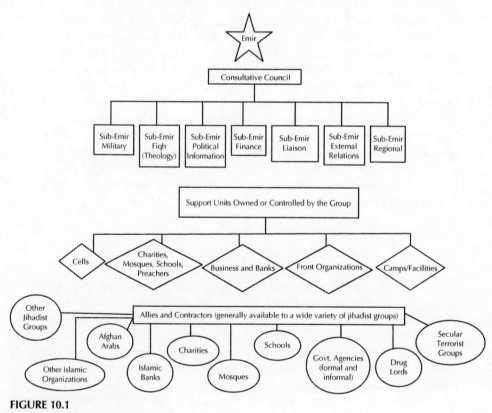

FIGURE 10.1
Typical jihadist organization

unit (Council of Islamic Jurisprudence), for example, consists of religious scholars, and ensures that the activities of the organization are in conformity with the Koran and Sunna. As noted in the preceding chapter, this is vital. Fighters being asked to sacrifice their lives must be absolutely convinced that their actions are sanctioned by Islamic law. Barring this, they will not reap their reward in heaven. Supporters, too, must be convinced that the jihadist cause is just and that the ends justify the most brutal of means, including the slaughter of innocent civilians. This is a difficult task that requires stretching Islamic law to the breaking point.[3]

The military branch is the heart of jihadist groups and is responsible for terrorists operations. In a few cases, they also maintain standing militias. During its prime in the mid-1990s, Algeria's le Groupe islamique armé (GIA), one of the largest and most brutal of jihadist organizations in the Islamic world, openly challenged the government on the battlefield. The military wing of the GIA was headed by the national military emir with the support of a variety of advisors and a council of *mujahedeen* (holy warriors). The national command gave way to regional and various local commands, and they to a variety of armored patrols, shock units, and suicide squads.[4] In times of crisis, the local units would dissolve into the population, while the leadership of the higher units would take to mountain base camps.

Al Qaeda: Variations on a Theme

The organization of Osama bin Laden's al Qaeda network followed a similar pattern, albeit on a more complex scale, with zones and regions being allocated on a global rather than a regional scale.[5] This suggests that the organizational structure of al Qaeda possesses much in common with a multinational corporation.[6] It now seems clear that bin Laden's military branch possessed separate units for the development of weapons of mass destruction. Some of bin Laden's chief sub-emirs had their own networks that they affiliated with al Qaeda, much as modern corporations "take over" their smaller competitors. Ayman al Zawahiri's branch of Egypt's Islamic Jihad, for example, merged with al Qaeda in 2001. A far larger number of groups allied with al Qaeda but retained their own identities and their independence of action.

Much like modern corporations, bin Laden outsourced much of his work to independent contractors. The 1995 car bomb attack on the National Guard barracks in Riyadh, Saudi Arabia, which killed seven people, including five Americans, was apparently contracted to the Islamic Movement of Change.[7] The subsequent 1996 attack on the Khobar Towers, according to a five-year investigation by U.S. authorities, was carried out by a Saudi branch of Hizbullah, with technical guidance by representatives of Hizbullah-Lebanon. Fingers were pointed to Iran as the Godfather of the Hizbullah movement, but ties to al Qaeda remain a matter of conjecture.[8] The bombing of the USS *Cole* in 2000 was apparently committed by three Yemeni groups enlisted by close aides of bin Laden: the Islamic Army of Aden-Abyan and two previously unknown groups, the Army of Mohammed and the Islamic Deterrence Forces.[9] The Yemenis did the detail work: setting up living quarters for the al Qaeda advisors, acquiring the boat and trailer used in the bombing, and even planning to film the event from a hillside.[10] The actual planning of the USS *Cole* bombing is attributed to Tawfiq bin Attash (and various aliases), a Yemeni man linked to al Qaeda. He is suspected of playing a role in planning the September 11 terrorist attacks. The bombing of the USS *Cole* itself was attributed to supporters of al Qaeda.[11] In much the same manner, the Islamic Army for the Liberation of the Holy Places claimed responsibility for the 1998 bombings of the American embassies in Kenya and Tanzania. A man who claimed bin Laden was his leader admitted to providing technical and logistical support to the bombers.[12]

The decentralization of al Qaeda operations increased dramatically in the aftermath of the September 11 terrorist attacks on the United States as bin Laden placed ever greater reliance on homegrown jihadist clones. In Bali, the group Jemaah Islamiya claimed responsibility for the 2002 bombing that killed more than two hundred people. The Imam Samudra of the Jemaah Islamiya claimed that his group robbed jewelry stores to finance the bombings. It was reported that he spent time in Afghanistan in the 1990s where he learned bomb-making skills.[13] He probably had al Qaeda contacts, but the Pakistani group Harakat ul-Mujahideen (HuM) also had extensive training camps in the region and was one of the main jihadist groups funded by the Central Intelligence Agency (CIA).[14] Credit for the 2003 Moroccan bombings has been shared between the Islamist group Assirat al Moustaquim (The Religious Path) and the extremist group Salafia Jihadia. All fifty suspects arrested in connection with the bombing had ties with the Salafist movement, which reportedly has ties with al Qaeda.[15] Initial reports indicated that the perpetrators of the attack were recently formed slum groups who resembled thugs more than religious devotees. Later reports seemed to implicate bin Laden, but it is possible that his role was one of inspiration rather than guidance.[16] The mujahedeen in the Arabian Peninsula claimed responsibility for the 2003 bombing of the western housing compound in Saudi Arabia. Saudi officials claim the terrorists were receiving orders from bin Laden, but to date the details remain fuzzy.[17] The same pattern continued with the attacks on the Madrid train stations and the London subway not to mention innumerable lesser attacks throughout the world.

Except for the September 11 terrorist attacks on America, then, al Qaeda provided funds and technical support, but local groups carried out the attacks. This pattern of loose affiliations and outsourcing makes it difficult to attribute blame with any degree of accuracy. After summarizing a long history of jihadist attacks on American and allied targets, a senior U.S. intelligence officer acknowledges that in most cases it is difficult to trace a clear line of responsibility to bin Laden. This, he continues, misses the point. "What is important is that the attacks fit the thematic parameters bin Laden has set for the 'guerilla' war he is waging and inciting against the crusaders and 'apostate' Muslim regimes. At a minimum, the attacks . . . suggest bin Laden's views and aspirations are shared by Islamists in many areas of the world."[18]

Like all analogies, the comparison of jihadist groups to a modern corporation is both insightful and deceptive. The organizational chart of the typical jihadist group does, indeed, resemble that of a modern corporation with its chief executive officers (CEOs) and layers of executives. This modern organizational framework provides the jihadists with the specialization they require to confront the power of modern governments, be they the secular regimes of the region or the United States and its allies.

There are, however, differences. The organizational structure of the jihadists reflects an all-consuming concern for secrecy and security, with few individuals in a position to identify more than a minor part of the organization. The structure of jihadist organizations also anticipates massive reprisals and can readily convert into a crisis mode until the pressure eases.

The essence of the jihadist organization, however, lies elsewhere. It is not the organizational framework of the jihadists that make them a lethal threat to America, but their patterns of leadership and the zeal of their employees. Neither follows the normal corporate pattern. Few Western CEOs court martyrdom by fire; few employees work for peanuts, endure excruciating hardships, and are willing to die for the firm. The jihadists are not about profits. They are about conversion, conquest, and destruction. But, above all, they are about personal salvation. A modern organizational structure is merely a means to an end. To focus on outward appearances is to profoundly miss the point.

Leadership in Jihadist Organizations

The authority that a jihadist emir exercises over his followers is a combination of religious authority and charismatic authority. Simple religious authority is based on the desire of individuals to gain salvation by following the rules of their religion, be it Islam, Christianity, or any other faith. Clergy are obeyed because of their superior knowledge of the faith and their ability to guide believers along the path of salvation. Many people, however, want more than guidance. They want a religious leader who possesses a clear sign of God's blessing, a leader who can work miracles and lead them to salvation. Leaders who possess God's blessing are said to be charismatic. They possess the gift of grace. When such a religious leader appears, the zealous follow him slavishly. This is most assuredly the case of the jihadists and their supporters.

Of course, one does not have to be a holy man to have the gift of grace. People under stress or living in unsettled times have always sought a hero or savior to lead them to salvation. More often than not, the desire for a savior has led to myth building, as people created heroes to provide them with a sense of security. Max Weber, one of the founding fathers of modern social science, thus coined the word charisma.

Charisma refers to a certain quality of [an] individual's personality by which he is set apart from ordinary men and treated as endowed with supernatural, superhuman or at least specifically exceptional powers and qualities. . . . In primitive circumstances this peculiar kind of deference is paid to prophets, to people with a reputation for therapeutic or legal wisdom, to leaders of the hunt, and heroes in war. It is very often thought as resting on magical powers.[19]

Hitler's mass rallies demonstrated the phenomenal power of a charismatic leader to guide a nation on the verge of collapse. People followed a maniac because they were desperate. As Hans Gerth sets the scene,

Persons whose career expectations are frustrated or who suffer losses in status or income in the intensive vocational competition of modern capitalism should be especially likely to accept the belief in the charismatic leader. Those placed on the disadvantaged side of life always tend to be interested in some sort of salvation which breaks through the routines associated with their deprivation. Such "unsuccessful" persons were to be found in every stratum of German society. Princes without thrones, indebted and subsidized landlords, indebted farmers, virtually bankrupt industrialists, impoverished shopkeepers and artisans, doctors without patients, lawyers without clients, writers without readers, unemployed teachers, and unemployed manual and white-collar workers joined the movement. National Socialism as salvationary movement exercised an especially strong attraction on the "old" and "new" middle classes, especially in those strata where substantive rationality is least developed, and will be most highly represented among those seeking salvation by quasi-miraculous means—or at least by methods which break through the routines which account for their deprivation.[20]

The people of the Islamic world are equally distraught, perhaps more so. Most are poor and oppressed and have little hope for a better future. It is only natural for them to seek salvation in their religion. That, after all, is the message of Christianity as well as Islam. It is also natural for them to seek a charismatic religious leader capable of leading them to the Promised Land. This is particularly true of the jihadists. Jihadists and their supporters are "true believers" who have an abiding need to identify with a charismatic religious leader capable of promising salvation. Perhaps this is due to the intensity of their religious training. It would also seem to have a great deal to do with the fears and anxieties that permeate the region as well as a culture that stresses blind obedience to the father.[21] In an *Al Jazeera* interview, Mansour al Zaiyat, perhaps the most famous of Egypt's Islamic lawyers, did his best to explain the relationship between the emir of a jihadist group and his followers. The emir in question was Omar Abdel-Rahman, the blind sheikh now incarcerated in a U.S. prison for his role in the 1993 bombing of the World Trade Center.

> INTERVIEWER: What did the Grand Sheikh Abdel-Rahman have to say about the truce declared in June of 1997?
>
> ZAIYAT: He learned of the initiative in prison in the U.S. He supported it a few days later saying, "They are youth who believe in who raised them." Only the Sheikhs of the Islamic Group can initiate actions. That is because of the deep esteem in which they are held by their sons [disciples], supporters, and admirers. It is much like a military commander gives orders to his soldiers. Only the sheikhs have that power, no one else . . . .
>
> INTERVIEWER: I didn't ask about the qualities of a leader, but about the military nature of the organization. . . . This relationship that makes an ordinary individual give his absolute loyalty—I don't want to say blind loyalty—to a man who is not a political leader. Isn't this dangerous even at the level of an Islamic state? Doesn't it create a problem when youth become so religious that they will consciously obey any order unto death? . . .
>
> ZAIYAT: No, it is not a military relationship. . . . It is spiritual. Maybe it is a relationship of love. It is a relationship of confidence. There are so many nonmilitary considerations in the relationship.[22]

It was the fusion of religious authority and charisma that enabled the Ayatollah Khomeini to mobilize the Iranian people against the Shah of Iran, and it was the same power that enabled his Islamic Revolution to inflame the Middle East. Far from being a mere grand ayatollah, the most exalted of religious ranks in Shi'a Islam, the Ayatollah Khomeini was viewed by many of his followers as the living embodiment of the Hidden Imam, or *marja-i-taq-*

lid uzma. This vision was justified by his smiting of the Shah, that most venerable of American allies. Lest more miracles be needed, U.S. helicopters sent to rescue American hostages captured by overzealous revolutionaries were mystically felled by sand in their engines, the stuff of miracles indeed.

The power of leaders such as Ayatollah Khomeini to sway the masses can only be understood with the realization that the relationship between a leader and his followers is a two-way street.[23] Khomeini's religious credentials had established him as an agent of the Hidden Imam and an object of emulation, while his years of revolutionary struggle had transformed him into a folk hero most assuredly blessed by God. This, however, was only part of the equation. The second part of the equation was that the Iranian masses were searching for a divinely inspired leader to lead them from the social, economic, and political decay of the Shah's regime. Many were willing to obey Khomeini's orders unto death because they believed in his mystical powers. Indeed, mass folklore elevated Khomeini to the stature of a minor deity precisely because they wanted a hero to believe in.[24]

Three decades later, his heirs perpetuate the myth of his sainthood in the hope that his charisma will shore up their flagging popularity. They have little choice. The Ayatollah Khomeini's successor, Ayatollah Khamenei, is neither charismatic nor a gifted religious scholar.[25] On the contrary, he was a lesser cleric rushed to the position of supreme guide in haste and compromise. There is no magic, and the Islamic Revolution has suffered accordingly.

Ayatollah Khomeini is the model that other jihadist leaders aspire to. Bin Laden has become a mythical folk hero of gigantic proportions but lacks the religious profundity of Khomeini. He has adopted the title of sheikh, but he is not a religious scholar. This fine point has been lost in the shuffle. The myth of bin Laden has become larger than life and fuels the jihadist movement of today much as the myth of Khomeini fueled the Islamic Revolution of the 1980s. Even his ability to escape the power of the United States has become the stuff of miracles. Everyone, including the Americans, is waiting for the next blow. In the meantime, psychological warfare has reached new levels. Each new terrorist alert in the United States and Europe has become a psychological victory in this most vicious game of cat and mouse.

Charismatic leadership, however, is only part of the jihadists' story. Religious authority is equally important. It is the religious authority of jihadist leaders that enables them to issue *fatwas* about what is or is not permissible in Islamic law. These *fatwas* are binding on the members of the group and are a key element in the power of the emir. As there are lots of religious leaders, there are lots of *fatwas*, many of which are contradictory. Some senior religious leaders have issued *fatwas* decrying the killing of innocent civilians. Others have embraced the jihadist position, decreeing that the killing of civilians is justified as long as it is necessary to protect the Islamic faith. The authority of *fatwas*, as the above example suggests, is binding only on the followers of the religious leader who issued it. The more popular the religious leader, the more powerful his *fatwas*. The *fatwas* of Ayatollah Khomeini became law in Iran and much of the Shi'a world.

Bin Laden has issued a variety of *fatwas* supporting his war against the United States, but even senior religious leaders who support his quest suggest that he lacks sufficient religious credentials to do so. Some have resolved the matter by issuing parallel *fatwas* of their own.[26] For bin Laden, however, it is his followers that count. In their view, bin Laden's successes are clear proof that he is divinely inspired. A sign of God's blessing supercedes theology.

Possessing mystical religious credentials also enables jihadist leaders to promise entry to paradise for those willing to risk their lives in the service to their faith. It is this power that enables the jihadists to recruit suicide bombers. Jihadist emirs have picked up this practice from the Shi'a despite the fact that Sunni Islam rejects the notion that high priests possess mystical powers. Ends, in their view, justify the means.

In much the same manner, mystical religious credentials give jihadist leaders the power to excommunicate their Muslim opponents by branding them as nonbelievers (*kafirs*). The leader of the Algerian GIA, that most bloody of jihadist organizations, used this principle to justify the mass killing of innocent Algerians.[27] By declaring them nonbelievers, he had signed their death warrant.

The jihadist style of leadership clearly has its advantages. CEO's and generals can praise, encourage, and bully, but they cannot guarantee a place in heaven nor can they dispatch errant employees to hell. Profit seeking is based on greed and status, while success is reflected in the ostentatious display of wealth. Jihadism, in contrast, is based on the desire for salvation. Status is gained by sacrifice and death. It's a whole different ball game.

The Downside of Jihadist Authority Patterns

Do the greater motivational advantages of jihadist leaders give them an insurmountable advantage in dealing with the West? Not at all. Jihadists simply have a different set of problems, many of which can easily be exploited in the war on terror. The effectiveness of a jihadist leader is proportional to his ability to establish absolute spiritual and psychological dominance over his followers. To be effective, he must convince them that he is, indeed, a divinely inspired vicar of the Prophet Mohammed. Barring this, his orders will be debated and his ranks depleted with defections as erstwhile followers seek a more inspired guide.

The founding fathers of jihadist organizations were invariably individuals of intense zeal and spirituality who, in the best biblical traditions, attracted a small group of disciples. As their movements grew, they consolidated their spiritual authority by launching ever-bolder raids against the infidel, trials by fire that demonstrated their prowess as generals and conveyed the impression of divine guidance. Mullah Omar, the leader of the Taliban, had established his intellectual and spiritual leadership among his student followers and consolidated that authority by leading the Taliban to victory after victory in the Afghan war against the Soviets.[28] To avoid any doubt, he symbolized his authority by wrapping himself in the cloak of the Prophet Mohammed, the most venerable of Afghanistan's religious treasures.[29]

In the case of bin Laden, the struggle for supremacy did not appear to be an issue. He was the hero of Afghanistan and Somalia and the probable author of the attacks on the American troops in Saudi Arabia—impeccable credentials indeed. He had also chosen his subordinates with great care, most of whom he had become acquainted with in Afghanistan or during his apprenticeship under al-Turabi. Bin Laden was influenced by his lieutenants, many of whom were renowned for their intellect and depth of religious knowledge, but it was he who brought all of the pieces together.[30] It was also he alone who had total knowledge of the al Qaeda network. As such, he could listen without being outflanked. But what happens when bin Laden is gone? He will become a saint in the eyes of his followers, but who will pick up the pieces?

The leadership of jihadist organizations also has its practical problems. The emir is the pope. He serves for life and remains inviolable. The doctrine of the organization is the religiously inspired vision of the founder. Apostasies cannot be tolerated, and those prone to sedition have to be purged. To avoid potential misunderstandings, disciples are kept at arm's length lest they steal the glory of the leader. Bin Laden has become a household word, but few people can name even one of his lieutenants. Information is carefully guarded and shared with subordinates selectively and sparingly. Only the leader has the full picture, and even information shared with subordinates could be of questionable quality or explicitly designed to create insecurities within the command structure. The practice of keeping potential competitors at arm's length is not unique to the jihadists but pervades all Arab organizations.[31]

All of the flaws inherent in the charismatic style of leadership are amplified by the process of succession. It is not easy to transfer God's special blessing, the gift of grace, to a subordinate who has been kept at an arm's length. Technically, selection of a new leader is accomplished by a vote of some sort among the dominant sub-emirs sitting as the *shura* (consultative council).

The aura, however, is gone. There is also the prickly matter of ideological conflict (for example, moderates versus conservatives), personal jealousies, and turf wars, all of which had been kept under control, if not encouraged, by the departed emir. All now burst into the open, with the losers either defecting with their personal entourage or biding their time while they wait for the opportunity to seize control of the movement. The primary goal of the newly proclaimed emir, for his part, is to consolidate his authority, a task best achieved by putting his own people in key positions. The position of the losers is further threatened, as is the potential for defection.

The selection process often finds the nod going to the more zealous of the fallen leaders' lieutenants, for zeal is the foundation of jihadist organizations.[32] Indeed, the jihadist movement was born out of impatience with the caution of the Muslim Brotherhood. The very concept of jihad implies action.

All signs suggest that al Qaeda is going through a similar process. Bin Laden might or might not be alive, but al Qaeda has gone to great lengths to assure the world that he is alive. In part, this is psychological warfare. Myth building buoys supporters, keeps al Qaeda in the public eye, and even sparks imitators. All drive Western security agencies crazy.

Zawahiri is often credited with being bin Laden's second in command, but this, too, is a matter of speculation. Zawahiri is bin Laden's personal physician and, by all accounts, played a major role in shaping bin Laden's philosophy of jihad.[33] These, however, are personal ties and do not convey the power to control other emirs once bin Laden has disappeared. Each emir has his own power base, and each, in all probability, aspires for dominance. It is also unlikely that Zawahiri possesses the keys to bin Laden's financial network, the complexities of which are mind boggling. He can control his own faction within al Qaeda but probably not much more. In part, this is a question of jealously, with growing reports of tensions and competition between the two men.[34] It is also a question of Zawahiri's prosaic religious credentials and relative invisibility. It is bin Laden who has taken the credit for his reputed genius. It is more than likely, accordingly, that the loss of bin Laden will have a depressing effect on the jihadist movement, much as the loss of the Ayatollah Khomeini led to confusion in Iran and the Shi'a world. Bin Laden will continue to inspire, but he will not continue to lead.

Other leadership problems abound. Security forces have exacted a heavy toll on the jihadist leadership. Some have been killed, while others have been arrested or forced into exile. This has disrupted the chain of command within jihadist organizations, spawned turf wars, and raised serious questions concerning precisely who is in charge.[35] In the case of the Islamic Group and Egyptian Jihad, Egypt's two largest jihadist organizations, the leadership is split three ways between the troops on the ground, those imprisoned, and those in exile, each with differing concepts of the strategy to be pursued.[36] While those in exile tend toward theoretical reflection born of isolation and experience, it is the troops on the ground who are taking the risks and making battleground decisions based on the realities of the moment.

The problem, however, is deeper. The culture of Islamic countries places a premium on age, with the older jihadist leaders demanding deference due to age, experience, and prior sacrifice. The younger leaders, having tasted power, are anxious to set the world on fire, both literally and figuratively. Many of the younger jihadist leaders simply find the orders of their superiors, presumably smuggled from the jail via Islamic lawyers, to be out of touch with the realities on the ground. The younger leaders also want more power. The veterans are reluctant to grant it.

While generational tensions within the jihadist organizations have been noted for some time, the crisis came to ahead in 2002, when the imprisoned leaders of the Islamic Group formally renounced violence. The younger jihadist leadership and many exiles slammed the decision and vowed to continue their jihad. This gave the appearance that the older leadership, while respected, had lost control of their organizations.[37] Up to now, the truce has held, although in 2007 a branch of Egypt's Islamic Group renewed its affiliation with al Qaeda. Independent jihadist groups have also proliferated and gained notoriety by launching high-profile attacks on Israeli tourists in Egypt.

In the case of al Qaeda, the depletion of the tight leadership circle forged in Afghanistan has been replenished by leaders of independent jihadist groups who have sworn unilateral allegiance to al Qaeda. By and large, they embraced al Qaeda to increase their own influence and legitimacy and were accepted by the parent organization to fill a void or extend its influence.[38] This was the case of Abu Musab al-Zarqawi in Iraq, Abu Hajar Abd al-Aziz al-Muqrin in Saudi Arabia, and al-Miquati in Lebanon, to mention but a few groups. Leaders of many of the affiliate groups have passed through al Qaeda training camps, but that is not the same as having strong personal ties with bin Laden. For all of al Qaeda's resemblance to a modern corporation, it is still the personal ties that bind. Others can be exploited, but only the closest of associates can be trusted. This is particularly important when the leadership is scattered and communications are tenuous. In some cases, the marriages of convenience have shifted the momentum to the people actually carrying out the attacks rather than to the central organization. Both al-Zarqawi in Iraq and al-Miquati in Saudi Arabia were far more anxious than bin Laden to use quasimilitary troops to seize territory and openly defied bin Laden in their attacks on Muslims.[39] This process can only increase as the jihadist leadership moves into its third, fourth, and even fifth generations. Generations in the jihadist world are not lengthy affairs. Affiliate leaders such as al-Zarqawi surface only to fall victim to the counterterror assaults. And yet, their numbers proliferate. It is almost as if the fragmentation of al Qaeda has made it easier for younger leaders to move to the fore, something that has been the bane of the radical moderates discussed earlier.

Unfortunately, these problems would seem to be of minimal importance as long as the current war plan of al Qaeda requires no more than an escalation of attacks on America and its allies. The real problems will arise as al Qaeda presses to regain control of its most elusive of networks in preparation for the next stage of the war plan. Not only will greater coordination be difficult to achieve, but also the next stage will suffer from the excesses of the present and the reassertion of past mistakes. Jihadists are again alienating supporters by attacking Muslims, the patience preached by bin Laden is giving way to adventurism, strategic consensus is eroding, personality conflicts abound as egos clash, cadres are poorly trained, and lapses of discipline have played into the hands of security forces.

The core of the jihadists' leadership problems, then, is the intense personalization of relationships between leaders and followers. Unlike modern corporations or armies in which reasonable similar cogs can be moved from one position to the next based on education and experience, authority patterns among the jihadists are overwhelmingly dependent on emotion, zeal, and psychological dominance. Individuals are not subservient to the institution. They are subservient to a particular leader. Replacements are found, but it takes time to establish new patterns of trust and loyalty. In the meantime, the strength of the organization is weakened. Also weakened are the complex communication systems of the jihadists, most of which rely heavily on personal contacts. Leadership transitions in the West are often difficult but not to the same degree.

Decision Making in Jihadist Organizations

The personalization of leadership, in turn, influences the ways in which jihadist organizations make decisions. Charisma requires that heroes remain active. Even the followers of bin Laden are looking for signs of God's continued blessing, not laurels of the past. Iraq has kept bin Laden in the limelight, but what comes next? Pressure to act, even rashly, is enormous.

This is just the beginning of the jihadists' problems. The wisdom of the emirs is not guaranteed, and few checks exist to curb errant whims. Emirs who speak with the inspiration of God are not easily defied. They also make poor listeners and have often been reluctant to build on the experience of others. This is particularly the case of homegrown jihadists anxious to make their mark in the world.

Emirs, like princes throughout history, have also found cooperation difficult. They meet and negotiate, but they are reluctant to relinquish sovereignty to competitors. Alliances are made, but they are the most fragile of alliances. Fear and distrust characterizes all Middle Eastern organizations, and the jihadists are no exception. Allies are essential, but few are trusted. Exceptional leaders such as the Ayatollah Khomeini and bin Laden can forge broad alliances, but they are few and their alliances seldom survive their passing. Moderate voices in the Islamic movement are now praying for the emergence of a charismatic Sunni cleric similar to the Ayatollah Khomeini to galvanize the Islamic movement.[40]

Given the above array of problems, charismatic decision making often results in ill-conceived projects that squander resources and alienate public support. Even the Ayatollah Khomeini made errors in judgment, the most cataclysmic of which was his refusal of Saddam Hussein's 1982 offer of peace in the Iran-Iraq War. The Iraqis were in retreat, and acceptance of Hussein's peace offer would have enabled the Ayatollah to bilk Saudi Arabia and Kuwait for billions of dollars in war reparations. Both Saudi Arabia and Kuwait had helped finance the war and had little option but to buy their way out of a venture that had gone terribly wrong. Similarly, it was errors by the jihadist emirs, particularly their excessive use of violence against Muslims, that alienated their supporters and placed them on the defensive. These same errors have kept the jihadists from developing a strong follow-up capacity that would enable them to better capitalize on their victories. Indeed, the whole pattern of jihadist history has been one of daring attacks with little follow-up. This will not achieve their goal.

The vulnerabilities inherent in the jihadist leadership style suggest that the easiest way to deal with their organizations would be to target their leaders at all levels. The arrest of senior leaders disrupts decision making; the arrest of midlevel leaders disrupts operations. Unlike modern organizations, jihadist organizations do not just keep on going. They revive, but it is an agonizing and debilitating process that seriously depletes the destructive capacity of the organization.

For the moment, this splintering has not dampened the jihadist war plan. Indeed, it has made it more difficult to contain. It will be a much different story as al Qaeda attempts to move to the next stage of its war plan. Attempts to do so could well lead to the destruction of the organization.

The Jihadist Soldiers: Who Are They, What Motivates Them, and How Good Are They?

In the final analysis, it is the cadres who are the core of any organization. Leaders plan; cadres execute. Elegant organizational structures and gifted generals go for naught if the troops can't get the job done. Are cadres the strength of jihadist organizations or a source of weakness to be exploited by America in its war on terror? Again, questions beget questions. Where do the jihadist cadres come from? What drives them? How are they trained and recruited? How good is their discipline and morale?

Where do jihadist cadres come from? The answer is simple: everywhere. Most are Muslims of Middle Eastern or Pakistani origin, but the Islamic populations of Bangladesh, Indonesia, and Malaysia are all well represented, as are Muslims from sub-Saharan Africa, Central Asia (the former USSR), Europe, and North America.

One reason that it is so difficult to establish a jihadist profile is that individuals migrate to the jihadist cause for different reasons. The ranks of jihadists who ignited the jihadist movement in Egypt included doctors, engineers, and other professionals. Many of the perpetrators of September 11 were the scions of wealthy Saudi families, albeit families of Yemeni or Palestinian origin. Some seethed with frustration about a corrupt regime; others appeared to be seeking greater meaning for otherwise hollow lives. Many European recruits feel a deep sense of humiliation resulting from social prejudice and harsh treatment by the police. In many cases their humiliation is transformed into hatred for Christians and Jews and by association. Sympathy for Palestinians and other oppressed Muslims populations become an excuse for violence. Some recruits have been moved by profound faith and knowledge of Islam. Others know little of their religion but have seized upon its slogans as a path to respectability and power.[41] Many of the jihadists who fueled the reign of terror in Algeria were little more than street thugs organized into religious gangs by local emirs.[42] Richard Reid, the infamous shoe bomber, was a lonesome drifter who sought belonging within the confines of a jihadist mosque.[43] The jihadists have also crossed the gender line, vastly expanding the size of the terrorist pool with female suicide bombers. The leaders are well educated, but most of the rank and file are drawn from the poor and destitute. Death in the name of God is their path to salvation.

Jihadists are recruited in a wide variety of venues, including Islamic student associations, mosques, cafes, prisons, Islamic welfare centers, and Internet chat rooms. Pop singers and music videos exhorting the virtues of jihad are also making their appearance.[44] A recent assessment suggested that some 80 percent of the jihadist cadres are now recruited via the Internet. We don't know how they arrived at this figure, but we thought it a scary one.[45] Recruits displaying the requisite zeal are gradually introduced into the rituals of the jihadists. The poor are provided with books and clothes, the lonely with belonging, the sinners with the hope of redemption, and the angry with outlets for their wrath. Algerian police psychologists suggest that many recruits are attempting to escape the scorn of low social status by establishing a new identity. Others yearn for power and view themselves as heroes of Islam or movie stars. Weapons and killing accentuate the thrill of power. In a few cases, the jihadists have simply been kidnapped and forced into service. Many accentuate their new identity by assuming a heroic name or referring to themselves as the father of a male child. Even unmarried jihadists assume this practice, which has the added advantage of confusing the police.[46] Jihadist recruiters are superb psychologists who spend hours ministering to the psychological needs of their recruits and assessing their psychological vulnerabilities.

In reality, the job of the jihadist recruiter is probably not that difficult. Incidental evidence suggests that most recruits already lean toward an authoritarian environment if not violence. Many recruits, inflamed by the Soviet attack on Islamic Afghanistan and the lure of everlasting salvation, sought out jihadist organizations and flocked to the ranks of the Afghan Arabs. Others were ferried to Afghanistan by the Muslim Brotherhood, Hizbullah, or as in the case of Saudi Arabia, by establishment mosques. Still other recruits have been introduced to the jihadists by friends or family. Many of the female jihadists are the wives or daughters of jihadists.[47] In any case, we could find no evidence suggesting that the supply of potential recruits was diminishing.

Once they have entered the ranks of the jihadists, recruits undergo an intense blend of religious indoctrination and technical training, much of the latter focusing on their role in terrorist operations. Of the two, religious indoctrination is probably the most important, for it is religious zeal and the promise of eternal salvation that drives the jihadist cadre. All doubts about the sanctity of their mission must be banished from their minds. To question that their mission has been ordained by God is to vacillate in the face of duty. It is also to question the authority of the emir and to jeopardize discipline within the jihadist organization. Doubt breeds disaster. Faith must also weld individuals from diverse backgrounds into a cohesive force and surmount the fears, jealousies, and personality conflicts that are the bane of all organizations in the Middle East.

Skill training is more prosaic and resembles training traditionally received by terrorists and guerilla groups throughout the modern era.[48] Bin Laden's training manuals differ little from U.S. intelligence manuals provided for use in the Afghan war against the Soviets. Indeed, Western security experts seized an eleven-volume encyclopedia of terror in the sweep of suspected al Qaeda sites in the aftermath of the September 11 terrorist attacks. Some six thousand plus pages in length, the encyclopedia is a self-help guide to the construction of everything from pipe bombs and booby traps to demolition of bridges and stadiums.[49] Also covered are first aid, map reading, weapons repair, construction of mines and mine fields, interrogation, sabotage, and the principles of war, including psychological warfare. Particularly frightening was the volume discussing the use of biochemical agents, including anthrax and ricin, both of which have been used by jihadist groups in the post–September 11 era. Ricin is a highly toxic chemical that, according to the London *Times*, was "used on the tip of an umbrella by a Bulgarian secret service agent to kill the Soviet dissident Georgy Markov in London in 1978."[50] More recently, the Russians have added plutonium to the list. Can al Qaeda be far behind?

A shorter training guide, entitled *Military Studies in the Jihad against Tyrants*, was seized in London in May 2000. Along with instructions on explosives, it advises potential terrorists on ways to assimilate in Western culture. The *New York Times* describes the volume, some 180 pages in length, as "part philosophical treatise, part training guide, part 'Spy vs. Spy' from a back issue of *Mad Magazine*."[51] The manual, with "Do Not Remove" stamped on the cover, was seized in a jihadist guesthouse. Other manuals have been disseminated in both book and CD format. PBS *Frontline* featured excerpts from the manuals captured on the person of an al Qaeda operative attempting to enter the United States from Canada. Among other things, the manuals stressed how members of cells and their leaders should behave to avoid detection in addition to other needed skills.[52]

Western experts have played down the significance of the training manuals, suggesting all of the materials that they contain are freely available on the Internet. One U.S. expert notes that "a visit to the U.S. Army's website offers scores of publicly available field manuals on everything from conducting psychological operations to sniper training and how to install Claymore antipersonnel mines."[53] The latest U.S. Marine antiterrorist manual came online in 2006. The web also provides instructions for building rockets for under three thousand dollars and once contained instructions for building an atomic bomb. The latter instructions were provided by a college student and are now no longer available online.

Prosaic as it might be, the training manuals speak volumes about the capacity of al Qaeda and other jihadist groups to inflict devastating damage on America and its allies. Brighter recruits are also sent abroad for more specialized training, the United States and Britain long being the venue of choice. That now is proving more difficult.

How Good Are the Jihadist Cadres?

The strength of jihadist cadres is their zeal. Indeed, it is doubtful that the personnel of any other organization on Earth can match the dedication and zeal of the jihadist cadres. They are ready to die for their cause and actively court death. The jihadists are also easily motivated. They are looking for salvation and openly seek the reassurance of their emirs. Secular organizations spend millions on motivational consultants with far less success. Jihadists who want to succeed in their deadly task are presumably anxious to acquire the necessary skills.

The jihadists also benefit from the diversity of their personnel. Aside from a rarity of blue eyes and blanched skin, the jihadists do not fit a common profile, a problem compounded by the growing number of East Asian, African, and female jihadists. A broad mix of skin colors, gender, training, and socioeconomic backgrounds makes it increasingly easy for the jihadist leadership to match personnel to the country and task at hand.

For all their zeal and sacrifice, the attitudes and work habits of the jihadist personnel are seriously flawed. In part, the problems besetting the jihadists are those that beset virtually all Middle Eastern organizations. Other problems reflect the venality of human nature, and still others are unique to the jihadist venture.

In the first category of problems is the general malaise that pervades virtually all Middle Eastern organizations: fear, loathing, and distrust are everywhere. Similar organizational tensions are illustrated in the somewhat humorous description of life in an Egyptian office. For those of serious purpose, the pervasiveness of this behavior is not a laughing matter.

> No sooner is an official promoted to the post of manager than he ceases to accomplish any constructive work. His primary concern is to receive the compliments indiscriminately leveled at him from every quarter, and to smile with condescending magnanimity at the servile flattery lavished at him by his former colleagues.
>
> Such a state of affairs has naturally developed out of a corrupt system of bureaucracy fostered and consolidated over the years, as a result of a deeply rooted fear in the hearts of juniors towards their superiors. Managers have actually capitalized on this fear in order to force more submission and humility on already humble juniors and to extort from them every possible kind of service and every conceivable kind of flattery.

With such material and moral accoutrements adorning the post of manager, it is only natural that officials should be vying with one another to attain this post through all the means available, not excluding hypocrisy, bribery, backbiting, double-dealing, and deception.[54]

Tensions within Middle Eastern organizations are eased by friendship rituals, the most prominent of which is the cigarette ritual. Colleagues sit around, sipping coffee or strong tea laced with sugar, offering each other cigarettes. There is seldom a need to exchange cigarettes, for everyone has some. The need is for an act of sharing. No one is fooled, but things go easier, at least until someone leaves the room and the gossip starts. The principle is not that different in the United States, but the bite is in the degree.

To survive in this environment, employees attach themselves to a patron or sub-emir capable of looking after their interests. The deal is a simple one: they support the sub-emir, and the sub-emir looks after their interests and facilitates their advancement. The patron needs people in critical places. They are his people and support him in his turf wars with other sub-emirs. If he wins, they win. If he bolts the organization in a test of wills, most of his supporters will also bolt, for their position in the parent organization has been compromised. If the sub-emir falls by the wayside, his clients scramble for a new patron, not a pleasant task for those who have bet on the wrong horse. This is not to suggest that patron-client networks are forged in iron, for an emir with fading power could find that his supplicants have gone elsewhere. One has to survive.

The result of this situation is that jihadist organizations tend to represent a mosaic of personal networks that reach their apogee in the grand emir. Loyalty to the organization tends to become secondary to the loyalty of the network. Clashes of policy and personality among the sub-emirs reverberate throughout the organization, sapping its cohesiveness. In some instances, conflict among rival patron-client networks leads to open violence.

This brings us to a second category of personnel problems decried by the jihadists in their self-analyses, that of the human failings of the cadres. Jihadists might be purer of heart than the average individual, but for all of their religious indoctrination, they remain human. Jealousy, greed, pride, and the lust for power pervade jihadist organizations much as they pervade most human organizations.[55] It was much the same among the Afghan Arabs in Afghanistan, with the human frailties of jihadist cadres being accentuated by bitter and enduring conflicts over fine points of doctrine. The latter, in turn, accentuated tendencies toward splintering and fragmented the cohesiveness of the Afghan Arabs.[56] Even one of bin Laden's key lieutenants was caught with his hand in the till. The jihadists, however, can less afford the consequences of human frailty than most other organizations. Secrecy requires they run a tight ship, and even minor glitches can spell disaster for a jihadist cell.

If the above problems apply to virtually all Middle Eastern organizations, the jihadists also have their own unique cross to bear, that being the overzealousness of their cadres. The same zeal that propelled the jihadists into the world arena possessed a cruel underside that saw killing become an end in itself. The excesses of the jihadists' rank and file have pushed potential supporters away from the jihadists and, in the eyes of many, justified governmental efforts to crush them. It was the jihadists, rather than the government, who had become the danger. The entire Islamic movement was in danger of becoming discredited.

The zeal of the rank and file has also made it difficult for the leadership to bide its time and play a waiting game. The troops demand action. Emirs who preach moderation find their ranks depleted as zealots flock to their more animated competitors. This has led to hasty and unwise decisions as divinely inspired emirs have found themselves running to keep ahead of their troops.

In much the same manner, the zeal of cadres defies compromise or even a willingness to adapt to the new realities imposed by the war on terror. The jihadist creed is founded on the fundamental belief that God will provide. There is no need for compromise. Recklessness and daring become substitutes for prudence and rational behavior.

It would also be a mistake to assume that zeal is uniformly intense across the spectrum of jihadist organizations. An infinitesimal number of jihadists have actually sacrificed everything to join the ranks of the Afghan Arabs or have willingly sacrificed their lives in suicide attacks. Many jihadists are now experimenting with truces while they search for a strategy that fits the new realities imposed on them by the war on terror. It also appears that many of the September 11 hijackers did not fully understand that they had embarked on a suicide mission—a dangerous mission, yes; suicide, no. Mohammed al'Owhali, a member of the al Qaeda team sent to destroy the American Embassy in Nairobi, got cold feet at the last moment and started running. He survived the bombing and is now in a U.S prison serving a life sentence without parole.[57] Suicide bombers, the ultimate weapon of the jihadists, are very scarce resources who must be carefully nourished and allocated with care.

Collectively, the above mix of personnel problems has created a debilitating crisis of morale within the jihadist organizations. Many jihadists are dispirited, especially those who lack the zeal and tenacity of the Afghan Arabs. Again, the problems are many. In part, the morale problems besetting the jihadists are merely the product of a daunting lifestyle. The hunters have become the hunted, cut off from their families and living in fear as they run from camp to camp. A few camps are elegant, but most are severe. Security forces also target relatives, adding to the anguish of the troops. These burdens were easier to bear during the heyday of the jihadist movement, but victories are no longer easy to come by and losses are high. The test of faith has become arduous, especially for those past the prime of youth. The authors of the jihadist truce in Egypt, for example, had spent long years in prison and longed to die in the arms of their families. The core of morale problems, however, lies within the internal dynamics of the jihadist organization. Distrust and insecurity among emirs and sub-emirs has led to purges and witch hunts, most fueled by innuendo and the all-pervasive rumor. Hard information is a rare commodity in the jihadist world, and one can never be too sure of one's colleagues. Adding to the tension is the pervasive conflict among patron networks and the ever-present fear of a defector or government spy. The intensity of Islamic indoctrination has not put an end to human venality.

Insecurity breeds harsh discipline, with the more severe infractions punished by flogging or other penalties common in early Arabia.[58] Taliban and al Qaeda troops opened fire on their colleagues when discipline wavered in the face of U.S. attacks.[59] Also severe are the loyalty rituals that, in extreme cases in Algeria, called for the murder of family members.[60] It is little wonder that idealists committed to an Islamic paradise of peace and prayer find themselves dismayed by the realities of jihadist organizational life.

The organizational environment of the jihadists, then, is essentially negative and conflictual. Zeal drives the jihadist during the attack mode, but internal dissensions sap the strength of jihadist organizations once the attack mode has passed. Like most emotional highs, the zeal of the jihadists has been difficult to maintain over long periods of time. Many simply drift back to a more conventional lifestyle or revert to a less demanding form of religious expression. Others lose focus, uncomfortable with the waiting game. The jihadist mentality is better suited to creating environments of chaos than to carrying out the mundane bureaucratic tasks required to transform the fruits of their violence into a broad-based mass organization. Conventional employees are less zealous than the jihadist warriors, but they are far better suited to the routine tasks required to sustain the organization over the long haul.

Finally, it should be noted that the jihadists are not the James Bonds they appeared to be in the aftermath of the September 11 terrorist attacks. The hijackers often bragged of planned exploits, perhaps feeling a need to bolster their spirits. In retrospect, their operations appeared clumsy, creating gross security breaches and littering the countryside with clear signs of their intentions. Unfortunately, U.S. security procedures were equally flawed.

The Physical Plant

Even the most dedicated jihadist organizations require a physical infrastructure of training camps, shelters, weapons depots, and supply lines if they are to carry out their bloody operations effectively. Early jihadist organizations were simple affairs, centered in friendly mosques, squalid slums, and sparse base camps secreted in remote hideouts. As jihadist ambitions increased, the infrastructure requirements increased proportionally. In the case of the larger jihadist organizations such as al Qaeda, physical plants now rival those of an army or multinational corporation. They have recruiting centers, training camps, supply networks, communications centers, sleeper cells, weapon dumps, laboratories, safe houses, and a secure headquarters for the leadership. They also maintain a variety of front organizations for contracting with suppliers, coordinating with sympathetic religious organizations, disseminating propaganda, dealing with outsourcers, and meeting with representatives of friendly governments. The task of describing the physical facilities of al Qaeda would, itself, require a book of several hundred pages and has been the stuff of minute investigations of al Qaeda camps in Afghanistan and elsewhere.

The advantage of the smaller, homegrown jihadist groups is the ability of their members to live off the land, take the bus to work, and remain indistinguishable from their neighbors. Most sport beards or wear the *hijab* (Islamic dress), but that is now the norm in the Middle East and merely enhances their cover in poorer neighborhoods. Many work for the government, including the police and the army. This is not exceptional, for most people in the Islamic world work for the government. Their jobs are usually not auspicious, but they do have access to sensitive areas and useful information. Other infrastructure demands are relatively minor. Most jihadists have their own military-type weapons, not a rarity in the Middle East, and materials for rudimentary explosives are not too difficult to come by. They are also easy to obtain in the United States.

The disadvantage of the smaller groups is their lack of size and reach. The disadvantage of larger networks such as al Qaeda is the size and complexity of their physical plant. Facilities are identified by security agencies and destroyed. They are rebuilt, but that takes time and money. Bin Laden has attempted to minimize his exposure to U.S. antiterrorist measures by placing much of his infrastructure in areas of chaos and decentralizing his leadership structure.

Much like the smaller jihadist groups, sleeper cells and front organizations are expected to be innocuous and self-supporting, with members of the sleeper cells often behaving in most non-Islamic ways to avoid suspicion: sex and booze in the name of God. The practice of disguising their true religious beliefs was perfected by the Shi'a to avoid the persecution of the Sunni majority and suits the needs of the jihadists admirably. Actually, it is remarkable how much the Sunni jihadists have adopted the tactics of the Shi'a.

Although the shift to homegrown cells and the decentralization of leadership has kept al Qaeda and its spin-offs active while it reassembles, its infrastructure is contracting and its dynamism has been blunted. This is of little solace to America and its allies, for much of the jihadist infrastructure remains in place and is likely to remain so for some time.

In sum, the main organizational strengths of the jihadists war machine are (1) leadership styles that inspire total devotion; (2) a cadre of fanatic followers who willingly sacrifice their lives in defense of Islam; (3) technological sophistication; and (4) a physical plant that provides for training, weapons, communications, logistics, and funding on a global basis. These strengths are balanced by (1) the highly personalized authority patterns that are disrupted by the loss of an emir; (2) the excessive zeal of cadres and lapses in morale that accrue during setbacks or periods of inactivity; (3) tensions and conflicts within and between competing jihadist organizations; and (4) the vulnerability of their physical plant to attack.

The most effective manner of combating the strengths of the jihadist war machine, accordingly, is to target jihadist leaders at all levels, to demoralize the jihadists by forcing them to suffer highly publicized defeats, and to constantly disrupt their physical plant. The more energy they expend on running and rebuilding, the less energy remains to attack America and its allies. Attacking the allies of the jihadists is equally important and is the topic we turn to next.

Notes

1. Kim Cragin and Sara A. Daly, *The Dynamic Terrorist Threat: An Assessment of Group Motivations and Capabilities in a Changing World* (Santa Monica, Calif.: RAND Corporation, 2004), at www.rand.org/pubs/monograph_reports/2005/MRF 182.sum.pdf (accessed December 12, 2006).

2. The model of a typical jihadist organization was pieced together from a wide variety of sources as well as extensive personal experience in working with Middle

Eastern organizations. The exact pattern will vary from group to group, but the basic format is the same.

3. Yousef Qaradawi, "Violence and the Islamic Groups, Part 1" [in Arabic], interviewed by Hamid Al Ansari, *Al Jazeera*, July 7, 2001.

4. Liess Boukra, *Algerie la terreur sacree* (Lausanne, Switzerland: Favre SA, 2002).

5. Rohan Gunaratna, *Inside Al-Qaeda: Global Network of Terror* (New York: Columbia University Press, 2002), 57.

6. Peter L. Bergen, *Holy War, Inc.: Inside the Secret World of Osama bin Laden* (New York: Free Press, 2001); Jason Burke, *Al Qaeda: Casting a Shadow of Terror* (London: I.B. Tauris, 2003).

7. Adnan Malik, "91 Killed in Saudi Arabia Terror Blasts," *Common Dreams News Center* 13 (May 2003), at www.commondreams.org/headlines03/0513-08.htm (accessed February 24, 2004).

8. U.S. Dept. of Justice, "Press Release: Khobar Towers," June 21, 2001, at www .fbi.gov/pressrel/pressrel01/khobar.htm (accessed July 19, 2003).

9. Sheila Carapico, "Yemen and the Aden-Abyan Islamic Army," *Middle East Report Online* 18 (October 2000), at www.merip.org/mero/mero101800.html (accessed July 19, 2003); "The Suspects," *Yemen Gateway*, December 12, 2000, at www.al-bab.com/yemen/cole7.htm (accessed July 19, 2003).

10. Daniel Klardman, Michael Isikoff, and Mark Hosenball, "Investigators Link Last Week's Attacks, Embassy Bombings in Africa and USS *Cole*," *Newsweek Web Exclusive*, September 20, 2001, at www.msnbc.msn.com/id/3066931 (accessed February 24, 2004).

11. "Alleged Cole, Sept. 11 Suspect Nabbed," *CBS News*, April 30, 2003, at www .cbsnews.com/stories/2003/05/15/attack/main553982.shtml (accessed August 2, 2003).

12. "The U.S. Embassy Bombings in Kenya and Tanzania," *Terrorism Update* (Fall 1998), at www.adl.org/terror/focus/15_focus.asp (accessed July 27, 2003).

13. "Imam on Trial for Bali Bombings," *Guardian*, June 2, 2003, at www .guardian.co.uk/print/0,,4681917-103681,00.html (accessed July 27, 2003).

14. B. Rahman, "Harkat-ul-Mujahideen: An Update," International Policy Institute of Counter Terrorism, March 20, 1999, at www.ictc.org.il/articles/articledet .cfm?-articleid = 85 (accessed March 20, 1999).

15. Malika Zeghal, *Les islamistes marocains: Le defi a la monarchie* [in French] (Paris: Editions La Decouverte, 2005).

16. "Moroccan Bombers Linked to Global Terrorism," *News Australia*, May 21, 2003, at www.newsaustralia.com/Morocco-V-Spain/Moroccan_bombers_linked_to_ global.htm (accessed July 15, 2003); Nicolas Marmie, "Morocco Arrests 19 Suicide Bomb Suspects," *Washington Post*, June 6, 2003, at www.washingtonpost.com/ wp-dyn/articles/A24422-2003June6.html (accessed June 6, 2003).

17. Al-Rais Saud, "Saudi Arabia: Lifting the Veil on Implicit Sympathy with the Extremists" [in Arabic], *Al-Wasat* (December 22, 2003): 11.

18. Anonymous, *Through Our Enemies' Eyes: Osama Bin Laden, Radical Islam, and the Future of America* (Washington, D.C.: Brassey's, 2002).

19. Max Weber, *The Theory of Social and Economic Organization* (New York: Macmillan, 1947), 328, 358–59.

20. Hans Gerth, "The Nazi Party: Its Leadership and Composition," *The American Journal of Sociology* 45 (January 1940): 526–27.

21. All are discussed at length by our colleague Michel Nehme, in *Fear and Anxiety in the Arab World* (Gainesville, Fla.: University Press of Florida, 2003).

22. Mansour Al Zaiyat, "Sharia and Life Series: Islamic Groups and Violence" [in Arabic], interviewed by Mahir Abdullah, *Al Jazeera*, August 11, 2002.

23. For an extensive discussion of the charismatic relationship, see Monte Palmer, *Dilemmas of Political Development*, 4th ed. (Itasca, Ill.: Peacock Publishers, 1989), 155–97.

24. Marvin Zonis and Cyrus Amir Mokri, "The Islamic Republic of Iran," in *Politics and Government in the Middle East and North Africa*, ed. Tareq Y. Ismael and Jacqueline S. Ismael (Miami: Florida International University Press, 1991).

25. Ali Banuazizi and Myron Weiner, eds., *The State, Religion and Ethnic Politics* (Syracuse, N.Y.: Syracuse University Press, 1986); Saskia Gieling, "The Marja'iya in Iran and the Nomination of Khamanei in December 1994," *Middle Eastern Studies* 44, no. 4 (December 1988): 777–87.

26. Bergen, *Holy War, Inc.*

27. Boukra, *Algerie la terreur sacree.*

28. Ahmad Rashid, *Taliban: Militant Islam, Oil and Fundamentalism in Central Asia* (New Haven, Conn.: Yale University Press, 2001).

29. Bergen, *Holy War, Inc.*

30. Rashid, *Taliban.*

31. Monte Palmer, Ali Leila, and El Sayed Yassin, *The Egyptian Bureaucracy* (Syracuse, N.Y.: Syracuse University Press, 1988).

32. Boukra, *Algerie la terreur sacree.*

33. Lawrence Wright, "The Man behind bin Laden," *New Yorker* 78, no. 27 (September 16, 2002): 1–46 (Infotrac February 7, 2004).

34. Craig Whitlock, "Keeping Al-Qaeda in His Grip," *Washington Post*, April 16, 2006, at www.washingtonpost.com/wp-dyn/content/article/2006/04/15 (accessed April 16, 2006).

35. Boukra, *Algerie la terreur sacree.*

36. Al Zaiyat, "Sharia and Life Series."

37. For conflict between sheiks who signed the truce and the exiles, see Jailan Halawi, "Rethinking Militancy," *Al Ahram Weekly*, 653, August 28, 2003, at http://weekly.ahram.org.eg/print/2003/653/eg6.htm (accessed August 30, 2003). For younger groups, see the emergence of a new Islamic Group branch reported in the *Middle East Times*, 35, August 30, 2003, at www.metimes.com/2k3/issue2003-35/eg/government_clamps_down.htm (accessed August 30, 2003).

38. Sherifa Zuhur, *A Hundred Osamas: Islamist Threats and the Future of Countersurgency* (Washington, D.C.: Strategic Studies Institute, 2005); Haiyan Naiyouf, "Experts Reveal to Arabiya.net Information on the Leaders of the al-Qaida in Lebanon," *Al Arabiya*, September 13, 2006, at www.alarabiya.net/Articles/2006/09/12/27406.htm (accessed September 13, 2006).

39. Michael Scheuer, "Al-Qaeda's Long March to War," *Asia Times*, May 31, 2006, at www.atimes.com/atimes/Middle_East/HE31Ak02.html (accessed May 31, 2006).

40. Qaradawi, "Violence and the Islamic Groups."

41. Farhad Khosrokhavar, *Quand Al-Qaida parle: Temoignages derriere les bar-reaux* (Paris: Bernard Grasset, 2006).

42. Boukra, *Algerie la terreur sacree*.

43. Stegeno Allievi, "Converts and the Making of European Islam," *The Netherlands ISIM Newsletter*, no. 11 (December 2002): 25–26.

44. For more on this topic, see *Al Arabiya*, August 31, 2006, at www.alarabiya.net/ (accessed August 31, 2006).

45. Alexis Debat, "Al Qaeda's Web of Terror," *ABC News*, March 10, 2006.

46. Hasan Awad, "Jihad Names for Armed Groups" [in Arabic], *Al-Wasat*, no. 622 (December 29, 2003): 10–11.

47. Sebastian Usher, " 'Jihad' Magazine for Women on Web," *BBC News Online*, August 25, 2004, at http://news.bbc.co.uk/2/hi/middle_east/3594982.stm (accessed August 25, 2004).

48. Omar Nasiri, *My Life with Al Qaeda: A Spy's Story* (London: C. Hurst & Co., 2006).

49. Nick Fielding, "Encyclopedia of Terror: Revealed: The Bloody Pages of the Al-Qaeda's Killing Manual," *Sunday Times* (London), November 4, 2001, at www.sunday-times.co.uk/news/pages/sti/2001/11/04/stiusausa02023.html (accessed November 4, 2001).

50. "Bulgaria Closes Markov Investigation," *BBC News Online*, September 20, 2000, at http://news.bbc.co.uk/2/hi/world/934326.stm (accessed May 8, 2004).

51. Alan Feuer and Benjamin Weiser, "Translation: The How to Book of Terrorism," *New York Times*, April 5, 2001, at www.library.cornell.edu.colldev/mideast/trmanx.htm (accessed February 12, 2002).

52. Oriana Zill, *Frontline*, PBS, February 19, 2007, at www.pbs.org/wgbh/pages/frontline/shows/network/alqaeda (accessed February 19, 2007).

53. John Pike, interviewed by ABC News, December 21, 2001, at www.abc news.com/ (accessed December 21, 2001).

54. *Egyptian Gazette*, March 24, 1982, cited in Palmer, Leila, and Yassin, *The Egyptian Bureaucracy*, 34.

55. Azam Al-Tamimi, "Failures of the Islamic Movement" [in Arabic], interviewed by Mahir Abdullah, *Al Jazeera*, November 11, 2001.

56. Mohammed Al Shafey, "The Story of Abu Walid al Masri: The Ideologue of the Afghan Arabs," *Asharq al-Awsat*, February 11, 2007.

57. "Dead Man Walking," *Guardian*, August 5, 2001, at www.guardian.co.uk/ (accessed August 5, 2001).

58. Boukra, *Algerie la terreur sacree*.

59. Jonathan Steele, "Stand and Fight, Fleeing Taliban Told," *Guardian*, November 14, 2001, at www.guardian.co.uk/waronterror/story/0,,593106,00.html (accessed November 14, 2001).

60. Boukra, *Algerie la terreur sacree*.

11

The Allies of the Jihadists

Those Who Make Terror Possible

A MERICA'S WAR ON TERROR is not merely a war against the jihadists. If only it were. It is also a war against those individuals, groups, organizations, and governments that support and finance jihadist operations. It is the allies of the jihadists who facilitate virtually every dimension of the jihadist war effort. This would certainly include recruitment, indoctrination (schools), training, logistics, communications, intelligence, shelter, protection (military), money laundering, documentation, and *wasta*, the Arabic word for connections. Little, if anything, gets done in the Islamic world without connections.

Without their allies, the jihadists would be no more effective than America's homegrown terrorists such as the neo-Nazis, leftist Weathermen, or violent religious cults such as the Branch Davidians. All remained isolated because they lacked a base of support sufficient to carry out their demented plans. The jihadists, however, do have allies. That's the rub. They have powerful allies who wittingly or unwittingly enabled them to challenge the most powerful nation that the world has ever known. The allies of the jihadists are seldom combatants, but it is they who make terror possible.

The allies of the jihadists can be categorized into three groups: the holy allies, the unholy allies, and the governmental allies. The holy allies include the legitimate Islamic institutions that have been infiltrated by religious extremists. Perhaps they also include the Muslim Brotherhood, Hizbullah, and other less radical Islamic groups that maintain a complex love-hate relationship with the jihadists. The unholy allies of the jihadists, in turn, consist of a broad array of non-Islamic groups ranging from secular terrorist groups to drug lords and weapons dealers. The governmental allies of the jihadists are the governments of the world that support terrorist operations. Some of that support is overt, some covert, some misguided, some inadvertent, and some simply the result of weakness.

In the present chapter, we take a closer look at the allies of the jihadists, their motivations, and the services they perform. We begin by examining the struggle to control the institutions of Islam and then move to an examination of the unholy allies of the jihadists. Finally, we turn to the governmental supporters of terror. They are the most dangerous of the jihadists' allies.

Holy Allies: The Struggle for Control of Islam

The clergy of Islam, much like the clergy of Christianity and Judaism, exhort the faithful to prayer and good works, inspire them to walk in the path of righteousness, and offer guidance in their personal affairs. It is also the clergy who alert the faithful to the dangers confronting their religion and who vilify its enemies. When danger lurks, it is they who suggest appropriate action and decide if and when terror is acceptable within Islamic law. How they decide these issues is critical to America's war on terror.

The clergy in Islam are collectively referred to as the *ulema*, or religious scholars. They are also referred to in the Arabic press as men of religion. Many are graduates of illustrious schools of religious education such as Cairo's Al-Azhar University, a venerable institution that traces its history to the tenth century. Others emerge as lay preachers, guided largely by their faith in God. They lead by zeal and inspiration rather than by the depth of their religious knowledge. The graduates of Al-Azhar preside over the elegant mosques that grace the skylines of Islamic cities, their minarets pointing heavenward in praise of God. The clergy of these glorious structures are government employees, and their sermons are closely watched by government censors. The popular men of religion often preach in mosques no larger than a garage or storefront converted to a place of worship. Quantity and zeal compensate for size and elegance. They are everywhere. Islam has also developed its own Billy Grahams, with Islamic tele-preachers becoming the stars of the region's many satellite networks. By and large, tele-preachers adopt the same tenor as the Muslim Brotherhood and other radical reformers. Zeal sells, but the censor is watching.

Fortunately for America's war on terror, the clergy of Islam are not of one mind on the most pressing issues of the day. Sunni clergy differ from their Shi'a counterparts over the most fundamental points of doctrine. Both, in turn, are divided into progovernment and antigovernment camps, with each camp being further divided between conservatives, moderates, and liberals, and they, by interminable personality conflicts and power struggles. Debates over the role of terror as a legitimate weapon in the defense of Islam are particularly bitter. Regardless of their conflicts, most preach that America has declared war on Islam.[1]

How does this play out for America's war on terror or "long war" as it is now called? The senior religious leaders of the Islamic world were virtually unanimous in their condemnation of the September 11 terrorist attacks on the United States. They have been almost as unanimous in the condemnation of the U.S. invasion of Iraq and in their support of the Palestinian cause. This said, the Islamic clergy have been sharply divided over the legality of Palestinian suicide attacks against Israeli civilians. The *mufti* (chief religious judge) of Mecca declared that attacks on innocent civilians are prohibited by Islamic law, a view echoed by the grand mufti of Saudi Arabia. Other Saudi clerics, however, were less certain on the issue.[2] The grand sheikh of the Al-Azhar Mosque in Cairo, the senior religious authority in Egypt, sharply condemned the suicide attacks against Israeli citizens, stating that Islam forbade "aggression against innocent civilians of any place, faith or nation."[3] He later changed his view to say that suicide attacks against Israelis that do not specifically target civilians are allowable in Islam. In the latter case, they are merely the victims of war.

The charge against this point of view was led by Qatar's Sheikh Yusuf al-Qaradawi, a leading television figure on Arab cable networks. In al-Qaradawi's view, Israel is a military society without civilians. There are no innocents in Israel. Similar views have been expressed by Lebanon's Mohammed Hussein Fadlallah, one of the most revered figures in Shi'a Islam and founder of Lebanon's Hizbullah.[4] The same logic was used by Osama bin Laden to justify the September 11 terrorist attacks on the United States.

The role of the Islamic clergy in the war on terror far exceeds the battle for the hearts and minds of the Muslim world. Clergy sympathetic to the jihadists actively recruit members for jihadist organizations. They also raise funds for jihadist activities, serve as a nexus for communications, disseminate jihadist propaganda, and possibly even establish jihadist training centers. The prime example of the role played by jihadist clergy is provided by Abu Hamza al-Misri, the now deposed leader of the Finsbury Park Mosque in London. The police maintained that the mosque had become a center for recruiting jihadists. Al-Misri had no formal religious training, but his sermons attracted a wide audience. Al-Misri's operations have been closed down, but others, less visible, have picked up the slack.

Projihadist clergy in the Islamic world are not protected by democratic freedoms, but their numbers and obscurity make them difficult to track. Most are found among the ranks of the popular "storefront" preachers who operate in relative freedom from governmental control. As the Egyptian security forces lament, "We don't have enough certified preachers to go around."[5]

The role of the establishment clergy, by contrast, is to counteract the influence of the jihadists among the masses, a thankless task at best. Most are too closely associated with corrupt regimes to be taken very seriously.[6] The clergy associated with the Muslim Brotherhood and other radical reform groups are a potential obstacle to the jihadists inasmuch as they offer political reform and religious salvation in a more moderate package. There is still plenty of fire and brimstone to go around, probably too much for most Americans. It would also be naive to believe that the jihadists are without supporters in the ranks of the government preachers. The same is true of the Muslim Brotherhood and other radical-moderate groups, all of which possess an extremist wing.

The clergy guide the faithful through the millions of the mosques that grace the Islamic world. Cairo alone has more than fifty thousand mosques, about thirty-two thousand of which are government mosques.[7] The remainder are popular mosques, many of which are controlled by either the Muslim Brotherhood or the jihadists. The message presented depends largely on the views of the clergy. Passivist and establishment clergy stress prayer and submission to the greater reason of God; jihadist clergy sound the call to battle. Clergy associated with the Muslim Brotherhood and other radical reformers stake out a fiery middle ground, urging vigilance against Islam's enemies and nonviolence in their pursuit of an Islamic state.

Islamic Education: Schools for Terror?

The mosque has long been the center for both religion and science, there being little distinction between the two. Religion was the foundation of all knowledge, scientific and otherwise. Members of the Islamic clergy were referred to as scholars or *ulema* in deference to their education. Much the same was true in the churches and monasteries of medieval Europe, although Muslim scholars made spectacular advances in mathematics and science far in advance of their European counterparts.

The principle remains the same today, although education in the mosque is largely restricted to the study of the Arabic language and religious texts. In the minds of the Arabs, their language is the language of God. Governments, not the clergy, are responsible for public education. Even here, however, the line between church and state is blurred. Cairo's Al-Azhar Mosque has expanded into a vast network of parochial schools, primary through PhDs, with branches throughout Egypt. All are part of Egypt's system of public education, with Al-Azhar itself boasting the same faculties as any other university, including a large medical school. Students in the Al-Azhar network receive a larger dose of religious training than students in other Egyptian schools but not without close supervision from the government.

Saudi Arabian students receive a far larger dose of religious instruction. Indeed, approximately one-third of the curriculum of elementary schools is devoted to Islamic topics. This ratio is more or less reflected throughout the Saudi education system, with approximately one-third of Saudi university students majoring in Islamic Studies.[8] Unlike Egypt, Saudi Arabia has an oversupply of certified religious scholars, many finding jobs with the religious police or filling the ranks of the unemployed.[9]

Pakistan, long an ally of the United States, possesses ten to thirteen thousand plus religious schools or *madrasas*, up from less than 150 just a few years ago, although these numbers vary dramatically from source to source.[10] Many are funded by Saudi religious charities intent on expanding the reach of the ultraconservative Wahhabi doctrine of Islam. Shi'a schools, a minority, receive indirect funding from Iran. The sharp rise in Islamic schools has been paralleled by an equally sharp rise in violent confrontations between Pakistan's Sunnis and its Shi'a minority.[11]

The role of religious schools in stimulating violence has been widely debated in the Middle East, with a recent debate on the *Al Jazeera* television network examining the topic in detail.[12] The debate covered all sides of the issue with the participants agreeing that all religions, Christianity and Judaism as well as Islam, teach the superiority of their faith and view nonadherents with a degree of suspicion. Until very recently, they recalled, Jews were condemned by the Vatican as the killers of Christ. It was also generally agreed that most holy works, including those of Islam, contained passages that could be interpreted as justifying violence.

The problem, according to the debaters, was not Islam but rather a perverted interpretation of Islam practiced by a minority of misguided zealots. There was little agreement on how widespread or severe the misguided teaching of Islamic principles had become, but there was recognition that the problem existed.[13]

Sheikh al-Qaradawi joined the fray by blaming both so-called government sheikhs and the young jihadist sheikhs for the perversion of Islamic doctrine. He referred to the *fatwas* of the jihadist sheikhs as "twisted jurisprudence" and suggested that they still had "soft bones," the Arab equivalent of being wet behind the ears.[14]

In any case, the United States is placing intense pressure on Egypt, Pakistan, Saudi Arabia, and other countries of the Islamic world to purge their educational curriculum of materials supportive of terrorism and anti-

America attitudes. This is probably a mistake. Tampering with Islamic education deepens the impression that America has declared war on Islam. It is also an extremely sensitive issue that smacks of both crusades and colonialism.

Merely forcing a politically correct curriculum on the countries of the Islamic world, moreover, will not solve the problem. Teachers supportive of the jihadists will preach terror and anti-Americanism regardless of the contents of the government curriculum. The Egyptian government has struggled to purge its education system of teachers sympathetic to the jihadists, but it is not clear that it is succeeding. As long as jihadists maintain a base of popular support, their message will find expression in the educational institutions of the Islamic world. Most of the hard-core indoctrination in the Islamic world, moreover, takes place in jihadists' schools that operate on the fringes of public education systems. Supervision is minimal. Pakistan's ten to thirteen thousand religious schools are matched by an equal number in Bangladesh, and secret intelligence reports put the number of Islamic *madrasas* in India at thirty thousand.[15] In Saudi Arabia, the entire education system is controlled by Wahhabi clerics and harshly criticized by the United States for stimulating violence, anti-Americanism, and hostility toward the Shi'a.[16] These charges prompted a Saudi survey of text materials with the Saudi foreign minister concluding that "5 percent of the material was considered 'horrible' and 10 percent questionable, while 85 percent called for understanding with other religious faiths."[17]

One must also question whether the act of attending an Islamic school dooms one to becoming a terrorist. Members of all faiths have received religious educations, only to emerge as agnostics or atheists. Some individuals, particularly those with strong authoritarian tendencies, will undoubtedly be swayed toward violence by religious indoctrination. Others will either become better Muslims or be pushed away from religion altogether. In a curious twist of irony, some Egyptian jihadists blame many of their mistakes on an inadequate understanding of Islam.[18] Most, it seems were the product of secular education systems.

Finally, one must question the ability of the United States to force a politically correct curriculum on the countries of the Islamic world. Few countries of the Islamic world are willing to risk pushing moderate Muslims into the hands of the jihadists by meddling with Islamic teachings based on the Koran and Sunna. The issue is simply too inflammatory in the wake of a growing wave of Islamic electoral victories. This is all the more the case when the educational reforms are being forced on them by the United States, a country increasingly viewed as the great Satan. The political leaders of the Islamic world are experts at survival and will not commit political suicide by capitulating to American pressure on an issue of this sensitivity. There will be lots of smoke and mirrors designed to please the United States, but there will be minimal hard action.[19] Even under the best of circumstances, altering Islamic education would be an arduous struggle that would take generations. Hopefully, the war on terror will be over by then.

The Money Trail of the Jihadists' Allies: Islamic Charities, Islamic Banks, and Islamic Businesses

Pre-Islamic Arabia, the era of ignorance in Muslim parlance, had degenerated into a society not far removed from Hobbes's state of nature: "All men," or so it seemed, "maketh war upon all men." Islam brought humanity a message of peace. It also sought to limit human turmoil by reducing its causes, not the least of which were social inequality and money gouging. Social inequality was to be addressed by obliging Muslims to give generously to the poor, and money gouging was dealt with by forbidding interest on loans.

Lest there be any doubt on the matter, the Koran imposes a 2.5 percent income tax, *zakat*, on all believers. Muslims are also required to pay an additional *zakat* to mark the ending of Ramadan, the holy month of fasting. *Zakat* is one of the five cardinal principles of the Islamic faith, and those who dodge this most holy of obligations must face the wrath of their maker.

Judging from the sums collected, few Muslims are willing to take this risk. The annual *zakat* in Egypt, one of the world's poorest countries, is estimated by Egypt's mufti to have reached five hundred million dollars on an annual basis, with an additional one hundred million dollars or so being donated to mark the end of Ramadan. In Indonesia, another poor country, donations marking the end of Ramadan were expected to reach a billion dollars.[20] "Just think what the *zakat* of 1.3 billion Muslims worldwide could do," said the Egyptian mufti.[21] Many mosques and clergy also receive informal donations from the pious, the sums of which can be quite generous. It is particularly common for Shi'a Muslims to contribute as much as one-fifth, or *kums*, of their wealth to senior religious scholars.

In earlier times, *zakat* was simply given to the needy on an impromptu basis or deposited in the *zakat* box at the local mosque. Most mosques have a *zakat* committee that determines how the charity funds will be allocated. Increasingly, however, charitable contributions are channeled through organized charities that minister to the Muslim poor. The Red Crescent Society is the Muslim counterpart of the Red Cross, the two organizations often cooperating to alleviate human suffering. Some of the larger charitable organizations such as the Society for the Cooperation of the Devotees of the Koran and Sunna have millions of members.[22] They also possess branches throughout the world and play a key role in channeling aid from the rich countries of the Persian Gulf to Islam's poor. It is hard to say how many Islamic benevolent associations exist, many being small and localized. The Saudis estimate that there are thousands of such charities in the Middle East, many operating with minimal supervision.[23] Online giving has also made its appearance, a process that will make it easier for the devout to give to the charity of their choice.

It is the Islamic benevolent associations and the Islamic banks in which they deposit their funds that have become the focal point of America's war on terror. According to *Islam Online*, an Islamic website reflective of the Muslim Brotherhood, the *zakat* can be spent on anything that serves the cause of God.[24] This includes charity for the poor, salaries of clergy and instructors in Islamic schools, and the maintenance of mosques, Islamic schools, hospitals, and shrines. *Zakat* can also be used for jihads to protect the faith and defend oppressed Muslims. This point was elaborated by Sheikh al-Qaradawi:

> If war is waged anywhere to achieve this goal, namely to free the occupied lands of the laws and the tyranny of disbelievers, it is undoubtedly a case of jihad for the sake of Allah. It thus needs to be financed from the money of *Zakat* the amount of which is to be decided based on the total sum of the charity, the requirements of jihad as well as the degree of the need of other potential recipients of charity. This is all to be decided by reliable scholars, if they are to be found.[25]

The grand mufti of Egypt, a key member of Egypt's government-appointed religious elite, openly urged Egyptian Muslims to send their *zakat* to aid Muslims in Chechnya. His reasoning follows: "Ramadan is supposed to be a blessed month, one of mercy and victory, but the enemies of Islam have turned it into the month of defeats and regression. At the beginning of last Ramadan, Iraq was bombed. In the beginning of this Ramadan, Chechnya was bombed. The Muslim nation must move before its borders totally deteriorate."[26]

These and a spate of *fatwas* from moderate Islamic leaders were issued well before the September 11 terrorist attacks on the United States and undoubtedly helped legitimize financial contributions to bin Laden's al Qaeda network. The fact that few have been repudiated remains a source of grave concern to the American government. How is financial support to the jihadists to be dried up when the most moderate of religious leaders openly urge support for jihadist activities? The Israelis have far greater cause for concern, for Palestine is the most symbolic of all Islamic jihads.

As always, much depends on who's in charge of collecting and administering charitable funds. If people sympathetic to the jihadists are in key positions, at least some funds are likely to find their way into jihadist hands. Do the jihadists attempt to infiltrate Islamic charities? Of course! It is a major source of their funding. A few charities exist specifically for channeling funds to the jihadists. British investigators, for example, suspect that the North London Central Mosque Trust falls into this category, but they have no proof.[27] The United States has put at least nine Islamic charities on its list of organizations that fund terrorism, including American branches of the Benevolence International Foundation.[28] The obvious offenders have been closed only to be replaced by less visible counterparts.

Even more reputable charities have discovered that certain branches have fallen under the control of the jihadists. As a recent Saudi Arabian report on jihadist terrorism noted,

> In March 2002, the U.S. Treasury Department and Saudi Arabia blocked the accounts of the Somalia and Bosnia branches of the Saudi Arabia-based Al-Haramain Islamic Foundation. While the Saudi headquarters for this private charitable entity is dedicated to helping those in need, the U.S. and Saudi Arabia determined that the Somalia and Bosnia branches supported terrorist activities and terrorist organizations such as Al Qaeda, AIAI (al-Itihaad al-Islamiya), Islamic Union, and others.[29]

Despite Saudi Arabian protestations of cooperation, the United States remains skeptical. The charities of Saudi Arabia and the Gulf are far wealthier than those of the West and appear to enjoy protection from within their respective governments. The United States accuses; the charities deny.[30]

A few Islamic charities are blatant in their support of the jihadists, but most are far more subtle. Grants are not made to jihadist groups per se but rather to legal front organizations maintained by supporters of the jihadists or to mosques that espouse the jihadist cause. The United States, for example has accused the Pakistani branch of Kuwait's Revival of Islamic Heritage Society of being a front organization for al Qaeda. The charity denies the accusations, presenting the Kuwaiti government with the names of some 2,870 orphans of the Afghan wars being supported by the charity.[31]

Many charitable organizations are also "networked" with "clean" organizations making grants to less scrupulous counterparts and those to more opaque charities directly linked to the jihadists. The money trail goes up in smoke, and neither the original charity nor its donors are aware of how their monies are being used. At the very least, they cannot be implicated. As the Saudi Arabian spokesman lamented when the wife of the Saudi ambassador to the United States was accused of funding terrorist organizations, "In the past, we may have been naïve in our giving and did not have adequate con-

trols over all of our donations. As a consequence, some may have taken
advantage of our charity and generosity. . . . This is now changing."[32]

Many charities, moreover, are the blameless victims of jihadist sympathizers who skim funds from legitimate projects and shift them to the jihadists
through one mechanism or another. Accounting mechanisms in the Middle
Eastern financial institutions are known for their flexibility, and a little skim-
ming is not unusual under the best of circumstances.

It is probable that Islamic charities help the jihadist cause in other ways as
well. The larger charities are international in scope and might well provide
vital communication links between jihadist groups. Whether they help in
logistics and the shifting of key personnel is difficult to ascertain. Their easy
access to areas of conflict enables them to do so. The prodigious sums of
money that flow through the hands of the Islamic charities also raises suspicion of money laundering. As the U.S. Drug Enforcement Agency (DEA) has
learned to its dismay, mingling good money with bad is not that difficult.
The point is not to attack the charities themselves but rather jihadist allies
within those organizations.

The picture becomes even more complex when one adds legitimate businesses to the fray. The business empire of Joseph Nada, foreign minister of
the Muslim Brotherhood empire, included a multitude of businesses that literally spanned the globe and earned him the title of "cement king" of the
Mediterranean.[33] Bin Laden's business empire included a daily newspaper,
the al-Shamal Islamic Bank in Khartoum, and the Tenar al-Mubaraka and
Wadi al-Aqiq companies that traded extensively in machinery and agricul-
tural produce—corn, sugar, sesame seeds, and fruit. To these were added various construction companies and a reported interest in Afghanistan's opium
trade. Proceeds from these and other businesses found their way into
accounts in Barclay's Bank in London, Girocredit in Vienna, and various
other banks in Hong Kong, Kuala Lumpur, and Dubai.[34] It was these legitimate businesses, in combination with friendly charities and cooperating
banks, Islamic and otherwise, that constituted a financial network that
spanned some twenty-five countries. This network has now been damaged,
but it still exists.

Beyond helping fund the jihadists, legitimate businesses provide jobs for
the jihadists, launder money, ship it around the globe, and provide cover for
operatives moving from country to country. Bin Laden's organization even
had its own travel agency. Legitimate businesses also fuel jihadist supply
lines, purchasing and storing materials until needed and then shipping them
on demand. Some businesses are more legitimate than others, the less savory
of which deal in drugs, arms, and stolen property. If a business is closed
down, it simply reopens under a new name.

Islamic banks, as the name suggests, honor the letter of the Islamic law by avoiding interest on loans and deposits. Depositors are rewarded by profit sharing and other techniques allowed by Islamic law. According to some estimates, Islamic banks have attracted approximately one-half of the individual savings of the Islamic world, and most global banks are now establishing Islamic affiliates.[35] Islamic investment companies have experienced similar growth, albeit on a smaller scale.[36]

It is the Islamic banks, according to the U.S. security agencies, that gather charity funds from individuals and organizations and distribute them through surreptitious channels to various jihadist groups. The Islamic banks are also accused of providing the jihadists and their allies with a full range of financial services, including the laundering of illegal money.

Joseph Nada, mentioned above, was once the world's leading Islamic banker. He staunchly denies that such transfers take place. His banks have been closed, but no charges have been brought against him. Depositors have reputedly lost large sums of money, a fact that probably adds to their resentment toward the United States.[37] Once again, there is no smoking gun. Even the non-Islamic banks of the region have a reputation for looseness, with the United States accusing some banks in the United Arab Emirates (UAE) of being the paymaster for bin Laden. Lebanon has also drawn its share of U.S. criticism, as has Israel. Ironically, many of the funds supporting terrorist groups in Israel are channeled through Israeli banks, raising a hue and cry for the reform of one of the world's looser banking systems.[38] In any case, loose financial institutions ranging from banks to money changers are a major component of money-laundering operations estimated to range from eight hundred billion dollars to as much as two trillion dollars on an annual basis.[39]

The latest twist in Islamic banking has been the introduction of the Islamic dinar. Guaranteed by the Dubai Islamic Bank and the Thomas Cook–Al Rostameni Exchange Company, more than one hundred thousand golden Islamic dinars were in circulation by 2002, with some four tons of gold being traded in e-dinars, the electronic equivalent of the gold dinar coins. While the Islamic dinar is unlikely to replace the U.S. dollar as the international currency of choice, another layer of complexity has been added to the money trail.[40] The linkup between the Dubai Islamic Bank and Thomas Cook, the venerable British travel and financial services company, illustrates just how effective the Islamic banks have become in penetrating the world's banking system.

In addition to exploiting Islamic banks and the looser elements of the world banking system, the jihadists have also honed the traditional *hawala* or *hundi* systems for transferring for laundering money.[41] The process is not complex and is often based on verbal commitments among trusted relatives. Your cousin, for example, might deposit ten thousand dollars in a business account of one of my friends in Pakistan. He later transfers it to one of my business accounts in the United States, and in turn, I write a check for ten thousand dollars to a bogus jihadist firm in Chicago. The transfer is virtually untraceable because no records are kept and the names of the bogus businesses keep changing.

The U.S. accusation that some charity funds find their way into the hands of jihadists is incontestable. Precisely how much money finds its way into the hands of the jihadists is difficult to estimate. No one knows, but even a small percentage of the billions given to charity each year is a substantial amount. Wealthy Gulf "angels" also funnel money to the jihadists through Islamic banks. Recent estimates by a consulting firm called Safron Advisors suggest that wealthy individuals in the Gulf region alone possess some 1.4 trillion dollars, much of which is dispersed around the globe.[42] With this amount of money, even a few "angels" can go a long way.

What is there to do? Once again, the United States is in a quandary. Because charitable giving is so central to the Islamic faith, attacks on charitable organizations reinforce the impression that the United States has declared war on Islam. Why else, Muslims ask, would the United States deprive the Muslim poor of much-needed aid?

It is also a profoundly difficult task to track the money.[43] No international enforcement agencies exist, and cooperation with the countries of the region has produced more smoke than fire. Some simply lack the capacity to keep their banks and charitable organizations in check. Others have blood on their hands or fear the uproar that would follow. Most also resent American intrusion into their internal affairs, perhaps fearing that the revelations might prove embarrassing to members of the ruling elite. Most multinational corporations, moreover, are wary of regulations that constrain their own financial operations, banking or otherwise. Ironically, the United States leads the world in money laundering, followed in order by Italy, Russia, China, and Germany.[44]

Finally, there is the question of religious freedom. How does one impose draconian restrictions on Islamic charities but not on Christian and Jewish charities? One way or the other, the political and social costs of closing down Islamic charities is profound and will inevitably hamper efforts to shut down the jihadist financial network.

Unholy Allies: Drug Lords, Mafioso, and Other Kindred Souls

Wars and revolution produce an insatiable need for weapons and war material, and the jihadist war against America is no exception. Charitable contributions and legitimate business activities help foot the bill, but they are only part of the money trail. Huge sums of money, no one knows how much for sure, result from the cultivation of opium and other drugs. In 2000, Afghanistan, then the stronghold of bin Laden's al Qaeda network, supplied about 70 percent of the world's opium. Subsequent U.S. efforts to squelch the Afghan opium trade have gone for naught as the most war-torn countries continue to new records in opium production.[45] Even more disconcerting has been the reassertion of Taliban and al Qaeda influence in the region. The *Wall Street Journal* reported that bin Laden's cut was 15 percent.[46] Lebanon, the base of the dominant Hizbullah network, has long been known as a major drug producer. Lebanese discuss the presence of drug cultivation in the Bekaa Valley as a matter of course. Many of the larger drug producers are reputed to be members of the Lebanese parliament or to be other major politicians. Just as drugs fueled the rebellion in Afghanistan, so did they fuel the fifteen-year civil war in Lebanon. The Lebanese government has made a number of highly publicized raids on drug producers, but most Lebanese remain skeptical.

Without users, of course, drugs would be worthless. The DEA estimates that Americans are spending some sixty-four billion dollars on illegal drugs annually. With figures this large, it is not clear what the DEA is enforcing.

The jihadists also acquire funds from the sale of illicit gems purchased from Sierra Leone, Angola, Liberia, the Democratic Republic of the Congo, and other gem-producing areas of Africa, most of which are threatened by civil war. The African rebels, too, are in urgent need of weapons, and raw gems mined outside of the De Beers cartel is what they have to sell. In the cases of Liberia and Burkina Faso, it was reportedly the presidents of the countries themselves who protected the terrorist agents. The former president of Liberia, Charles Taylor, reportedly received a one-million-dollar bribe for his services.[47] Once acquired, the gems are processed by allied businesses in Antwerp and other processing centers. Some ten million dollars' worth of gems were processed in the run-up to September 11, 2001, according to sources in Antwerp.[48] Given estimates that the September 11 terrorist attacks cost bin Laden's al Qaeda network something in the range of five hundred thousand dollars, a few million dollars can go a long way.[49]

Gems also provide the jihadists with a safe haven for their funds. Bank accounts can be frozen, but gems simply increase in value. They also are immune from airport metal detectors, are easily shipped from place to place without detection, are readily convertible to cash, and provide a ready-made avenue for laundering drug money. How does one trace the trail of gems sold for cash?

Gold has also become a favorite of the jihadists, finding easy outlets in discount centers and providing a hedge against banking sleuths and frozen accounts. In retrospect, it now appears that bin Laden converted many of his financial assets into gold in the days before the September 11 terrorist attacks on the United States.

Inevitably, these activities bring the jihadists in league with drug lords and other criminal networks. In the elegant phrasing of Asa Hutchinson, director of the DEA, "Drug traffickers and terrorists work out of the same jungle, they plan in the same cave, and they train in the same desert."[50]

The Russian Mafia appears to top the list of jihadist allies in the criminal world. Among other things, they process the jihadists' raw opium, distribute it in Europe and the United States, and provide them with weapons of all varieties. Foreign intelligence sources suggest the list also includes the sale of a small nuclear device stolen from the arsenal of the former Soviet Union, but details remain sketchy. What is not sketchy is the fact that the collapse of the Soviet Union opened a vast black market in weapons and weapons technology of all varieties.[51]

In addition to facilitating the flow of money and weapons, the unholy allies of the jihadists often provide them with logistics, shelter, training, intelligence, and most other services required for covert operations. This is all the more possible because the Mafia and drug rings are international in scope and operate with relative impunity in their home territories. They are also adept at building networks in the West and in avoiding detection. Could they assist in smuggling operatives and weapons into the United States? As senior officials in the U.S. Department of State note,

Relationships between drug traffickers and terrorists benefit both. Drug traffickers benefit from the terrorists' military skills, weapons supply, and access to clandestine organizations. Terrorists gain a source of revenue and expertise in illicit transfer and laundering of proceeds from illicit transactions. Both groups bribe corrupt officials whose services provide mutual benefits, such as greater access to fraudulent documents, including passports and customs papers. Drug traffickers may also gain considerable freedom of movement when they operate in conjunction with terrorists who control large amounts of territory.[52]

Not only is the link between the jihadist and organized crime frightening, but if America's uphill war against drugs is any indicator, it will be impossible to stop. Billions of dollars are involved, and the complexity of the linkages between the terrorists and the criminals defy the imagination. In one recent case, for example, an Israeli arms dealer in Panama sent an e-mail message to a Russian arms dealer in Guatemala saying his customers needed everything from assault rifles to rockets and rocket launchers. The weapons, presumably paid for with drug money, were to be supplied to the Nicaraguan army. The target country was Liberia, with officials speculating that their final destination "was somewhere else."[53]

Governments as Allies of Terror

Of all of the allies of the jihadists, none are more vital to their cause than the governments of the world that directly or indirectly support terrorism. It is governments of the world that fund, shelter, train, arm, and encourage the terrorist at every turn, even to the point of assisting with the recruitment of jihadist cadres. It is also the governments of the world that allow the allies of the jihadists to operate with relative impunity, be they firebrand preachers, friendly charities, corrupt banks and businesses, criminal organizations, or other symbiotic terrorist organizations. Not all governments do everything, but most, including the United States and Britain, do their part. Few things in the war on terror are certain, but one thing is: the war on terror will not be won unless state support for the jihadists is sharply curtailed. We would like to say eliminated, but that is probably an impossibility.

Which countries support terrorism? The answer is devastatingly simple. Virtually all of the countries in the world have supported terrorism in one form or another, not the least of which is the United States. The United States made little secret of its support for the jihadists in the struggle to liberate Afghanistan from Soviet rule. The United States had always looked to Islam as a bulwark against the spread of communism, and Afghanistan was no different. Both feared the Soviets. U.S. support for the jihadists in Afghanistan also differed little from earlier American support for the Contras in Nicaragua's long and bloody civil war and a host of similar "interventions" in the affairs of Latin America. All were part of American's war against communism. The trouble with Afghanistan was that things went terribly wrong. With the Islamic world free of the communist threat, the jihadists turned against their former ally and launched a new jihad to rid the Islamic world of American domination.

The United States also recruited, trained, and armed opposition (terrorist) groups in Iraq in the hope of overthrowing Saddam Hussein and establishing a moderate Iraqi government compliant with the wishes of the United States. The term democracy was bantered about, but few people familiar with the history of Iraq or the ninety some opposition groups quarreling over Saddam's carcass had little hope in the matter. No sooner had Saddam Hussein been put to flight than the United States began arming the Mujahedeen Kalq, the MKO, an anti-Iranian terrorist group sheltered by Saddam Hussein, as a weapon against Iran.

The story of the MKO well illustrates the murky relationships between the West and terrorist groups in the Middle East. The MKO emerged in 1965 as one of a spate of leftist groups opposed to the Shah's rule. A brief flirtation with Ayatollah Khomeini's government ended in 1981 when Khomeini, then firmly in power, turned on the leftist groups that had supported the revolution. Key leaders of the MKO, including Massoud Rajavi, fled to Paris where the organization reconstituted itself as a terrorist group dedicated to overthrowing the Islamic regime in Iran. France, however, was more interested in developing economic ties with Iran than fighting the mullahs, and in 1986, Saddam Hussein became Rajavi's new patron. Iraq was still in the throes of its bloody war with Iran, and Saddam Hussein needed all the help he could get. The MKO, some five to ten thousand strong, fought the Iranians and, following Iraq's defeat in the first Gulf war (1991), helped Saddam Hussein crush uprisings by the Kurds and the Shi'a. The MKO also unleashed a bloody war of terror against Iranian targets in Iran and abroad.[54] With Saddam scuttled, Washington again embraced the MKO as a key weapon in its undeclared war against Iran. However, this venture was short lived. The MKO was a powerful weapon against Iran, but its presence on the U.S. list of terrorist organizations proved embarrassing. Washington backed off, but the use of MKO against Iran continues to be debated in administration circles.[55]

As a practical matter, it is not a question of who is using terror but of whose ox is being gored. The United States feels that it is justified in using all means at its disposal, including terrorism, to protect itself and the free world from the jihadists and all other threats to the stability of the world. Heading the list of other threats are pariah states intent on developing weapons of mass destruction. The jihadists feel equally justified in opposing U.S. domination of the region, including Israeli occupation of Palestinian territories. This view has few dissenters in the Muslim world.

Why Governments in the Islamic World Are Allies of Jihadist Terror

Why do many countries in the Islamic world aid and abet anti-American terrorism? Why does Lebanon give Hizbullah free reign? Why does Pakistan's Inter-Services Intelligence (ISI) play a key role in supporting jihadist groups in Kashmir? Why do Saudi Arabia and sheikdoms of the Persian Gulf turn a blind eye to charities that are the taproot of the jihadist money tree? Why does Israel continue to expand settlements in the Occupied Territories when they constitute a major stimulus for Palestinian terror? These are vital questions in America's war on terror, for it is hard to cure a problem without understanding its cause. Unfortunately, there are probably as many reasons for resisting America's war on terror as there are countries in the region. The following reasons are among the most prominent.

1. *Public Opinion.* As a general principle, anti-American sentiment in the Islamic world is so intense that the leaders of the region are reluctant to give their full support to America's war on terror. The Islamic world is not democratic, but its leaders do fear the masses. This became evident in the run-up to the invasion of Iraq, when even staunch allies such as Egypt, Turkey, and Saudi Arabia opposed the U.S.-British strike against Iraq. It was not Saddam Hussein who their leaders were worried about but rather their own thrones.

2. *Religious Pressures.* Supporting America's war on terror also places the leaders of the Islamic world in direct conflict with the Islamic movement in all of its various incarnations. Most Muslims have little difficulty with the United States hunting down the jihadists who committed the September 11 terrorist attacks, but they are deeply offended by U.S. pressure to reform Islamic education and curtail the activities of Islamic charitable organizations. It is truly difficult for the leaders of the Islamic world to give full cooperation to America's war on terror when most of their subjects believe that America has declared war on Islam. Indeed, the leaders of the Sudan, Bangladesh, and Saudi Arabia, among others, openly curry mass popularity by supporting the more moderate elements in the Islamic movement.

3. *Differing National Interests.* Even countries that firmly support America's war on terror often find that American demands conflict with their own national interests. When President Reagan vowed to get the Israelis out of Beirut in 1982, for example, Prime Minister Menachem Begin of Israel responded, "Jews do not kneel but to God."[56] Ariel Sharon and his successors have been equally contentious in their determination to expand Jewish settlements in the Occupied Territories. The struggle between Washington and Tel Aviv over settlements continues and is far from being resolved. Washington believes that the settlements fuel anti-Americanism and serve as a provocation for terror. Many Israelis believe that they are a vital step in building a Greater Israel that encompasses most of the Occupied Territories.

4. *Terror as Foreign Policy.* Beyond having national interests that differ from those of the United States, many countries in the Islamic world find terrorist organizations to be powerful weapons in their foreign policy. Syria, for example, has long supported Hamas and the Palestinian Islamic jihad in the hope of forcing Israel to make peace with Syria on

equitable terms. The deal is a simple one: withdraw from what remains of occupied Syrian territory, and we will withdraw our support for Hamas and Islamic Jihad. The picture is much the same in regard to Syria's links with Hizbullah. Pakistan similarly relies on jihadists in Kashmir to liberate what it claims to be a Pakistani province.

5. *Business Is Business.* One of the hardest nuts to crack in America's war on terror has been clamping down the business and financial centers that launder jihadist money and filter funds to the terrorists. The biggest offenders, according to American sources, are Dubai, Sharjah, the UAE, Lebanon, and Israel.[57] Israel has subsequently been removed from the list. The United States also accuses the UAE of being a major center for criminal gangs involved in drug and gunrunning, presumably in cahoots with the jihadists. All protest their innocence but resist altering banking practices in the name of free-market economics and economic survival.

6. *Terrorists Are Part of the Power Structure.* In some parts of the Islamic world, terrorist and other extremist organizations are so powerful that they actually constitute part of the ruling power structure. This was very much the case of the Sudan during al-Turabi's heyday and is very much the case in Lebanon today. Hizbullah is one of the major actors in Lebanese politics, and it is the only group in Lebanon allowed to maintain its own militia. Attempts to close down Hizbullah would threaten a renewal of Lebanon's long and bloody civil war, a prospect that is unacceptable to the vast majority of Lebanese. This said, the situation remains tense and has become a major theme on Lebanese talk shows.

Perhaps the most interesting case of government agencies supporting terror is that of the Pakistani ISI. The ISI, the Pakistani equivalent to the Central Intelligence Agency (CIA) and the Federal Bureau of Investigation (FBI), possesses a long history of orchestrating jihadist activities in Afghanistan and Kashmir. It has also defied control by Pakistan's political leaders and is variously described as Pakistan's "invisible government," "kingdom within a state," and "our secret godfathers." During periods of civilian rule, about half of Pakistan's history as an independent state, the ISI was used by Pakistan's generals to keep tabs on civilian politicians. In some cases, it might have plotted their removal from office. It was the ISI that channeled American aid to bin Laden and the Taliban during the Afghan rebellion against the Soviets. It is the ISI that stands accused of funneling weapons and money to the jihadists in Kashmir and setting up spy networks in India. Other charges against this most complex of organizations focus on its complicity in the development of Pakistan's nuclear weapons and its ties with North Korea. General Pervez Musharaf has removed the director of the ISI, a former ally, and has attempted to bring the "invisible government" under his control. This will not be an easy task. The ISI has a reported ten thousand members including a massive core of informers.[58] Its tentacles also penetrate all sectors of Pakistan's political life. While blackmail is too strong a word, the capacity of the ISI to embarrass Pakistan's elite is virtually unlimited.[59]

The U.S. case against Pakistan does not differ markedly from its case against Iraq and Iran, the main distinction being Pakistan's willingness to allow U.S. Special Forces to operate in Pakistan. Pakistan has also promised to terminate state support for the jihadists and bring Islamic schools and charitable organizations under control. The United States has praised these efforts but notes that Pakistan must stop being a "platform for terrorism."[60]

7. *States Are Too Weak to Stop Terrorism.* Americans intuitively assume that all sovereign governments are in control of their people and territory. This is not the case in most areas of the Islamic world. The frontier regions of Pakistan are under the control of tribal sheiks who rule much as they see fit. They are openly supportive of the jihadists and are now imposing Taliban-style rule on the region. According to some reports, bin Laden T-shirts are a big hit.[61] Far worse, the United States begrudgingly acknowledges that al Qaeda base camps are now being established in the region.[62] Attempts to crush the Taliban in the region have failed. The Pakistani government has made a deal with the Taliban to keep the situation under control.[63] The U.S. government is unhappy with this arrangement, but what can it do? The territories are simply too mountainous and too remote to be effectively patrolled by the army. Pakistan also lacks the resources to do so. The situation is much the same in Yemen, a mountainous country whose remote tribes have historically been in various degrees of revolt against the central government. The government controls the cities and the flatlands. The mountain tribes are best controlled by bribes. Yemen has allowed U.S. Special Forces to operate in its territory, but the sledding is tough.

8. *Collusion with Government Officials.* Jihadist sympathizers exist in all strata of society including senior government officials and leading members of the clergy. Some are open in expressing their views; most are not. Some work in the government bureaucracy; others are members of the army and police. Still others are wealthy businessmen well skilled in the art of bribing venal government officials. We asked a well-placed official if he ever accepted bribes. "My family doesn't take bribes," he replied with contempt, "we give them." The numbers of

jihadist supporters increase as one descends the hierarchy of power. So do their invisibility and the ability to apprehend them. One way or another, officials are shifting resources to the jihadists and other extremists groups and turning a blind eye to their activities. People in high positions also provide a modicum of protection to those at lower levels. This, of course, is the story of Iraq.

9. *Delusions of Grandeur.* We add megalomania to the list of reasons for supporting terror because it is difficult to find another explanation for Colonel Muammar Qadaffi's long history of supporting terrorist operations. Qadaffi believes that he inherited the mantle of Arab leadership from Abdul Nasser and has spared no efforts to portray himself as the champion of Arab causes. This has included support for a variety of terrorists, including the infamous Abu Nidal. No sooner did the world's media ignore the Libyan leader than a new crisis began brewing. Sometimes it was terror; other times it was a renewed drive to unite the Arabs or the sedition of one of his neighbors. During the 1970s, he even sent money to America's Black Muslims in the hope that it would trigger a revolution in the United States. Always believing himself to be something of a religious saint, he sparked outrage among Muslim clerics when he changed the beginning date of the Muslim calendar from the death of Prophet Mohammed to the date of the Prophet's birth. Even in his youth he had organized revolutionary cells, shaving the heads of disciples who disobeyed his orders.[64] Qadaffi's zeal calmed precipitously following the U.S. bombing of Libya in 1986, and the Libyan dictator eventually acknowledged that Libyan agents had been involved in the bombing of Pan American Flight 103 over Lockerbie, Scotland. Qadaffi himself denied knowledge of the affair but agreed to pay reparations to the families of the victims. Always unpredictable in his search for notoriety, he has joined the war on terror and embarrassed former friends by revealing the aid they provided to his nuclear weapons program. Of these, none was more embarrassed than Pakistan, a core state in America's war on terror.

There can also be little doubt that Saddam Hussein suffered from bouts of megalomania. By and large, the role of the Iraq media was to transform Saddam Hussein into a living god. Cults of personality are not rare in the Middle East, but few could match those of the Iraqi dictator. The opponents of the Ayatollah Khomeini also claimed that he had deluded himself into believing that his actions were divinely inspired. Delusions of grandeur are dangerous. Rational politicians back down in the face of overwhelming odds. They are also willing to negotiate for the best deal. Those suffering from the delusions of invincibility do neither. Others simply can't admit that they were wrong. One way or the other, the only solution is defeat. This problem, of course, is not limited to the Islamic world.

Countries with More than One Reason for Supporting Terror

Countries with a single reason for supporting terror are relatively easy to deal with. Syria's support of terrorism, for example, is overwhelmingly motivated by a desire to keep Israel at bay and regain the Golan Heights. Washington might have accepted this rationale in the hope that Syria's support of anti-Israeli terror will go away once a comprehensive Arab-Israeli peace settlement is in place. At the very least, Washington has been reluctant to attack Syria for fear of igniting a regional conflagration.

The picture is much different for countries with multiple reasons for supporting terror. As a general principle, the more reasons a country has for supporting terror, the more it will defy America's efforts to stamp out the jihadists. This applies to friends of the United States as well as to its enemies. This point is well illustrated by Saudi Arabia and Iran, two key countries in America's war on terror.

The case against Saudi Arabia is threefold. First, Saudi Arabia sponsors a broad network of religious schools throughout the Islamic world. These schools, by and large, adhere to a Wahhabi doctrine known for its hard-core fundamentalism. It is also a xenophobic doctrine that lends itself to anti-Americanism. Both, in the view of the United States, promote jihadism. Second, the Saudis contribute generously to Islamic charities linked to extremist groups. Some contributions are direct. Some are inadvertent. The result, according to Washington, is the same. The jihadists receive the funds they need to carry out terrorist attacks against America and its allies. Third, Saudi Arabia funds jihadist groups attacking Israel. Israeli sources claim that 50 percent of Hamas's funds come from Saudi Arabia.[65] Saudi Arabia has also been the major financial backer of the Palestinian struggle for an independent country.

None of the above points are a matter of much dispute. The pertinent question is why does Saudi Arabia, a longtime ally of the United States, continue to pursue policies that undermine America's war on terror? The answer, in a nutshell, is that most of the motives for supporting terror reviewed above are applicable to Saudi Arabia. To begin with, Saudi Arabia is a tribal monarchy whose main claim to legitimacy lies in its support of Islam. Lest there be doubt on the matter, the title of the Saudi king is "his majesty, the custodian of the two sacred holy places." Supporting Islam has always been and continues to be a cardinal principle of Saudi foreign policy.

Saudi sponsorship of Islamic schools symbolized that policy, as did Saudi-sponsored Islamic alliances designed to serve as a counterweight to Arab nationalism.

The legitimacy of the Saudi regime has also been purchased by providing Saudi citizens with a cradle-to-grave welfare system. Schooling is free, and home loans, seldom repaid, are available for the asking. All are funded from the kingdom's lavish oil revenues. Both pillars of Saudi rule have now begun to fray. Well educated and increasingly vocal, Saudi citizens are demanding that a royal family known for its corruption and lax morals clean up its act. Bin Laden, a friend of the royal family before his exile in the Sudan, was one of its foremost critics.[66] His message was basically "reform or perish." Even government clerics have become critical of the corruption and ineptitude of the family.[67]

More than ever, accordingly, the royal family feels compelled to stress its Islamic credentials and support Islamic causes. This involves charity giving of all varieties, much of which is collected by charities that operate with minimal supervision. It also means supporting the Palestinian struggle, the most visible of Arab and Islamic causes. This is all the more the case because Saudi cooperation in the U.S. strike against Saddam Hussein was profoundly unpopular in Saudi Arabia. It will be recalled that a Saudi intelligence survey of popular attitudes toward the war against Iraq found that 95 percent of the respondents opposed it.

In much the same manner, strident anti-Americanism in Saudi Arabia makes it difficult for the Saudi government to grant U.S. agents free reign in investigating jihadist attacks on American sites in the kingdom. Part of this reluctance is the pervasive fear and distrust that pervades all areas of life in the kingdom. The royal family, estimated to be between five and thirty thousand in all, also fears that these investigations might produce unpleasant surprises. Many of the family members have been known for their sympathy for Islamic causes, including the jihadists. As the royal family controls almost everything worth controlling in Saudi Arabia, some collusion is inevitable. All things considered, it is probably impossible for the United States to dry up Saudi support for Palestine, fundamentalist education, and Islamic charities without jeopardizing the Saudi regime itself. That might also mean jeopardizing Saudi oil resources. If the royal family goes, it could well be the jihadists who come next.

The American case against Iran returns to 1979 and the Ayatollah Khomeini's overthrow of the Shah of Iran. Proclaiming an Islamic Revolution against the United States and everything American, the hand of Ayatollah Khomeini was seen everywhere: in the seizing of U.S. diplomats in Tehran, in attempted coups in Bahrain, in the attack on the holy mosque in Mecca, in the attacks on the American Embassy and marine barracks in Beirut, in the development of Hizbullah organizations throughout the Shi'a world, and in the funding of Sunni jihadists everywhere. The Islamic Revolution lost some of its steam with the death of Ayatollah Khomeini, but support of terror continued unabated. Iran was a key player in al-Turabi's network and continues to provide funding and arms to Hizbullah, various Iraqi Shi'a militias, Hamas, and the Palestinian Jihad. Iran's connections with bin Laden remain more conjectural, but there can be little doubt of Iran's role in resisting the U.S. occupation of Iraq.

Iran is motivated to support terror against America and its allies by most of the reasons outlined above. Public opinion in Iran continues to be anti-American, and a shaky Islamic government feels compelled to convince its population that it's not backing down in the face of U.S. threats. Iranians, it appears, see little hope for a rapprochement with the United States and are preparing for the worst. Threatened U.S. and Israeli attacks on Iran have merely added fuel to the fire.

Iranian foreign policy continues to oppose a strong U.S. presence in Iraq, Saud Arabia, and the sheikhdoms of the Persian Gulf. It is in Iran's national interest to do so. All serve as an obstacle to expansion of the Iranian Revolution. All could also be used as a springboard for an American attack against Iran. President Bush has openly discussed the possibility of such a strike, and the Israelis have urged him to do so. Iran's inability to match the United States militarily leaves it with two basic choices: (1) it can capitulate to U.S. demands that it dismantle its nuclear facilities and Hizbullah networks, or (2) it can attempt to drive the United States from the region by means of terror and subversion. The first choice would humiliate the Islamic regime and call its survival into question. The alternative is dangerous but might be necessary for the survival of the regime—hence the rush for nuclear weapons.

Notes

1. This assessment is based on many years of watching a variety of Muslim telepreachers on diverse Arabic television channels.

2. "Saudi Grand Mufti Condemns Killing of Non-Muslims," *Middle East News*, October 25, 2001, at www.middleeastwire.com/Saudi/stories/20011025_meno.shtml (accessed October 25, 2001).

3. "Egyptian Cleric Clarifies Words on Suicide Attacks," *Ha'aretz*, April 15, 2002, at www.haaretz.com/hasen/pages/ShArt.jhtml (accessed April 15, 2002).

4. "Qaradawi Launches Sharp Attack on Sheikh Al Azhar," *Middle East Online*, December 4, 2001, at www.middle-east-online.com/ArabicNews/Palestine/Dec2001/Qardawi_azhar.html (accessed December 5, 2001).

5. Hamidi D. Zaqzuq, "Interview with the Minister of Wafqs" [in Arabic], *Al-Wasat* (January 4, 1999): 23–25.

6. Francis Cabrini Mullaney, *The Role of Islam in the Hegemonic Strategy of Egypt's Military Rulers 1952–1990* (Ann Arbor, Mich.: UMI Dissertation Information Service, 1995).

7. Diana Digges, "All Preachers Meek and Mild," *Cairo Times* 1, no. 15 (September 18, 1997), at www.cairotimes.com/content/issues/Islists/preach 15.html (accessed July 21, 2003).

8. Joseph Nevo, "Religion and National Identity in Saudi Arabia," *Middle Eastern Studies* 34 (July 1998).

9. Hani A. Z. Yamani, *To Be a Saudi* (London: Janus Publishing, 1998).

10. Febe Armanios, "Islamic Religious Schools, Madrasas: Background," Congressional Research Service, Library of Congress, October 29, 2003, 4; Christopher M. Blanchard, "Islamic Religious Schools, Madrasas: Background," CRS Report for Congress, Order Code RS21654, updated January 23, 2007.

11. "Unfulfilled Promises: Pakistan's Failure to Tackle Extremism," *International Crisis Group Asia Report* 73 (January 16, 2004): 1–21.

12. Mohammad Kharishan, "Changing the Arab Educational Program at the Request of the U.S." [in Arabic], *Al Jazeera*, December 22, 2001, at www.aljazeera.net/ (accessed December 22, 2001).

13. Kharishan, "Changing the Arab Educational Program."

14. Yousef Qaradawi, "Violence and the Islamic Group, Part I" [in Arabic], interviewed by Hamid Al Ansari, *Al Jazeera*, July 7, 2001, 2–3, at www.aljazeera.net/programs/shareea/articles/2001/7/7-07-1.htm (accessed August 24, 2002).

15. S. Gurumurthy, "Madrasas and Jihad," *Papers Online*, May 1, 2002, at http://sathyavaadi.triod.com/truthisgod/papers/020501.htm (accessed June 20, 2003).

16. Michael A. Prokop, "Saudi Arabia: The Politics of Education," *International Affairs* 79, no. 1 (2003): 78–79.

17. John Duke Anthony, "The American-Saudi Relationship: A Briefing by HRH Prince Saud al-Faisal," *Gulfwire Newsletter* (October 13, 2002), in Febe Armanios, "Islamic Religious Schools, Madrasas: Background," Congressional Research Service, Library of Congress, October 29, 2003, 4.

18. Kemal As-Said Habib, "The Experience of the Islamic Movement in Egypt" [in Arabic], *Al Manara* 12 (2000), at www.almanara.net/issues/12/121.htm (accessed December 13, 2001).

19. Faye Bowers, "On a Dagger's Edge: Saudi Students Face a Changing System," *Christian Science Monitor*, January 12, 2004, downloaded from Saudi-U.S. Relations Information Service, at www.saudi-us-relations.org/newsletter2004 (accessed January 14, 2003); Mohammed Kharishan (moderator), "Changing the Arab Educational Program at the Request of the United States" [in Arabic], panel discussion, *Al Jazeera*, December 22, 2001, at www.aljazeera.net/program/first_Cent_wars/articles/2001/12/12-22-1.htm (accessed December 29, 2001).

20. "Indonesia Expected to Collect a Billion Dollars of Zakat Fitr," *Islam Online*, December 4, 2002, at www.islamonline.net/complete search/English/mDetails.asp (accessed December 21, 2002).

21. "Indonesia Expected to Collect a Billion Dollars."

22. Hala Mustafa, *The Political System and the Islamic Opposition in Egypt* [in Arabic] (Cairo, Egypt: Markaz Al-Mahrusa, 1995).

23. "Saudi Arabia Announces Counter-Terrorism Measures," Saudi Arabian press release cited in *Gulfwire*, December 9, 2002, at www.saudi-american-forum.org/Newsletters/SAF_News_09.htm#A1 (accessed December 9, 2002).

24. "Fatwa Bank: Salaries to Imams from Zakat," *Islam Online*, December 1, 1999, at www.islamonline.net/fatwa/English/FatwaDisplay.asp (accessed December 9, 2002).

25. "Fatwa: Spending Zakat Money on Jihad," *Islam Online*, April 11, 2002, at www.islamonline.net/completesearch/English/FatwaDisplay.asp (accessed April 11, 2002).

26. Mujahid Mleji, "Mufti of Egypt Calls on Muslims to Send Zakat to Chechnya," *Islam Online*, December 12, 1999, at www.islamonline.net/compeltesearch/English/mDetails.asp (accessed December 12, 1999).

27. Patrick Butler, "Muslim Cleric Banned from Charity Role," *Guardian*, December 16, 2002, at http://society.guardian.co.uk/charitymanagement/story/0,8150, 861058,00.htm (accessed December 16, 2002).

28. "Terrorist Finance: Follow the Money," *Economist*, June 1, 2002, 67.

29. "Saudi Arabia Announces Counter-Terrorism Measures."

30. "Kuwait Permits Benevolent Associations to Gather Monetary Contributions," *Al Arabiya*, September 21, 2006, at www.alarabiya.net/ (accessed September 21, 2006).

31. "Kuwaiti Islamic Charity Denies U.S. Terrorist Charges," *Middle East News*, January 11, 2002, at www.middleeastwire.com/Kuwait/sotries/20020111_meno.shtml (accessed January 13, 2002).

32. "Saudi Arabia Announces Counter-Terrorism Measures."

33. Joseph Nada, "Dimensions of the American Attack of Islamic Financing" [in Arabic], *Al Jazeera*, November 29, 2001, at www.aljazeera.net/programs/no_limits/articles/2001/11/11-19-1.htm (accessed November 29, 2001).

34. Borzou Daragahi, "Financing Terror," *Money* 30 (November 1, 2001): 120 (Infotrac A79304052, accessed November 2001).

35. Gamal Essam El-Din, "A Financial Jihad," *Al Ahram Weekly*, November 21–27, 2002, at www.alahram.org.eg/weekly/202/613/ec2.htm (accessed November 21, 2002); "Les banques islamique veulent seduire les clients Europeans" [in French], *Le Monde*, August 17, 2004, at www.lemondec.fr/web/imrimer_article/0,1-0@2-3234,36-375768,0.html (accessed August 17, 2004).

36. For more on this topic, see *Al Jazeera*, 2005, at www.aljazeera.net/ (accessed March 29, 2005).

37. Nada, "Dimensions of the American Attack."

38. Amos Harel, "Israel Does Little to Stop Money Flow to Terror: Shin Bet Sets up New Unit," *Ha'aretz*, December 29, 2003, at www.haaretz.com/asen/spages/377358.html (accessed December 30, 2003).

39. James Anderson, "International Terrorism and Crime: Trends and Linkages," William R. Nelson Institute for Public Affairs, James Madison University, Harrisonburg, Va., n.d., at www.jmu.edu/ (accessed January 4, 2003).

40. "Islamic Dinar Gathers Momentum," *Middle East Times*, 2002, at www.metimes.com/ (accessed November 9, 2002).

41. Douglas Farah, "Al Qaeda's Road Paved with Gold: Secret Shipments Traced through a Lax System in the United Arab Emirates," *Washington Post*, February 17, 2002, at www.washingtonpost.com/wp-dyn/articles/A22303-2002Feb16.html (accessed February 17, 2002).

42. UAE Ministry of Information & Culture, "Rich Investors from UAE 'Park $266b Abroad,'" *Emirates Bulletin* 25 (February 5, 2002), at www.columbia.edu/ (accessed February 21, 2004).

43. "Financing Terrorism," *Economist Special Report*, October 22, 2005; Eben Kaplan, "Rethinking Terrorist Funding," Council on Foreign Relations, January 31, 2007, at www.cfr.org/publication/12523/crethinking_cterrorist_financing (accessed February 18, 2007); Eben Kaplan, "Tracking Down Terrorist Financing," Council on Foreign Relations, April 4, 2006, at www.cfr.org/publication/10356/tracking_down_terrorist_financing (accessed February 18, 2007).

44. Nick Kochan, "The Washing Machine: How Money Laundering and Terrorist Financing Soils Us," excerpts from *Observer*, June 5, 2005, 3.

45. Declan Walsh, "Afghan Fury over UK Troops Telling Farmers They Can Grow Poppies," *Guardian*, April 28, 2007, at www.guardian.co.uk/ (accessed April 28, 2007).

46. "Al Qaeda's Balkan Links," *Wall Street Journal*, November 1, 2001, at http://online.wsj.com/public/us (accessed November 1, 2001).

47. Douglas Farah, "Report Says Africans Harbored al Qaeda: Terror Assets Hidden in Gem-Buying Spree," *Washington Post*, December 29, 2002, at www.washingtonpost.com/wp-dyn/articles/A8929-2002Dec28.html (accessed December 29, 2002).

48. Amelia Hill, "Bin Laden's $20m African 'Blood Diamond' Deals," *Guardian*, October 20, 2002, at www.observer.co.uk/international/story/0,6903,815450,00.html (accessed October 20, 2002).

49. Hill, "Bin Laden's $20m African 'Blood Diamond' Deals."

50. Eric Lichtblau, "U.S. Raids Foil Plots to Send Arms to Al Qaeda and Others," *New York Times*, November 6, 2002, at www.nytimes.com/ 2002/11/07/ international/ asia/ 07HOMG.html (accessed November 7, 2002).

51. Bill Gertz, "Al Qaeda Appears to Have Links with Russian Mafia," *Middle East Times*, reprinted from the *Washington Times*, October 10, 2001, at www.metimes.com/ (accessed October 10, 2001).

52. Senate testimony, Rand Beers, assistant secretary for International Narcotics and Law Enforcement Affairs, Francis X. Taylor, ambassador-at-large for Counter-Terrorism, March 13, 2002.

53. Farah, "Report Says Africans Harbored al Qaeda."

54. "U.S.-MKO Deal a Breach of Bush's Anti-Terrorism Campaign," *Payvand's Iran News* 36 (April 2003), at www. payvand. com/ news (accessed April 26, 2003).

55. Elizabeth Rubin, "The Cult of Rajavi," *New York Times Magazine* 4 (July 13, 2003).

56. *Time*, August 16, 1982, cited in Monte Palmer, *Politics of the Middle East* (Belmont, Calif.: Peacock Publishers/Wadsworth, 2007), 132.

57. Judy Pasternak and Stephen Braun, "Emirates Looked Other Way while al Qaeda Funds Flowed," *Los Angeles Times*, January 20, 2002, at www.latimes.com/ news/ nation world/world/ la-012002uae.story.htm (accessed July 26, 2002).

While few Muslims hold a brief for jihadist terror, most believe that the United States has declared war on their religion. In their minds, America's unequivocal support of Israel and its brutal war in Iraq are testimony to this fact. Anti-Americanism is rampant throughout the Islamic world and places very real constraints on how closely Muslim leaders can cooperate with the United States without being branded American puppets. Such fears caused the expulsion of U.S. forces from Saudi Arabia, and seldom a week passes without the Egyptian press proclaiming that President Husni Mubarak is not a tool of the Americans.

The leaders of the Islamic world, in turn, complain that the United States is insensitive to their domestic problems and is unwilling to help matters by easing its heavy-handed attacks on Islam and by bringing Israel to heel. Both, they argue, would do wonders to ease anti-Americanism in the region. They also find it quixotic that the United States is pushing them to be more democratic and humane at the same time that it is asking them to crush extremist groups and their supporters.

Islamic Strategies for Fighting Terror and Extremism

How, then, do the Muslim countries balance these realities in their struggles against Islamic extremism in its various manifestations?

The process begins by making a clear distinction between the jihadists and the radical moderates such as the Muslim Brotherhood, Hamas, and Hizbullah. The jihadists test the limits of Islamic theology, while the radical moderates come perilously close to being mainstream. The jihadists strike and run. They can't win elections, nor can they occupy territory. Their support base is narrow, and for the most part, they are feared by the population. This is not so for the Muslim Brotherhood, Hizbullah, and other radical moderates. They can win elections, and it is they who have penetrated all reaches of society including the military and security services. It is also they who have the capacity to field militias and send the country spiraling into civil war. The jihadists advocate violence as the only avenue to an Islamic state. The radical moderates are pragmatic and flexible. Violence is the weapon of last resort. The jihadist vision of an Islamic state bears much in common with the Spanish Inquisition. The radical-moderate vision of an Islamic state is seductively modern.

It is precisely these differences that make the radical moderates such a threat to the pro-American regimes of the Islamic world. This does not mean that the jihadists are not viewed as a threat but merely that they are less of an immediate threat than the radical moderates. America's Islamic allies, accordingly, have developed separate strategies for dealing with each. There is some overlap but not much.

Islamic Anti-jihadist Strategies

Initial Muslim struggles against the jihadists relied on brute force including relentless torture and collective punishments against any and all groups remotely suspected of terrorist links. The jihadists were crippled, but as in the Israeli case, the indiscriminate use of force alienated a broad section of the population and threatened to create more terrorists than it was eliminating. Threats of a broader insurrection also loomed as soldiers and police, many with deep religious convictions, became restive with the task of killing innocent Muslims. Prisons bulged and became training grounds for terror. Also as in the Israeli case, brute force produced only a stalemate. While the Israelis could continue to pursue a punitive strategy against alien (Arab) terrorists, most Muslim countries found the reliance on force to be both risky and counterproductive. The enemy within was too deeply rooted in their societies to be easily eradicated. In some cases, jihadist leaders became folk heroes and objects of emulation. When internal pressure became too great, the jihadists simply managed their affairs from the neighboring countries or Europe. Even government successes had as much to do with jihadist errors as they did with military genius. Alternative strategies became essential.

This does not mean that force has ceased to be a key element in the Muslim struggle against jihadist terror. It has not. The need for alternative strategies was merely recognition of the fact that force alone could not stem the jihadist threat. Abductions and assassinations remain commonplace, and suspects continue to rot in ghastly jails without trials. Torture has been refined to an art form—so much so that the United States regularly sends suspects to Egypt, Syria, and other Islamic countries for interrogation, a process referred to as rendition.[1] The image that comes to mind is that of Saddam Hussein at the funeral of a departed comrade, his palms raised as testimony that his hands were free of blood.

This said, brute force has been balanced by a variety of "softer" tactics. Key to this process have been efforts to attack the jihadists on theological grounds. Jihadist interpretations of the Koran and Sunna stretch Islamic dogma to the breaking point and have left them vulnerable to charges that they are heretics intent on destroying Islam. Both government and radical-moderate clerics have been relentless in pursuing this theme, with particular emphasis being placed on Koranic injunctions against killing Muslims and innocents. Government sermons also stress Koranic verses praising peace, tolerance, and submission to political leaders, however unjust.[2] Attacks on jihadist theology are matched by gory descriptions of the chaos that the jihadists have wrecked in Algeria and the living hell created by the Taliban in Afghanistan. "What is their program?" the government clergy ask. "They have none," comes the answer. "Only violence." The message is clear. Don't be deceived. Your life today is far better than anything that the jihadists have to offer.

The news media, in turn, variously portray the jihadists as criminals, anarchists, or insane madmen addicted to violence and intent on destroying the Islamic faith. Indeed, there are a few woes in Islamic society that are not blamed on the jihadists. Criminalizing the jihadists is important, for even the slightest suggestion that they were men of religion would enhance their status and cloud government efforts to suppress them.

At the same time secular regimes attack the jihadists, they attempt to steal their thunder by making themselves appear ever more Islamic. Books are banned, bars closed, and dazzling new "government" mosques dot the landscape. The government-controlled media has also become pro-Islamic with an endless array of religious programming. The number of state-sponsored Islamic radio and TV stations has also mushroomed. In a variation on this theme, popular televangelists have been encouraged as long as their message is one of nonviolence.[3]

Egypt's senior religious leaders have also become proactive, condemning the brutality of Israeli efforts to crush the Palestinian uprising, calling for charity donations to be channeled to Muslim forces in Chechnya, and calling for a jihad against the American attack on Iraq.[4]

The picture was much the same in Saudi Arabia, with a senior Islamic cleric issuing a *fatwa* from Mecca, Islam's holiest city, forbidding Saudi Muslims from participating in a strike on Iraq: "Not by word and not by deed, not by guidance and not by gesture, not with supply and not with support."[5]

Both the Egyptian and the Saudi *fatwas* were issued in the tense days leading up to the U.S. attack on Iraq, and neither *fatwa* could have been made without a nod from their respective governments. The United States was not pleased with these statements, but both Egypt and Saudi Arabia faced a critical choice. They could allow government clergy to oppose the war, or they could leave the field open to more radical groups, including the jihadists. The situation was much the same throughout the Islamic world.

The leeway given to establishment clergy in Egypt and other areas of the Islamic world is symptomatic of a broader effort by the secular governments of the regions to fight terror by distancing themselves from American and Israeli policy. Egypt's President Mubarak has been strident in his verbal attacks on Israeli suppression of the Palestinians and has led the charge in

leading Arab condemnation of the U.S. occupation of Iraq. Leaders throughout the Islamic world have followed suit. In their view, American policy
toward Iraq and Israel is fueling terrorism, and little is to be gained by deep-
ening the chasm between themselves and their populations. Lest there be any
doubt on the matter, the Saudi king has declared the U.S. role in Iraq
"illegal."[6]

Simultaneously, timid efforts have been made to cleanse the content of
school curricula and sermons. Islamic institutions and charities that support
jihadist terror are being closed, albeit without great enthusiasm. Most Islamic
countries are also attempting to bring mosques and religious schools
(*madrasas*) under government supervision and to assure that clergy have
been properly trained. Pakistan has expelled all foreign students from its religious schools and plans to bring unlicensed religious schools under government control as soon as possible.[7] This is proving difficult. The Egyptians,
too, are finding it difficult to control mosques and religious schools, with
thousands left unregistered.[8] As a practical matter, mosques are too numerous to be easily controlled, and most Islamic countries lack an adequate supply of qualified preachers to ensure moderate content of their sermons.[9]
Saudi Arabia is an exception to this rule and possesses an oversupply of graduates from its religious universities. The question is, are they moderate?

Much the same is true of efforts to cripple the financing of the jihadists.
Bold initiatives are announced, only to fade with time and popular opposition.[10] Saudi Arabia, for example, attempted to ban illegal charity collections
in schools, but the practice has resumed. Efforts to control Islamic banking
have proven particularly difficult.

At the individual level, Saudi Arabia has announced great success with religious reeducation programs designed to "reprogram" captured jihadists and
return them to society as useful citizens. According to Saudi press reports,
some four hundred former jihadists have been successfully reeducated, a success rate of some 90 percent. No details were provided on the evaluation procedures or the long-term effectiveness of the program.[11] Also at the
individual level, the Saudi Public Security Administration is experimenting
with techniques for shielding its members from extremist ideas. Coincidently, they are also trying to make their members more positive in their
dealings with the public.[12]

Divide and Conquer: Playing the
Moderates against the Jihadists

A growing number of Islamic countries are attempting to weaken the jihadists by strengthening the more moderate groups within the Islamic move-

ment. Moderate Islamic political parties in Morocco, Kuwait, Pakistan, and Turkey have been allowed new scope in an effort to give devout Muslims a peaceful alternative to the jihadists.

Egypt has been ambivalent on the strategy of accommodation, vacillating between attempts to use the Muslim Brotherhood as a counterweight to the jihadists and fears that an unrestrained Brotherhood would prove too popular to control. Recent experiments with moderate Islamic parties in Turkey, Morocco, Kuwait, and Pakistan have justified Egypt's apprehensions. All have seen Islamic parties emerge as a dominant political force in their respective parliaments, and Islamic parties have claimed the premiership in Turkey. In the meantime, the Muslim Brotherhood and Hizbullah follow the strategy of championing democracy and criticizing the obvious failings of their respective governments.

Countries such as Yemen, Somalia, Iraq, Nepal, Afghanistan, and Pakistan have a long tradition of maintaining order in remote regions by bribing tribal leaders, a practice that has been extended to the struggle against the jihadists. The only other option is to assault the tribes directly, a dangerous strategy that threatens to transform the war against the jihadists into a civil war.[13]

Muslim defenses against the jihadists have also increased in sophistication. Cooperation among security forces has increased, and modern technology has been brought into play.[14] Kuwait, for example, has installed eight thousand security cameras to fight terror, and Saudi Arabia, taking a page from the Israelis, is building a massive security fence along the Iraqi border to slow the infiltration of jihadist terrorist from that war-torn country.[15] The Saudi Commission for Virtue and Prevention of Vice (the religious police) is similarly upgrading the technological skills of its personnel. Hackers and other violators face penalties of a year in jail and heavy fines.[16]

This blend of brute force and soft tactics has maintained a stalemate between the jihadists and the secular governments of the Islamic world but not a great deal more. In the process, the governments and the jihadists exhaust each other, while the Muslim Brotherhood and its radical-moderate counterparts grow stronger. If this trend continues, it will be they who rule.

The Egyptians came to this realization in the late 1990s and declared a truce with its major jihadist groups, a topic discussed at length in chapter 3. That process has now become a rush. Yemen released one hundred prisoners in 2007, including convicted terrorists who had fought with al Qaeda in Iraq. All were given one thousand dollars to start a new life.[17] In 2006, Tunisia released key jihadists accused of attempting to overthrow the government by force as part of a general amnesty of some 1,600 prisoners.[18] The same year Algeria released two thousand jihadists arrested during the insurgency of the 1990s as a step toward national reconciliation.[19] Pakistan, the most venerable of America's Islamic allies, vacillates between military strikes against tribes supporting the Taliban and al Qaeda and the formal truces that have resulted in the release of hundreds of Taliban and al Qaeda militants from prison.[20] Kuwait, for its part, has long turned a blind eye to jihadists as long as they operated outside of the country.[21]

Both sides seem to win. The government is free to martial its efforts against the Muslim Brotherhood or other radical moderates, while the jihadists have time to regroup and rearm. The jihadist threat remains, but no one seems terribly concerned as long as their venom is directed against external targets. No one, that is, except the United States, Saudi Arabia, Israel, and Europe.

How long can the truces last? As we have seen in earlier chapters, the jihadist movement is in the process of reshaping itself. As long as the jihadists focus on the United States and its allies, truces in the Islamic world could well last for several years. This does not appear to be the case. Groups tentatively affiliated with al Qaeda have made a resurgence throughout the Islamic world and have resumed attacks on Muslims. Branch leaders of al Qaeda have also argued for renewed efforts to overthrow America's allies in the Muslim world, a move resisted by the central al Qaeda leadership intent on the broader war with the United States, Israel, and Europe. Kuwait and Saudi Arabia are clearly nervous.

Anti-Radical-Moderate Strategies

At least for the moment, however, it appears that truces are reducing the incidence of jihadist terror in the Islamic world. The United States is unhappy, but the governments of the region have gained time to contain the very real threat to their survival posed by the radical moderates. The question is, how is this to be done at a time when the popularity of the radical moderates is surging?

The Muslim Brotherhood, Hizbullah, and other radical moderates are hard to challenge on theological grounds because their doctrines are widely accepted as being mainstream—nor can they be attacked as wild-eyed reactionaries intent on enslaving the Islamic world in a time warp of the seventh century. In reality, they are more forward looking than most of America's allies in the Islamic world. They also provide better services to the poor than befuddled and self-serving bureaucracies of the region. Their main crime is being too popular.

Egypt has confronted the Muslim Brotherhood by attempting to rip off its mask, if such there is. Egypt's government-controlled press has been relentless in casting the Muslim Brotherhood as jihadists masquerading as guise moderates. The early violent history of the Muslim Brotherhood is recounted in gruesome detail as is the fact that the jihadist movement itself was an off-spring of the Brotherhood.[22] Even the brother of Hassan al-Bana has been enlisted in the struggle. His message is simple. He states that he grew up with these people and that they are not what they seem. In much the same manner, Hizbullah and its Iraqi clones are attacked as being tools of Iran. Turkey's generals have allowed the Islamic Justice and Development Party to rule but issue dire warnings that its leaders are secretly conspiring to undermine the country's secular traditions.

Limited force can be used against the radical moderates to be sure, but that risks bloody confrontations if not civil war. Security forces in the Islamic world have been infiltrated by the radical moderates, and their loyalty is suspect. The Egyptian government has set the stage for a showdown with the Muslim Brotherhood by condemning it as a threat to the security of the nation. Alas, such bombast is little more than a pretext for bludgeoning Brotherhood supporters at the polls and arresting a few leaders and financiers. Far from being an all-out war, they are a plaintive warning shot across the bow of the Brotherhood. It is not clear that the Brotherhood is listening. The Jordanians, Saudis, and Kuwaitis are even more timid. In the case of Hizbullah in Lebanon and its Iraqi clones, force can't be used. They are part of the government. This said, Hizbullah has accused elements of the Lebanese security forces of conspiring with the Israelis during the Second Lebanon/Hizbullah War. Key figures in the Lebanese government have also expressed the hope that the international force that now separates Israel and Hizbullah would disarm the latter. It has not. Armed confrontations have also become common between Hamas and al-Fatah in Palestine, with the Israelis facilitating the shipment of arms to the latter.

Alternatively, governments of the Islamic world have turned to democracy to blunt the appeal of the radical moderates. Leftist parties, once banned, are now encouraged to field electoral candidates as are reform parties of the center. By and large, such efforts have been stillborn. The leftists are passé, and the reformists embarrass pro-American governments with their calls for human rights and true democracy. Key American allies such as Egypt don't want competition from any source, right, left, or center. Once a secular opposition party shows signs of popular support, it is crushed by the government. The radical moderates, accordingly, remain the only game in town. They have also become very skilled politicians.

Turkey, Morocco, and Pakistan, by contrast, appear willing to accept participation by the radical moderates in the political process as long as they operate as political parties and renounce violence. Militias are not allowed, although this is a gray area in Pakistan. Saudi Arabia's religious establishment is far more conservative than the Muslim Brotherhood, which is generally accepted as a counterweight to the jihadists. The Brotherhood is also accepted in Kuwait, Jordan, and most of the Gulf sheikhdoms. Hizbullah and Iraqi clones now represent the most powerful force in their respective countries. Both are operating within a democratic framework, but that could change. Iraq is in a state of chaos, and Lebanon is moving in that direction.

Lessons of the Islamic Experience in Fighting Islamic Extremism and Jihadist Terror

Why, then, have the governments of the Islamic world found it increasingly difficult to contain Islamic extremism in both its jihadist and radical-moderate forms? The answer to this question starts with the fact that none of the causes of extremism and terror discussed in chapter 2 have eased. Indeed, they are growing worse. People are demanding more and, for the most part, are sinking deeper into despair.[23]

It has also become obvious that force alone cannot stop Islamic extremism whatever its form. This was the conclusion of the Israelis, and it is also the conclusion of Turkish generals who have been fighting terror by the Kurdistan Workers Party (PKK) for decades.[24] Virtually all countries in the Islamic world now acknowledge that there has to be a political solution to the problem.

The difficulty with political solutions is that they require existing governments to make compromises that they find unacceptable. The Egyptian regime is unwilling to accept a diminution of its power. The Israelis are unwilling to accept a Hamas government that refuses to recognize the right of the Jewish state to exist. The Turks refuse to give the Kurds an independent homeland. Much the same is true of Saudi Arabia and the other Gulf monarchies. No one wants to relinquish land, privilege, or power.

Letting the people decide won't work because few regimes in the Islamic world will commit suicide by allowing free elections. If the awesome list of victories for the radical moderates is any indication, the results are a forgone conclusion. Ironically, even the United States, once a beacon of freedom and democracy, has become afraid of democracy in the Islamic world. This means, in effect, that there are few mechanisms for political adjustment in the Islamic world other than confrontation and violence. Violence begets violence, and the pageant of carnage continues.

Notes

1. Richard Norton-Taylor, "CIA Tried to Silence EU on Torture Flights," *Guardian*, October 26, 2006, at www.guardian.co.uk/ (accessed October 26, 2006).

2. Elie Elhadj, *The Islamic Shield* (Boca Raton, Fla.: Brown Walker Press, 2007).

3. Stephen Ulph, "Jihadi after Action Report: Syria," Combating Terrorism Center, West Point, N.Y., November 2006.

4. "Al Azhar Calls for Jihad in Case of an Attack on Iraq" [in Arabic], *Al Jazeera,* March 10, 2003, at www.aljazeera.net/news/arabic/2003/655/eg7.htm (accessed September 13, 2003).

5. Al-Auda, Sheik Suliman ben Fahd, "Saudi Religious Scholar Forbids Participation in U.S. Strike on Iraq" [in Arabic], *Al Jazeera,* March 6, 2003, at www.aljazeera.net/new/Arabic/2003/3/3-6-7.htm (accessed March 6, 2003).

6. Hassan M. Fattah, "U.S. Iraq Role Is Called Illegal by Saudi King," *New York Times,* March 29, 2007, at www.nytimes.com/ (accessed March 29, 2007).

7. "Foreign Students Ordered Out of Pakistan Madrassas," *Guardian,* July 29, 2005, at www.guardian.co.uk/pakistan/Story/0,2763,1539053,00.html (accessed July 29, 2005).

8. Mohammed Samaha, "The War of the Random Mosque" [in Arabic], *Rosa al Yousef,* July 14, 2007, at www.rosaonline.com/ (accessed July 14, 2007).

9. Nabil Daroush, "Morocco Tightens Regulations for Building Mosques," *Asharq Al-Awsat,* January 17, 2007.

10. Dania El Sabban, "Illegal Charity Collectors Return to Saudi Schools," *Asharq Al-Awsat,* March 19, 2007.

11. "90% of Arrested Extremists Re-Evaluate Their Beliefs" [in Arabic], *Al Arabiya,* February 19, 2006.

12. "Saudi Public Security Launches Plan to Shield Personnel from Extremism," *Asharq Al-Awsat,* April 23, 2007.

13. Syed Saleem Shahzad, "Pakistan Crosses a Dangerous Boundary," *Asia Times,* March 28, 2007, at www.atimes.com/ (accessed March 28, 2007).

14. Nahid Andijani, "Saudi Religious Police Tackle Cyberspace," *Asharq Al-Awsat,* March 27, 2007.

15. "8,000 Cameras: Kuwait Hopes to Guarantee Security" [in Arabic], *Al Arabiya,* October 25, 2006.

16. "Egypt Government Say Amendments Passed," *Asharq Al-Awsat,* March 27, 2007.

17. "100 Muslim Extremists Freed in Yemen," *Asharq Al-Awsat,* March 5, 2007.

18. "Tunis Declares Amnesty for 1600 Prisoners, among Them 70 Militant Leaders" [in Arabic], *Al Arabiya,* February 25, 2006.

19. "Algeria Frees Islamic Insurgents Jailed in '90s," *Washington Post,* March 5, 2006, at www.washingtonpost.com/wp-dyn/content/article/2006/03/04/AR2006030401332.html (accessed March 5, 2006).

20. Jim Lobe, "'War on Terror' Returning to Its Cradle," *Asia Times,* October 5, 2006, at www.atimes.com/ (accessed October 5, 2006).

21. Nicholas Blanford, "Gun Battles Force Kuwait to Take Closer Look at Influence of Islamic Extremism," *Daily Star* (Lebanon), February 21, 2005, at www.dailystar.com.lb/ (accessed February 21, 2005).

22. "Hassan Al-Bana Gave Birth to Generations of Deception and Religious Perversion," *Rosa al Yousef,* October 21, 2006.

23. *Arab Human Development Report 2004* (New York: United Nations Development Program, 2005).

24. "Military Option No Way Out," *Turkish Daily News,* November 18, 2006, at www.tdn.com.tr/ (accessed November 18, 2006).

14

America, Islamic Extremism, and Jihadist Terror

Few Americans were concerned about the threat of Islamic extremism in the years prior to World War II. Independence movements were the order of the day, and Islam, whatever its form, seemed to be something of an anachronism. The struggle for the future would be between Western democracy and authoritarianism in its various forms. With the Nazis defeated in World War II, it was the seductive ideologies of socialism and communism that swept the Islamic world. Indeed, the Islamic world was awash with leftist coups. Few were communist, but most looked to the Soviet Union for support.

How was America to parry the leftist threat? Freedom and democracy were the answer, but they were dangerous. The United States was locked in a struggle to the death with the Soviet Union, and it was folly to allow the leftists to vote themselves into power. Besides, America's staunchest allies in the Middle East were dictators and tribal kings, none of whom had the slightest interest in democracy. The answer seemed obvious: Islam. Only Islam, the predominant religion of the Middle East, could serve as a counterweight to the leftist slogans of freedom, equality, and development. But, was Islam powerful enough to stem the leftist tide? Perhaps it could be strengthened.

Thus, American policy toward Islamic extremism during the long years of the Cold War became one of nurturing and support. Little thought was given to the virulent new jihadist strains that were evolving throughout the Islamic world. Perhaps they were just what the doctor ordered to stem the communist tide.

This policy reached its peak with the Soviet invasion of Afghanistan in 1979. Alarmed by fears that its invasion of Afghanistan signaled a new Soviet offensive in the Middle East, U.S. support for the jihadists poured into Afghanistan, much of it managed by Pakistani Inter-Services Intelligence (ISI). They, after all, understood the territory, and the United States would be spared the risk of confronting the Soviet Union directly.

All of this changed dramatically with the September 11, 2001, terrorist attacks on the United States. America suddenly found itself in a deadly war unlike any other that it had ever encountered. There were no massed armies to bomb or front lines to fortify, only shadows that dissolved into throngs of the innocent. The enemy wore no uniforms except, perhaps, the ubiquitous beard, but even that could be abandoned for holy purposes. It was also the most psychological of wars. The jihadists fought for neither national pride nor wealth. They fought for God and an eternal paradise. That was the reward of those who died in defense of their faith. It was also a global war without limits. The jihadists were poised to strike anywhere and everywhere at a time and place of their choosing.

U.S. Policy in Fighting Terror and Islamic Extremism

What was there to do? The U.S. military was designed to counter the dual threat of conventional war against massed armies and the even deadlier threat of a nuclear conflagration with the Soviet Union. Little serious thought had been given to the possibility that a global war of terror could strike at the heart of the United States.[1] Time was of the essence. The United States had to strike, and it had to strike with force. But where were they to strike and at whom? Afghanistan was easy. That was the headquarters of bin Laden and al Qaeda. But what about after that? To make matters worse, the newly elected Bush administration was still settling in and had little experience in international affairs.[2]

America's antiterrorist strategy in the aftermath of the September 11 terrorist attacks focused on striking the jihadists with maximum force. Parallel efforts were made to forge an international antiterrorist alliance, strengthen the capacity of allies to fight terror, punish countries that supported terror, dry up the breeding grounds that sustained the terrorists, close down the jihadist supply lines, stem their funding, and strengthen America's domestic defense against terrorist attack. The need to eliminate the causes of terror was also discussed, but that was a long-term process that would have to wait until the jihadist threat had been countered.

America's antiterror guidelines were right on target. The jihadists were identified as the enemy, and all components of American antiterrorist strategy focused on their destruction. But, how were these guidelines to be implemented in a manner that put maximum pressure on the jihadist enemy without shattering international cooperation or strengthening the jihadist cause by alienating the Islamic world? A daunting challenge at best, perhaps it was impossible.

Intuitively, President Bush turned to the Israelis for guidance. The Israelis were the world's leader in fighting terror and had generations of experience in dealing with Arabs and other Muslims. They knew the territory. The president also had high regard for Ariel Sharon, the hard-nosed Israeli prime minister and ex-general. Sharon had little but contempt for Arabs and Muslims. Force, in his view, was the only thing they understood.

Perhaps influenced by Sharon's example, President Bush came down hard on the side of force. The United States, he vowed, would not sit idly by while the jihadists plotted their next move. Much like the Israeli model, potential threats would be dealt with by preemptive strikes before they could reach American targets. Labeled the Bush Doctrine, the threat of preventive strikes represented a major change in American policy.[3] It also represented a declining concern for civil rights as well as a disregard for civilian casualties resulting from U.S. antiterrorist policies. Terrorists, according to the Bush Doctrine, had no human rights, and it was the terrorists who were responsible for the suffering of Muslims, not the United States. Much of the same applied to the United Nations and international law including conventions on the rights of sovereign states. The United States, like Israel, had the right to defend itself, the fictions of international sovereignty or no. Also, as in the case of Israel, the Bush Doctrine declared that it would be the United States who determined guilt. There was no need for international tribunals unless they served the purpose of the United States. International support was appreciated but not essential. The United States would do what the United States had to do and would not be deterred by international pressure from defeating the jihadists. Mistakes could be sorted out later.

Overlooked by American infatuation with Israel's antiterrorist strategy was the fact that the Israeli model wasn't solving Israel's Palestinian problem. Things were getting worse, not better. Israel's antiterror strategy, moreover, was not designed to fight either Islamic extremism or jihadist terrorism. Both had only come to the fore in the recent years and were in large part responsible for the upsurge in anti-Israeli terror.

Be this as it may, the United States embraced Israel's list of terrorist organizations as its own. The list included Hamas, Hizbullah, and the Muslim Brotherhood. In line with Israeli policy, no distinction was drawn between the jihadists and the radical moderates. All had been implicated in supporting terrorist attacks against Israel, and all continued to pose a clear and present danger to the Jewish state. America's clearly defined war against jihadist terror had suddenly become a struggle against Islamic extremism in all of its manifestations.

This, too, represented a major break with America's long-standing tradition of working with Islamic extremism. The world had simply changed. The Soviets were gone, and the jihadists had turned on their former benefactor. The radical moderates did not attack the United States directly, but they were fueling the waves of the anti-Americanism that were surging throughout the Islamic world. As such, they were part of the problem.

U.S. strategy was also colored by President Bush's neoconservative advisors who urged that he forge a new Middle East based upon peace, the rule of law, religious tolerance, prosperity, and democracy. The causes of terror would be eliminated, and the world, including Israel, would be free from the scourge of terrorism and Islamic extremism. This was to be a long-term process that began with the elimination of the world's main supporters of terror and, by implication, the main threats to the United States and Israel. The list was headed by Iraq, Iran, and North Korea and became the foundation of President Bush's "axis of evil." Syria soon became an honorary member of this most illustrious group.

How Well Is America Doing in Its Struggle against Jihadist Terror and Islamic Extremism?

America's war on terror and Islamic extremism, now renamed the long war, is approaching the second decade with no end in sight.[4] Rather than containing jihadist terror, it appears to be spawning it. That, at least, is the conclusion of the American intelligence community in a recent report on the trends of global terrorism that stated, "Although we cannot measure the extent of the spread with precision, a large body of all-source reporting indicates that the activists identifying themselves as jihadists, although a small percentage of Muslims, are increasing in both number and geographical dispersion."[5]

A new Middle East is being forged, but it bears little resemblance to the Middle East of peace, prosperity, and democracy promised by the White House and its neoconservative advisors. If present trends continue, the new Middle East will be a Middle East of religious extremism pockmarked by the swamps (failed states) in which jihadist terror breeds. The list is long and growing: Iraq, Somalia, the Sudan, Algeria, Chechnya, Palestine, Kashmir, the wilds of Pakistan, Lebanon, and Afghanistan are the names that dominate the news, but they will soon be joined by others. Israel has promised a new war with Hizbullah and threatened to strike at Iran's nuclear facilities if the United States doesn't. Neither the United States nor Israel has ruled out the use of nuclear weapons. The United States is struggling to keep Turkey from invading the emerging Kurdish state in northern Iraq, while jihadist terror and lesser forms of religious extremism have spread to the length and breadth of the Islamic world, including the vast Muslim populations of Europe and Asia. The United States remains vulnerable to terror attack as do all of its allies. According to some analyses, the United States is a disaster waiting to happen.[6] The intelligence community seems to agree.

Why Is the Struggle Going Poorly?

What has gone wrong? Why all of the problems? The debate is interminable, but several points would seem incontestable.

The policies formulated to fight terror and Islamic extremism in the aftermath of the September 11 terrorist attacks were rushed, confused, and contradictory.[7] This could be excused given the urgency of the moment, the inexperience of the new administration, the limited and flawed information available about the nature of the jihadist threat, and the general unpreparedness of the security services to come to grips with the crisis at hand. All are discussed in length in the *Final Report of the National Commission on Terrorist Attacks on the United States* and require little elaboration at this point.[8] Unfortunately, not much has changed. America's efforts to stem terror and Islamic extremism remain confused and contradictory, perhaps even more so.

The core of the problem is that a war designed to eradicate a narrow group of jihadist assassins has mushroomed into a war against all forms of Islamic extremism and from there into a grandiose plan to forge a new Middle East free of terror and extremism. The White House stresses that all three are linked. The United States and Israel, in its view, will never be safe from terror as long as business in the Islamic world continues as usual. This could well be true.

The difficulty is that each of Washington's three goals requires a different strategy. Eliminating the jihadists focuses on attacking a miniscule if elusive target with maximum force. Because the jihadists are international in scope, they can only be eradicated through international cooperation. Going it alone won't work. It also requires keeping the jihadists on the run and separating them from their support base. This can only be accomplished by the active support of the world's 1.3 billion Muslims. They are America's natural allies in the war against jihadism and must be mobilized in the struggle to eliminate it. Defeating the jihadists similarly requires a strong emphasis on civil defense. They can't be allowed to score cheap victories against the

United States, their prime enemy. Washington, according to official policy statements, aspires to all of the above. Words, unfortunately, have not been reflected in deeds.

Eliminating the radical moderates including the Muslim Brotherhood, Hizbullah, and Hamas is a much trickier proposition. A frontal attack is probably impossible because they are either part of the government or would be if there were free elections. They are also too deeply embedded in their respective societies to be isolated as criminals or heretics. Most are heavily armed, which makes them even more dangerous. The only effective way to ease Islamic extremism, as Washington acknowledges, is to ease the poverty and oppression that breed extremism and to allow democracy to function. It sounds great, but generations of foreign aid had failed to dent the poverty and despair that breed extremism in the Islamic world.[9] Democracy might encourage the moderation of the radical moderates as it seems to have done in Turkey, but it simultaneously threatens America's traditional allies including Israel, Egypt, and Saudi Arabia, all of whom refuse to play.

As a result, confusion in dealing with the radical moderates reigns. The United States praises the election of the radical moderates in Turkey as an important step toward democracy in the Islamic world and has almost single handedly arranged the election of pro-Iranian Hizbullah clones in Iraq. Egypt and Saudi Arabia are pilloried in the world press for not being more democratic, but the United States turns a blind eye while Egypt makes a mockery of democracy and pleads with Saudi Arabia to modify a Wahhabi religious doctrine that makes the Muslim Brothers seem like flaming liberals. Simultaneously, the United States props up a military dictator in Pakistan, staunchly supports Israel's attempts to force a popularly elected Hamas out of office. It also encouraged the Jewish state's 2006 attack on Hizbullah. The United States even pressured Israel to keep the war alive after it had been lost.[10] Hizbullah is verboten, but the Supreme Council for the Islamic Revolution in Iraq (SCIRI), its Iraqi clone, is supported as a key element in Iraq's ruling coalition. This seems strange given the fact that Hizbullah is isolated while SCIRI is Iran's main force in Iraq and shares an open border with the Islamic Republic. If American reports are accurate, Tehran is funding, training, and arming Iraq's Shi'a militias. Names remain vague, but the most pro-Iranian of Iraq's militias is SCIRI's Badr Brigades. What will be the role of SCIRI and other Hizbullah clones in reshaping the Middle East once the United States exits Iraq? Does the United States expect gratitude?

The State Department explains that it deals with the radical moderates on a case-by-case basis, depending on the circumstances and the needs of the moment.[11] As the circumstances of the moment are constantly changing, this comes perilously close to having no policy toward Islamic extremism at all.

It clearly flies in the face of U.S. vows to counter extremism with democracy and radicalizes the region by reinforcing the impression that the United States has declared war on Islam. This, of course, fuels anti-Americanism and scuttles U.S. efforts to mobilize the Muslim support it so desperately needs in its struggle against jihadist terror.

The task of containing Islamic extremism pales in comparison to the challenge of building a new Middle East of peace, prosperity, and democracy allied with the United States and supportive of Israel. While it is difficult to find a clear blueprint of America's plan for building a new Middle East, its major components have been discussed at length. Countries accused of supporting terror and extremism are to be dispatched, Israel is to serve as the cornerstone of the U.S. operations in the region, Islam is to be reshaped into a moderate faith that lives in partnership with its sister religions, and the Middle East and the broader Muslim world are to be integrated into a global political and economic system guided by America.[12] Along the way, the causes of terrorism and extremism will be eliminated, oil will flow, and Israel, as former prime minister Ehud Olmert promised upon taking office, will again be a fun place to live.

In reality, American plans for forging a new Middle East are more of a grand vision than a coherent plan. It is also an elusive vision of several authors and many parts. The vision begins with a very realistic assessment that neither jihadist terror nor Islamic extremism can be contained if the Middle East continues on its present course. Decades of patching and fixing on a case-by-case basis have only made things worse and have placed America and its allies in jeopardy. Nothing short of radical surgery will do. As the leader of the world and its overwhelmingly most powerful country, according to diverse versions of the neoconservative vision, it is America's obligation to right a situation that is spiraling toward chaos. This, at least according to Richard Perle and David Frum, might require the secession of Saudi Arabia's oil-rich Eastern Province unless Riyadh shapes up. They also see little need to "cure the vast malaise in Muslim civilization by carving a Palestinian state out of the Judean hills."[13] From the tenor of the Perle vision of a new Middle East, America would have to be at war with Islam to achieve its objectives. This was not a matter of idle chatter, for Perle was an assistant secretary of state during this critical juncture in the formation of American antiterrorist policy.

Tragically, the architects of America's vision of remaking the Middle East supported their realistic assessment of the ineffectiveness of U.S. policies toward terror and extremism with a number of questionable assumptions about the ability of the United States to perform radical surgery on this most complex and volatile of regions. Of these, the most lethal was the assumption that air power and the overwhelmingly technological superiority of American troops would be sufficient to topple the rogue states of the region and intimidate laggards into compliance. This was matched by the assumption that the Arabs and their Muslim neighbors were realists whose bravado would collapse in the face of overwhelming force. Democracy, it was further assumed, would spring from the ashes of defeat much as it had in Germany and Japan in the aftermath of World War II. Islamic moderation would follow suit. Crowning these assumptions was infinite faith of the Bush administration in the ability of global capitalism to eradicate the despair that fueled terror and Islamic extremism.

As in all good visions, dreams of forging a new Middle East were deeply rooted in the emotions of the populace. Beyond promising a painless solution to jihadist terror and Islamic extremism, the neoconservative vision of a new Middle East fired crusader zeal and called upon America to kick ass and stop being a wimp.

Questions were raised about the capacity of an American intelligence community condemned for blowing the September 11 terrorist attacks to forge a new Middle East, but they were brushed aside by assurances that glitches had been fixed. Greater reliance would also be placed on the private sector and nongovernmental organizations (NGOs).

Fears were also raised that efforts to forge a new Middle East would galvanize the world's 1.3 billion Muslims against the United States and ignite a war of religions. These fears, too, were brushed away with assurances that most Muslims would welcome liberation from oppression and backward-looking extremists. The important thing was getting started. Time was of the essence. The more America dithered, the more painful the solution.

But where should they start? Why, Iraq, of course.

The War in Iraq and the Wars against Terror and Islamic Extremism

It was under the urging of the neoconservatives that Iraq became the centerpiece of U.S. antiterrorist and antiextremist strategy. As senior members of the Bush team who had long been pushing for preemptive strikes on rogue states openly admitted in the lead-up to the Iraq War, "Without Sept. 11, we never would have been able to put Iraq at the top of our agenda. . . . It was only then that this president was willing to worry about the unthinkable—that the next attack could be with weapons of mass destruction supplied by Saddam Hussein."[14]

With Saddam Hussein gone, the neoconservatives argued, Israel, Saudi

Arabia, and Kuwait would be safe from Iraqi weapons of mass destruction. The terrorists would be denied access to the same Iraqi weapons, world oil supplies would be brought under American control, rogue states would shy away from supporting terror, and a launching pad would be established for an inevitable attack on Iran, the prime supporter of jihadist terror and Islamic extremism. Military personnel also noted that taking out Saddam Hussein was the only way that the United States could extricate itself from a decade-long burden of patrolling the no-fly zones established to protect Iraq's Kurds and Shi'a from Saddam's vengeance. Both had revolted against Saddam's regime in the first U.S.-Iraqi war, and Saddam Hussein was the most vindictive of individuals.

The intense Shi'a and Kurdish opposition to Saddam Hussein—they represented 80 percent of the Iraqi population—made Iraq the logical first move in a domino strategy for toppling the other rogue states of the region. Saudi Arabia and Kuwait would provide launching bases, as would Turkey. There was no question of the Iraqi army resisting American military power, the first American venture against Saddam Hussein having lasted only one hundred hours. Whatever resistance existed would be softened up by air and naval bombardments. American casualties would be incidental, and the costs of the war would be more than compensated for by Iraqi oil revenues. The Iraqi people would welcome American troops as liberators and show their gratitude by becoming willing allies of the United States in its war against Iran.

All that was required was an excuse. That came with much-flawed intelligence estimates indicating that Saddam Hussein was supporting al Qaeda and building nuclear weapons.[15] The intelligence was inconclusive, but it was enough for the White House and Downing Street to run with it. It proved false on both counts. Saddam Hussein's claim of nuclear weapons was a bluff to keep the Iranians and Israel at bay. A U.S. government report later confirmed that he had none[16]—nor, according to the Office of Inspector General of the Department of Defense, did he have ties with bin Laden and al Qaeda.[17] Saddam was not above working with bin Laden, but it appears that bin Laden had little interest in working with an Iraqi dictator that he despised.

There were dissenting voices, but there always were. General Colin Powell, the only member of the Bush team with experience in the region, argued against the attack, as did key generals and Central Intelligence Agency (CIA) officials. In 2002 Powell informed the president, "You are going to be the proud owner of 25 million people. . . . You'll own it all."[18] The warnings of the naysayers were countered by enthusiastic Israeli support for the war and the staunch support of Britain and the other Anglos. The Canadians were a bit skittish, but then, they always were—probably the French influence. The

Bush administration was not in the mood for naysayers. Besides, it didn't matter. The United States had more than enough power to destroy Saddam Hussein without the support of the Arabs, Turks, and Continental Europeans.

There was also a bright side to the perfidiousness of America's erstwhile allies. Turkish intransigence provided further proof, if need be, that Islamic governments could not be trusted, regardless of their pretense at moderation. As for the hostility of Saudi Arabia and Egypt toward the war, what better evidence was there of the need for a new Middle East? The Egyptians had already made peace with the jihadists, and the Saudis were the purveyors of the most virulent strain of Islam. Enough was enough. The Europeans, for their part, would not share the exploitation of Iraqi oil and the massive rebuilding contracts expected at the end of the war. To the victor go the spoils, and that would be an Anglo affair. Perhaps a piece of the pie would even go to the Israelis. Anyway, the time had come for action.

As expected, Saddam Hussein was dispatched with undo difficulty. America and its allies, however few in number, were welcomed as liberators by much of the population. And then came the hard part. What should they do next? Iraq was less of a country than a mosaic of hostile religious and ethnic groups pieced together by the British at the end of World War I. A semblance of unity was maintained by a series of tyrants, the last of whom was Saddam Hussein. With Saddam gone and his ruling apparatus destroyed, it was now the United States who was in charge of maintaining order among Iraq's three major groups. The elder President Bush had been within walking distance of Baghdad a decade earlier but had stopped when someone asked him the most perplexing of questions: what are you going to do when you get there?

Iraq, Terror, and Islamic Extremism

There is little need to harp on America's debacle in Iraq other than to note that the optimism of the president's neoconservative advisors was misplaced, their assumptions flawed, and the fears of their critics justified.

The only part of the Iraqi project that went according to plan was the invasion. This said, even the military's plans had anticipated little sustained opposition to the occupation of Iraq. The stabilization phase, according to military planners, would take two to three months and require 270,000 troops, decreasing to 165,000 troops at the end of the phase. The recovery phase would take eighteen to twenty-four months and would see the existing core of 165,000 troops decrease to 25,000 by the end of the phase. The final transition phase would take an additional twelve to eighteen months and would see the existing core of 25,000 troops reduced to 5,000 by the end of December 2006.[19] Little if any thought was given to how the recovery and transition phases were to be managed. Such plans either did not exist or were ignored.[20]

The military assumed that the State Department would handle it, but there was little coordination.[21] A former American general was placed in charge of the transition to civilian rule but lasted only a year. His replacements ranged from scholars to diplomats, none with experience in the Middle East, and were changed faster than Salome changed veils.[22] Much the same was true on the Iraqi side as a series of handpicked puppets gave way to a government beholden to Iran. Even this was mismanaged as the CIA and the Department of Defense battled over which Iraqi puppet to put in place. This was merely symbolic of broader turf wars raging within the administration. Colin Powell, the only figure with substantial military experience and knowledge of the Middle East, gave way to theoretical warriors and yes-people. Condoleezza Rice, with a distinguished career in teaching and university administration, served as the president's national security advisor during his first term and then replaced Powell as secretary of state. According to her official biography she possessed no experience in Middle Eastern or Islamic affairs.[23] The remaining naysayer in the administration had disappeared.

Surprised by an unanticipated Iraqi resistance to the U.S. occupation, American troops were rushed into a guerilla war for which they were untrained. Many vehicles lacked adequate armor to protect them from rockets and roadside mines. Iran and Syria were blamed for providing weapons to anti-American forces, but they were hardly necessary. U.S. military documents released in 2007 revealed that Iraq was littered with ammunition dumps, most poorly guarded.[24]

Why this should have been a surprise remains a mystery to those familiar with Iraq and the Middle East including intelligence agents, foreign service officers, and scholars. But then, they weren't asked.

In the meantime, contractors enlisted to rebuild the Iraqi infrastructure overcharged the government billions of dollars, many for projects that were never completed.[25] When the findings were disclosed by the government agency responsible for oversight of the contractors, the agency was abolished.[26] The money came directly from the U.S. Treasury. Iraqi oil revenues that were to foot the bill had yet to materialize. Indeed, Iraqi oil production has yet to reach prewar levels, and much of what is produced is bottled up by exploding pipelines.

Nation-building efforts in Iraq were equally flawed. Efforts to strengthen Iraq's civilian infrastructure did not take shape until 2005 with the establishment of Provincial Reconstruction Teams. They had no armor at all, and in many cases, they lacked pencils.[27]

Why didn't Iraq, with all of its oil wealth, blossom like Japan and Germany had at the end of World War II? That, after all, was the plan. Sadly, this was another flawed assumption that came a cropper. Germany and Japan were advanced economic powers with an intense sense of national identity before their defeat in World War II.[28] Both also possessed dedicated bureaucracies with long experience in running the affairs of the country. Iraq, sadly, was lacking on all scores. Sectarian and ethnic loyalties overwhelmed tepid feeling of Iraqi nationalism, there was little industry, and Iraq's oil revenues had been squandered on a series of failed wars. Even the massive security-bureaucratic apparatus that had kept Saddam Hussein in power was abolished with the U.S. occupation. Far from blossoming into a model for a restructured Middle East, Iraq dissolved into civil war. The United States refused to acknowledge the existence of a civil war and clung desperately to a pro-Iranian government best known for its massive corruption and death squads.

The Kurdish regions of northern Iraq were the one bright spot in the occupation. Americans were applauded and the economy was booming. At long last, the Kurds had achieved self-rule replete with their own parliament and own flag. It was merely a matter of time before they declared their independence, the Kurdish flag having long ago replaced the Iraqi flag in the northern provinces. Turkish troops are massed on the Kurdish-Iraqi border and have threatened to invade if Kurdish independence is declared. The Kurdish president, for his part, has threatened to fuel the Kurdish (Kurdistan Workers Party [PKK]) revolt in Turkey unless Ankara backs down from its threatened invasion. Whose side will the United States be on if the Turks invade: the Kurds or their traditional allies, the Turks? The Israelis are already training the Kurds despite their strong ties with the Turks, and the Turks and Iranians have formed an anti-Kurdish alliance bolstered by growing economic ties. It is all very confusing.

Afghanistan has gone about as well as Iraq. Civil war rages, and the Taliban has reasserted its control over large areas of the country. Support for al Qaeda has increased apace as have cover-ups of the glitches. American and allied casualties continue to mount, an unfortunate number being killed by friendly fire. Many friendly fire victims are honored as the victims of al Qaeda terrorists to spare the military and the administration unneeded embarrassment.

In the spring of 2007, hoping to come to grips with a situation spiraling out of control, the White House sought a grand czar to ride herd over both the Iraqi and Afghani wars. The task proved challenging as the White House's initial choices for the position, all retired four star generals, declined the honor. Marine General John J. Sheehan, a former commander of the North Atlantic Treaty Organisation (NATO), was particularly vocal in rejecting the position, stating, "The very fundamental issue is, they don't know where the hell they're going." He also noted a deep conflict within the administration between the hawks who want to remain in Iraq to the bitter end, and the pragmatists who are looking for a way out.

The Consequences of the War in Iraq for American Struggles against Jihadist Terror and Lesser Forms of Islamic Extremism

You get the picture. Suffice it to say that the Iraqi model will not defeat jihadist terror, quell Islamic extremism, or strengthen the national interests of the United States and Israel in the region. The fallout from Iraq will continue for at least a decade, but the main points listed below are now obvious, and most are outlined in some detail in the report of the Iraq Study Group, a blue ribbon commission of senior members of both the Republican and Democratic parties established by President Bush to find a solution to the Iraqi mess.[30]

1. The war in Iraq has diverted money, military resources, and energy from the war on terror and the parallel struggle against Islamic extremism. It has similarly diverted resources away from the Homeland Security Agency, a vital element in America's defenses against jihadist terror.

2. The U.S. military has been strained to the breaking point and will find it difficult to sustain its positions in Afghanistan, invade Iran, stabilize Somalia and the Sudan, or pursue the jihadists into the wilds of Pakistan and Africa where they are establishing training bases.[31] Using military force to quell the radical moderates requires invasion and is no longer feasible.

3. Dissension within the American government created by the war in Iraq has spilled over into America's domestic politics. As the war in Iraq was the centerpiece of the wars on terror and Islamic extremism, the climate for dealing with both has been further confused.

4. The international community has been so soured by Iraq that it will take a long time to rebuild a coordinated global effort against jihadist terror based upon trust and mutual confidence. Even the British, the staunchest of U.S. allies, have bailed out of Iraq and are questioning their special relationship with the United States.[32]

5. Poor planning and bureaucratic confusion have enabled al Qaeda and other jihadist groups to score cheap victories against U.S. forces. This

has bolstered their morale and credibility while simultaneously compromising America's aura of invincibility, a critical psychological component in the struggle against terror and extremism. Both the jihadists and the diverse Hizbullah organizations now believe that they can prevail against America's might. President Bush added to the problem by blaming U.S. problems in Iraq on al Qaeda, an organization that didn't have a presence in Iraq prior to the war. It does now. Like it or not, the United States has created another swamp in which terror breeds.

6. The jihadists in Iraq attracted recruits from throughout the Middle East. They are now returning home to create their own cells. Even the Turks are feeling the pinch.[33] Saudi Arabia, as noted, is building a wall to keep them out. Good luck. Rather than reducing jihadist terror, the war in Iraq has facilitated it.

7. Iran, far from being threatened by a U.S. invasion from Iraq, is now consolidating its position in its neighboring Shi'a country. With the threat of a U.S. invasion (but not air strike) vastly reduced, Iran has also been emboldened in its efforts to develop nuclear weapons. Whether there be a Shi'a Crescent or not, Iran has been strengthened and Iraq's Hizbullah clones can be expected to extend their influence throughout the Gulf.

8. Iran is now by far and away the dominant power in the Gulf region. Saddam Hussein had been kept in office for the precise purpose of countering Iranian power. That check no longer exists.

9. The chaos created in Iraq could well serve as the catalyst for yet another Middle Eastern war. The Saudi Arabians are supporting the Sunni militias, the Iranians are supporting the Shi'a militias, the Turks are threatening to obliterate the Kurdish militias and perhaps occupy northern Iraq, and the Israelis have threatened to attack both Iran and Hizbullah. This is not really what the United States had in mind.

10. The Iraq war triggered soaring oil prices, which have strained a world economy already short of oil. Iraq wasn't the only cause of increased oil prices, but it clearly did its part. The regional instability caused by the Iraq war promises more of the same.

11. Saudi Arabia and Jordan now worry about the consequences of a rapid U.S. withdrawal from Iraq. They also worry about a continued U.S. presence in this most war torn of countries. Their fears are justified. Everything in the Middle East is connected to everything else.[34]

The Consequences of the Iraqi War for Israel

The consequences of the Iraq War for Israel are also part of the equation because the policies of the United States and Israel are so intertwined that they are difficult to disentangle. Israel's survival was a key component in the neoconservative vision of a new Middle East that fueled the war. Israelis were also vigorous advocates of the war as well they should have been. They had tasted Saddam's rockets and were in little mood to question intelligence reports of weapons of mass destruction, however flawed.

The Israelis are now pondering the results of the war on their own security. On the plus side, the immediate threat of Iraqi missiles is gone as is the threat of a conventional war with Saddam Hussein's massive army. Threats of conventional war with an increasingly fragile Syrian regime have also decreased.[35] Libya, for its part, saw the writing on the wall and dismantled its nuclear program.

The negative side of the ledger, however, continues to grow. The U.S. defeat in Iraq has only served to replace Saddam Hussein with a Shi'a regime beholden to Iran. Thoughts of a U.S. invasion of Iran, strongly favored by Israel, are no longer on the table. Iran's nuclear program has been advanced by the Iraqi war as has the threat of a resurgent Hizbullah.

A more subtle casualty of the Iraqi war has been Israel's enduring attempt to disassociate the Palestinian conflict from America's struggle against jihadist terror and lesser forms of Islamic extremism.[36] That ended with "The Iraq Study Group Report: The Way Forward—A New Approach." The report of the blue ribbon committee convened by President Bush candidly warned, "The U.S. will not be able to achieve its goals in the Middle East unless the U.S. deals directly with the Arab-Israeli conflict."[37] This was followed by a similar warning in former president Jimmy Carter's book entitled *Palestine: Peace Not Apartheid*.[38] The British Parliament concurs: "The Committee identified the continuing failure to achieve a peace settlement acceptable to both Israel and the Palestinians as a contributory factor in the spread of militancy among sections of Muslim society worldwide."[39] George Soros, the Jewish billionaire philanthropist, joined the fray by accusing the American Israeli Public Affairs Committee, one of the most powerful lobbies in Washington, of pushing President Bush toward a hopeless strategy toward the Palestinians.[40]

Finally, Israel is confronting the probability that a U.S. withdrawal from Iraq will lead to a new Middle East profoundly adverse to the interests of the Jewish state. As former prime minister Olmert expressed these concerns, "Those who are concerned for Israel's security, for the security of the Gulf states and for the stability of the entire Middle East should recognize the need for American success in Iraq, and a responsible exit."[41] He went on to predict that Jordan could be the first casualty of the Iraqi War. All in all, a war that was to increase the security of the Jewish state has done just the opposite.

The Neoconservatives: Right or Wrong?

Who's to blame? The president blames bin Laden. The neoconservatives blame the president for botching their glorious vision of a new Middle East.[42] The Democrats blame the Republicans for prosecuting a flawed war and accuse the president of being in a state of denial over Iraq. The Republicans blame the Democrats for scuttling the war effort. The CIA is pilloried for bad intelligence, while intelligence officers blame the then director of the CIA for pandering to the president's desire for a war in Iraq rather than providing him with accurate assessments of their reports. The buck, it seems, doesn't stop anywhere.

This said, the neoconservatives remain unrepentant. The problem, in their view, was not their vision of a new Middle East but rather the way that the Bush administration botched the war in Iraq. As Uri Lubrani, an advisor to the Israeli Ministry of Defense recently lamented, "Let us close our eyes and imagine how the Middle East would look had the United States been success-ful in Iraq, instead of the humiliation that it has. . . . Such a victory could have changed the entire region."[43]

Actually, the Bush administration didn't botch the war. The U.S. military carried out its task in exemplary fashion. It was what came afterward that was the problem. The imperial dreams of the administration's neoconservative advisors—they were part of the planning process—was a key element in the Iraqi debacle.

The neoconservatives were, however, correct on two key points. First, U.S. antiterrorist strategies weren't working. At the very least, they weren't ade-quate to stem the terrorist threat. Second, as leader of the free world, the United States had to take decisive action to stem the terrorist threat to the United States, Israel, and just about everyone else. Ironically, the debacle in Iraq has made the need for decisive U.S. action against jihadist terror more urgent than ever.

From Here We Start Doing What to Whom, When, and How?

What is there to do? There is really only one option. The United States should try a strong dose of realism based upon its own experience and that of its allies including Israel and the governments of the Islamic world. No grand visions, just adjusting to the realities of the real world.

And where should they begin? First and foremost, accept the reality that the United States, for all of its military power and technological sophistication, cannot fight the entire world all of the time. If it could, the United States wouldn't be engaged in a long war against jihadist terror, licking its wounds in Iraq, wringing its hands of North Korea's nuclear weapons, or waffling over Iran's pursuit of the same.

This being the case, it is necessary to make realistic assessments of what the United States can do to whom, when, and how.[44] There is no question of America's ability to obliterate the world with its nuclear arsenal or defeat a conventional enemy in a war with massed troops and clearly demarcated positions. What is at question is its ability to strike an elusive terrorist enemy that shelters in swamps (failed states in military jargon) and hides among civilian populations. Air strikes don't work, and occupation breeds hostility and terror. The perils of occupation are bad enough in their own right, but they are compounded when efforts are made to transform the Occupied Territories into docile pawns willing to sacrifice the interests of their own people for those of the occupying power. This clearly has been the lesson of the Israeli occupation of the Occupied Territories and the U.S. occupation of Iraq. Also in question is the administrative capacity of the U.S. government to implement grand plans that require the coordinated efforts of hundreds of agencies (or is it thousands) at different levels of government on a global basis over a sustained period of time.

Because there are realistic limits to what America can do to whom, when, and how, the United States must be in a position to focus its resources, military and otherwise (diplomatic and economic), on those enemies that pose the greatest threat to America's security. Those enemies must be clearly identified so that they can be dealt with effectively across the broad spectrum of government agencies. Each agency can't have its own list of enemies, nor can there be hidden agendas that key government figures pursue while pretending to do something else. It just doesn't work, and everyone loses. This has been the failed history of America's long war to date.

Identifying America's enemies is not enough. They must also be listed in terms of the severity and immediacy of their threat to the United States. The most deadly and immediate of enemies must be given priority over those who pose less of a threat to the United States. This does not mean that the others should be ignored, but they cannot be allowed to divert vital resources from the main threat. If stemming the main threat fails, everything else is moot. This point was very clear during the Cold War struggle against the Soviets but has faded in the mishmash of the long war.

Even giving priority to America's enemies is not enough. Each must be countered with suitable strategies. Barring this, America's finite resources will be fragmented and squandered. Coordination among America's hundreds of security-related agencies, problematic in the best of times, will become virtually impossible.

Who, Then, Are the Enemies of the United States?

The foremost enemies of the United States are the jihadist terrorists and their supporters. They, at least, are the top priority of America's sixteen security organizations including the Justice Department, CIA, Federal Bureau of Investigation (FBI), and Joint Chiefs of Staff as collated in the "National Counterintelligence Strategy of the United States of America, 2007."[45] They are followed in turn by countries pursuing weapons of mass destruction, the two most immediate offenders being Iran and North Korea. Lesser forms of Islamic extremism are not addressed in the report, although many radical-moderate groups do appear on the U.S. list of terrorist organizations. This suggests concern but little sense of urgency.

Strategies for Fighting Jihadist Terror

The "National Counterintelligence Strategy" report begins by noting,

> The struggle against jihadist inspired terror is a global one, without 'fronts' in a conventional sense. It will necessarily be a long one, which cannot be won by military operations alone. Terrorists have grown more diverse in their inspirations, more sophisticated and adaptive in their tactics, and possibly more numerous. The difficulty of our mission to defeat them can hardly be overstated.[46]

Because the number 1 priority of America's intelligence community is protecting the United States, the report calls for massive improvements in the operations of America's intelligence community. The list is long and includes an urgent call for improvements in the collection, analysis, integration, access, sharing, and utilization of intelligence data. This will not be easy as 50 percent of the relevant personnel have less than five years experience, minimal linguistic ability, and little exposure to cultural diversity—nor do the diverse components of the intelligence community find it easy to communicate with each other. According to the report, "Each agency and department runs legacy systems that were planned and in many cases deployed long before the Internet age. They were not built to talk to one another, and the technical challenges involved with making them communicate . . . have proved daunting."[47] As a result, information gets stovepiped. Improvements are being made but, as the report stresses, must be done in a manner consistent with U.S. laws and the protection of privacy and civil liberties. The intelligence community also worries that its technological advantages are "under siege." Particularly important was the report's call on the intelligence community to learn from past mistakes.

As the struggle against jihadist-inspired terror cannot be won by military operations alone, the report stresses the need to bolster the growth of democracy and to sustain peaceful democratic regimes. This, without being stated, is recognition that the radical moderates will have to play a role in any political solution to jihadist-inspired terror. How could it be otherwise? The radical moderates are winning all of the elections. By implication, the report addresses the corresponding need to eliminate the "failed states" in which terror breeds. Other military publications address this problem directly and point out that the leaders of failed states have so little control over what goes on in their countries that they cannot cooperate effectively in the struggle against jihadist terror. Failed states also create an adverse environment for the collection of intelligence data and often result in unreliable information.[48]

Because the struggle against jihad is a global war, the report stresses that the American intelligence community "cannot win against our adversaries on its own."[49] Great emphasis, accordingly, is placed on the need to build stronger relationships with foreign intelligence agencies. As a step in this direction, the United States and Britain have now begun to share classified intelligence data on Iraq and Afghanistan.

All in all, we found the report to be a work of art. In one fell swoop it manages to work within the guidelines established by the White House, forge agreement among sixteen diverse security agencies (the military and Homeland Security each count as one), make the intelligence community look good, and tell the truth about the fragility of America's ability to fight jihadist-inspired terror with faint praise and promises to do better in the future.

The magnitude of the administrative and operational problems discussed in the report help to explain why the war on terror has become the long war. They also make it patently evident that the U.S. intelligence community, including the military and the State Department, do not possess the capacity to challenge lesser forms of Islamic extremism or to forge a new Middle East.

On the plus side, pursuing the strategies and correcting the problems outlined in the report will go a long way toward defeating the jihadists. These are thoughtful people with a great deal of experience, and their views should be weighed carefully.

Missing from the report are the things that the intelligence community cannot say. The White House and Congress make decisions; the security community executes them. The president is the commander in chief, and his orders are to be obeyed, not contradicted. This being the case, we shall take the liberty of stating the obvious for them.

First, stay focused on the jihadist terrorists and the containment of weapons of mass destruction that might soon be used by the jihadists against the United States and its allies.

Second, do not dilute this most vital of efforts with vague and uncoordinated visions of defeating the radical moderates or remaking the Middle East. According to the report, America's intelligence community has enough problems fighting the jihadist terrorists as it is. We are not judging the desirability of these other objectives, merely accepting the reality that the United States does not possess the capacity to achieve them. Wishing will not make it so.

Third, because force alone cannot stop jihadist terrorism, it is necessary to balance force with political solutions. Democracy, the third priority of the report after fighting the jihadist terrorists and containing weapons of mass destruction, is a step in this direction. Economic development must also be added to the equation.

Democracy and economic development, while vital, are long-term political solutions to jihadist terror. There must also be political solutions that address the immediate flash points fueling jihadist terror. Of these none are more important than bringing a swift conclusion to the holy jihads that have become the feeding trough for the jihadist movement. Palestine and Iraq lead the parade (more on this shortly).

Fourth, the United States would be well advised to stay out of civil wars and movements of national liberation that have little to do with jihadist terrorism. The experience in Iraq, Palestine, and Afghanistan all demonstrate that American involvement in civil wars and movements of national liberation only ends up fueling jihadism and Islamic extremism.

Is Iraq really in a civil war? The president says not yet. Unwilling to contradict the commander in chief, a second National Intelligence Assessment entitled "Prospects for Iraq's Stability: A Challenging Road Ahead" did the next best thing. It said that Iraq was worse than a civil war.

> The Intelligence Community judges that the term 'civil war' does not adequately capture the complexity of the conflict in Iraq, which includes extensive Sunni-on-Shi'a violence, al-Qa'ida and Sunni insurgent attacks on Coalition forces, and widespread criminally motivated conflict, including the hardening of ethno-sectarian identities, a sea change in the character of the violence, ethno-sectarian mobilization, and population displacements.[50]

Fifth, it is vital that the United States stop transforming bin Laden into a folk hero by blaming al Qaeda for America's problems in Iraq and elsewhere.[51] This inspires recruits, strengthens the morale of jihadist cadres, spawns homegrown jihadist cells throughout the world, and demoralizes intelligence agencies. Much the same can be said of President Bush's ill-timed references to crusades and Senator John McCain's quip that the United States should "bomb, bomb, bomb, bomb, bomb" Iran. McCain's comments had produced two hundred thousand hits on YouTube by the following afternoon.[52] All of this plays well in the United States, but it terrifies our allies and enables jihadist and Islamic extremists to claim that the United States has, indeed, declared war on Islam. The senator said that he was merely joking, but the Muslim world was not laughing. Perhaps that is because U.S. bombs are the core of its policies in Iraq, Afghanistan, Palestine, and Lebanon.

Strategies for Fighting Islamic Extremism

The best way to stop the radical moderates is to hold fair elections. As Secretary of State Rice addressed the students at the American University of Cairo in 2005, "For 60 years, my country, the United States, pursued stability at the expense of democracy in this region, here in the Middle East, and we have achieved neither." She also called on the Egyptian government to "put its faith in its own people."[53]

The United States soon backed away from its infatuation with democracy, but the advice was sound. If the radical moderates win, so be it. It will be they who bear the brunt of solving the social and economic problems of their countries. Gone will be the days of reaping popular support based upon popular revulsion against the greed, oppression, and incompetence of America's pet dictators in the region. Let people see the radical moderates for what they are. If they can bring stability and development within a moderate Islamic framework, God bless them. If they fail, the populous will become disenchanted.

The threat of a sweeping victory by the Muslim Brotherhood and other radical moderates can also be parried by allowing a visible secular opposition to develop. Secular parties exist, but at the first sign of life they are either crushed as subversives or bought off by the regime. As things stand now, the radical moderates represent the only serious opposition to corrupt, inept, and oppressive dictators. Much of their popular support is a protest against dictatorship and oppression with a hint of "here's to ya, America."

If present trends are any indication, the probability of radical-moderate victories is very high. If they win, they must be allowed to rule. Little is to be gained by allowing the radical moderates to assume power only to force them out of office with violence and economic sanctions. As the case of the Hamas in Palestine had demonstrated, this merely leads to radicalism, forces them into alliances with the supporters of terror, and provides a ready-made excuse for their probable failures. We agree with Shlomo Ben-Ami, the former Israeli foreign minister, who argues that the best way to deal with radical

moderates is to make them effective. This places America in the strong position of building democracy, supporting responsible Islam, building hope,
and isolating the jihadists. Besides, efforts to force the radical moderates out
of power doesn't work and only serves to expand the base of their popular
support. Heavy-handed efforts to crush a popularly elected radical-moderate
government also reduce the legitimacy of successor regimes by making them
appear as puppets of the United States and Israel.

Democracy, moreover, is unlikely to be effective unless it is combined with
serious efforts to addressing the economic desperation of much of the Islamic
world. The administrative and operational problems that beset the U.S. intelligence community pale in comparison to the chaos that reigns in the global
efforts to bring economic development to the Third World.[54]

Risky Business?

It is risky, to be sure! Among other things, it probably means sacrificing the
curious kings and aging dictators who have served America so poorly for so
long. They are, after all, part of the problem. It is doubtful that Islamic
extremism, whatever its variety, could have reached its present level without
them. The more the United States keeps them in power, the worse things will
get. Don't forget, most of the dictators have made peace with the jihadists,
the number 1 enemy of the United States. Is this really what Washington
wants?

Then why risk it? The answer is simple. Everything else America has tried
has failed. Why not go with democracy? That, after all, is America's strong
suit. If America has to intervene in the region, it should intervene on the side
of democracy, human rights, religious freedom, and economic development,
not the other way around.

Does this mean selling out Israel? Not at all. It means saving Israel by
doing what is best for the long-term security of both countries. For all of
the talk about security fences and unilateral Israeli withdrawal to defensible
borders, the debate about how to solve the Palestine-Israeli conflict revolves
around two basic poles. The first is a return to Israel's 1967 borders. The
other is transfer, alias ethnic cleansing.[55] A solution to the Israeli-Palestinian
conflict based on a return to Israel's 1967 borders came near to being a reality
prior to the assassination of Yitzhak Rabin in the run-up to the 1996 Israeli
elections and was widely discussed during the premiership of Ehud Barak a
decade later. This solution was unanimously accepted by the Arab states in
2007 and represents a position that is minimally accepted by a majority of
the populations on both sides of the issue.

Barring an acceptance of some version of this plan, the Palestinian-Israeli conflict will continue indefinitely to the detriment of both Israel and America's war against extremism and terror.

Pressure for transfer will increase apace, the repercussion of which in terms of terror and Islamic extremism defy calculation. Sadly, a recent opinion poll found that some one-half of Israel's Jewish citizens favored "encouraging Arab emigration."[56] Israel's extreme right wing has also strengthened its position in the Israeli Cabinet.

Clearly, it is in the interests of the United States and Israel to find a solution to the Palestinian crisis based on the 1967 borders. The Arab world will be able to bury an issue that haunts it like none other, and the United States will be able to participate in the rebuilding of Palestine. If this requires working with Hamas, as former Israeli foreign minister Ben-Ami suggests is necessary, so be it. The wind will be taken out of Hizbullah and Iranian sails, and the United States will be free to concentrate on jihadist terrorists.

Does this provide an ironclad guarantee of Israel's security? Of course not. There are no guarantees in the Middle East. What is certain is that present Israeli and American policies are only making things worse and that time is on the side of the enemy. The best guarantee of an Israeli demise is a continuation of present policies of confusion interspersed with alternate spasms of gratuitous violence and retreat behind new borders to be defined by Israel, a policy that Ben-Ami ridicules as "Israel playing chess with itself."[57] The former builds anger, anti-Americanism, and Islamic extremism. The latter builds confidence among the jihadists that terror works. Do you have doubts on the issue? Read the Israeli press. It is all there in spades.

And what about Iraq? It's simple. Leave with the minimal loss of lives on all sides, and allow the UN to sort things out.[58] The war has been lost. The Shi'a clones of Hizbullah are taking over the south and east, the Kurds have transformed the north into an independent country, and what remains of Iraq has become a jihadist swamp that is exporting terrorists and destabilizing the region. A broader Middle Eastern conflict looms, but the United States has demonstrated that it lacks the ability to stabilize the situation. It surely doesn't want to be in the middle of it.

The advocates of staying in Iraq warn of appeasement, but they obviously haven't studied history, nor are they very good poker players. Appeasement occurs before a conflict when countries fold their cards out of fear. This is not the case in Iraq. All of the cards are on the table, face up. There are no hidden hold cards to bluff with, and the United States is merely putting good money after bad. More to the point, it is sacrificing needless American and Iraqi lives for a cause that can only help the jihadists and fuel Islamic extremism.

Notes

1. The 9/11 Commission, *Sept. 11 Commission Report: Final Report of the National Commission on Terrorist Attacks on the United States* (New York: W.W. Norton, n.d.).

2. Richard A. Clarke, *Against All Enemies* (New York: Free Press, 2004); George Tenet, *At the Center of the Storm: My Years at the CIA* (New York: HarperCollins, 2007).

3. Bob Woodward, *Plan of Attack* (New York: Simon & Schuster, 2004); Bob Woodward, *Bush at War* (New York: Simon & Schuster, 2004).

4. John Mills, "It's Now 2007, So Where Are We in the Long War?" *Strategic Insights* 6 (2) (March 2007).

5. "Trends in Global Terrorism: Implications for the United States," Declassified Key Judgments of the National Intelligence Estimate, April 2006, at www.global security.org/intell/library/reports/2006/nie_global-terror-trends_apr2006.htm.

6. Stephen E. Flynn, *The Edge of Disaster* (New York: Random House, 2007); "The Terrorist Threat to the U.S. Homeland," *National Intelligence Estimate*, National Intelligence Council, July 2007.

7. Clarke, *Against All Enemies*; Tenet, *At the Center of the Storm*.

8. *Sept. 11 Commission Report*.

9. Angela Balakrishnan, "Poor Countries 'Suffering from Aid Chaos,'" *Guardian*, September 22, 2006, at www.guardian.co.uk/aid/story/0,,1878591,00.html (accessed September 22, 2006); United Nations Development Program, "Arab Human Development Report, 2004," New York, 2005.

10. Hani Bathish, "U.S. Gave Israel Time to Continue War," *Daily Star* (Lebanon), March 23, 2007, at www.dailystar.com.lb/ (accessed March 23, 2007).

11. Manal Lutfi, "The Brotherhood and America Part One," *Asharq Al-Awsat*, March 14, 2007.

12. Jim Lobe, "Perle-Frum Book Updates Neocon ME Agenda," *Daily Star* (Lebanon), January 12, 2004, at www.dailystar.com.lb/ (accessed January 12, 2004).

13. Lobe, "Perle-Frum Book Updates Neocon ME Agenda," 1.

14. Steven R. Weisman, "Pre-emption: Idea with a Lineage Whose Time Has Come," *New York Times*, March 23, 2003, at www.nytimes.com/2003/03/23/international/worldspecial/23PREE.html (accessed March 23, 2003).

15. Craig R. Whitney, ed., *The WMD Mirage: Iraq's Decade of Deception and America's False Premise for War* (New York: PublicAffairs, 2005).

16. Douglas Jehl, "U.S. Report Finds Iraqis Eliminated Illicit Arms in 90's," *New York Times*, October 7, 2004, at www.nytimes.com/2004/10/07/politics/07intel.html (accessed October 7, 2004).

17. U.S. Department of Defense, "Review of Pre Iraqi War Activities of the Office of the Under Secretary of Defense for Policy," Report No. 07-INTEL-04, February 9, 2007.

18. Woodward, *Plan of Attack*, 150.

19. Joyce Battle and Thomas Blanton, eds., "Top Secret Polo Step: Iraq War Assumed Only 5,000 U.S. Troops Still There by December 2006," National Security Archive Electronic Briefing Book No. 214, February 14, 2007.

20. Michael E. Gordon and Bernard E. Trainor, *Cobra II: The Inside Story of the Invasion and Occupation of Iraq* (New York: Pantheon Books, 2006); Tommy Franks with Malcolm McConnell, *American Soldier* (New York: Regan Books, 2004); Thomas E. Ricks, *Fiasco: The American Military Adventure in Iraq* (New York: Penguin Press, 2006); Woodward, *Plan of Attack*; David C. Hendrickson and Robert W. Tucker, "Revisions in Need of Revising: What Went Wrong in the Iraq War," Strategic Studies Institute, December 2005, at www.StrategicStudiesInstitute.army.mil (accessed December 5, 2006); W. Andrew Terrill, ed., "U.S. Military Operations in Iraq: Planning, Combat, and Occupation," Strategic Studies Institute, April 2006, at www.StrategicStudiesInstitute.army.mil (accessed April 3. 2007).

21. Michael R. Gordon, "A Prewar Slide Show Cast Iraq in Rosy Hues," *New York Times*, February 15, 2007, at www.nytimes.com/2007/02/15/washington/15military. html (accessed February 15, 2007).

22. L. Paul Bremer III, *My Years in Iraq* (New York: Simon & Schuster, 2006).

23. "Biography of Dr. Condoleezza Rice, National Security Advisor," White House, 2001, at www.whitehouse.gov/nsc/ricebio.html (accessed October 26, 2003).

24. Davi M. D'Agostino, "Operation Iraqi Freedom: DOD Should Apply Lessons Learned Concerning the Need for Security over Conventional Munitions Storage Sites to Future Operations Planning," Testimony before the Subcommittee on National Security and Foreign Affairs, Committee on Oversight and Government Reform, U.S. House of Representatives, U.S. Government Accounting Office, 2007, at www.gao.gov/ (accessed April 4, 2007).

25. Erik Eckholm, "Memos Warned of Billing Fraud by Firm in Iraq," *New York Times*, October 23, 2004, at www.nytimes.com/2004/10/23/politics/23whistle.html (accessed October 23, 2004); Griff Witte, "Contractors Rarely Held Responsible for Misdeeds in Iraq," *Washington Post*, November 4, 2006, at www.washingtonpost .com/ (accessed November 4, 2006).

26. James Glanz, "Congress Tells Auditor in Iraq to Close Office," *New York Times*, November 3, 2006, at www.nytimes.com/ (accessed November 3, 2006).

27. Shawn Dorman, "Iraq PRTs: Pins on a Map: Focus on War Zone Diplomacy," *Foreign Service Journal* (March 2007): 21–39; U.S. Special Inspector General for Iraqi Reconstruction, "Iraq Reconstruction: Lessons in Program and Project Management," March 2007, at www.sigir.mil/reports/pdf/lessons_learned_March21pdf-iraq report (accessed March 29, 2007).

28. Monte Palmer, *Political Development: Dilemmas and Challenges* (Itasca, Ill.: Peacock, 2001).

29. Peter Baker and Thomas E. Ricks, "3 Generals Spurn the Position of War 'Czar,'" *Washington Post*, April 11, 2007, at www.washingtonpost.com/ (accessed April 11, 2007).

30. James Baker and Lee Hamilton, "The Iraq Study Group Report: The Way Forward—A New Approach," U.S. Government Report, n.d.

31. Mark Thompson, "Why Our Army Is at the Breaking Point: Exhausted Troops, Worn-out Equipment, Reduced Training, the Lessons of Iraq and Afghanistan—and How to Undo the Damage," *Time*, April 16, 2007, 28–41.

32. Mary Jordan, "Blair Announces Plans for Troop Drawdown in Iraq," *Washington Post*, February 21, 2007, at www.washingtonpost.com/ (accessed February 21, 2007).

33. Selcan Hacaoglu, "Turkey Fears New Terror Threat if Homegrown Militants Return from Fighting in Iraq," *Turkish Daily News,* November 16, 2006, at www.tdn.com.tr/ (accessed November 16, 2006).

34. Monte Palmer, *Comparative Politics: Political Economy, Political Culture, and Political Interdependence* (Belmont, Calif.: Thomson/Wadsworth, 2006).

35. Jonathan Spyer, "The Impact of the Iraq War on Israel's National Security Conception," *Middle East Review of International Affairs* 9, no. 4 (December 2005), at http://meria.idc.ac.il/ (accessed December 10, 2005).

36. Nathan Gutmann, *The Other War: Israelis, Palestinians and the Struggle for Media Supremacy* (San Francisco: Encounter Books, 2005).

37. Baker and Hamilton, "The Iraq Study Group Report," 39.

38. Jimmy Carter, *Palestine: Peace Not Apartheid* (New York: Simon & Schuster, 2006).

39. House of Commons Foreign Affairs Committee, "Foreign Policy Aspects of the War against Terrorism: Fourth Report of Session 2005–06," Stationery Office Limited, London, June 21, 2006, 71.

40. Ed Pilkington, "Soros Takes on U.S. Pro-Israeli Lobby," *Guardian,* April 17, 2007, at www.guardian.co.uk/ (accessed April 17, 2007).

41. Shmuel Rosner and Aluf Benn, "Israel Fears U.S. Iraq Exit Could Topple Jordanian Regime," *Ha'aretz,* March 16, 2007, at www.haaretz.com/hasen/spages/83 8396.html (accessed March 16, 2007).

42. Julian Borger, "Neocons Turn on Bush for Incompetence over Iraq War," *Guardian,* November 4, 2006, at www.guardian.co.uk/ (accessed November 4, 2006).

43. Yaakov Amidror, "Analysis: Lebanon II, the Fallout," *Jerusalem Post,* January 17, 2007, at www.jpost.com/servlet/Satellite?cid = 1167467749510&pagename = J Post/JPArticle /ShowFull (accessed January 17, 2007).

44. Harold D. Laswell, *Politics: Who Gets What, When, How* (New York: World Publishing, 1958).

45. Director of National Intelligence (DNI), "National Counterintelligence Strategy of the United States of America, 2007," at www.dni.gov/reports/NCIX_Strategy_2007.pfd (accessed April 19, 2007).

46. DNI, "National Counterintelligence Strategy," 9.

47. DNI, "National Counterintelligence Strategy," 18.

48. Thomas Dempsey, *Counterterrorism in African Failed States: Challenges and Potential Solutions,* Strategic Studies Institute, April 2006, at www.StrategicStudies Institute.army.mil/ (accessed December 12, 2006).

49. DNI, "National Counterintelligence Strategy," 18.

50. DNI, "Prospects for Iraq's Stability: A Challenging Road Ahead," *National Intelligence Estimate,* January 2007, at www.dni.gov/press_releases/20070202_release.pdf, 2.

51. Peter Walker, "Bush Blames al-Qaida for Iraq Violence," *Guardian,* November 28, 2006, at www.guardian.co.uk/ (accessed November 28, 2006).

52. Mark Rice-Oxley, "Q: What to Do about Iran, Senator McCain? A: As the Beach Boys Said: Bomb, Bomb, Bomb, Bomb," *Guardian,* April 21, 2007, at www.guaridan.co.uk/ (accessed April 21, 2007).

53. Anthony Shadid, "Egypt Shuts Door on Dissent as U.S. Officials Back Away," *Washington Post*, March 19, 2007, at www.washingtonpost.com/ (accessed March 19, 2007).

54. "Foreign Aid: The Non-Aligned Movement," *Economist*, April 7, 2007, 57–58.

55. Ilan Pappe, *The Ethnic Cleansing of Palestine* (Oxford: Oneworld Publications Unlimited, 2007).

56. Yoav Stern, "Poll: Half of Israeli Jews Think State Should Encourage Arab Emigration," *Ha'aretz*, March 28, 2007, at www.haaretz.com/ (accessed March 28, 2007).

57. *Jerusalem Post*, April 10, 2006, at www.jpost.com/ (accessed April 10, 2006).

58. Steven N. Simon, "After the Surge: The Case for U.S. Military Disengagement from Iraq," Council on Foreign Relations, CSR No. 23, February 2007.

Index

About the Authors

Monte Palmer has had more than forty years of experience working in the Middle East including his recent tenure as the director for the Center for Arab and Middle Eastern Studies at the American University of Beirut. His earlier associations include the Al-Ahram Center for Strategic and Political Studies in Cairo, as well as associations with the bir-Zeit University in the West Bank and Libya's Arab Development Institute. He is currently professor emeritus at Florida State University. His recent publications include *At the Heart of Terror*, with Princess Palmer (2004); *Politics of the Middle East* (2007); *Political Development: Dilemmas and Challenges*, fifth ed. (2001); and *The Egyptian Bureaucracy*, with Ali Leila and El Sayed Yassin (1988).

Princess Palmer has traveled extensively in the Middle East and has taught at numerous schools in the area including Cairo American College, the American Community School at Beirut, and the Lebanese American University. She has also served as a consultant for the World Bank and as director of the Florida State University Reading Clinic. Her specialty is reading and education in the Arab world. She is the coauthor, with Monte Palmer, of *At the Heart of Terror* (2004).

3m